BEHOLD THE WALLS

KARLOS K. HILL
General Editor

BEHOLD THE WALLS

Commemorative Edition

CLARA LUPER

Edited by Karlos K. Hill and Bob L. Blackburn

University of Oklahoma Press : Norman

Publication of this book is made possible in part through the generous
assistance of the Oklahoma Historical Society.

Library of Congress Cataloging-in-Publication Data
Names: Luper, Clara, 1923–2011, author. | Hill, Karlos K., editor. | Blackburn,
    Bob L., 1951– editor.
Title: Behold the walls / Clara S. Luper ; edited by Karlos K. Hill and Bob L.
    Blackburn.
Description: Commemorative edition. | Norman : University of Oklahoma
    Press, [2023] | Series: Greenwood Cultural Center series in African
    diaspora history and culture ; volume 3 | Includes index. | Summary:
    "Originally published in 1979, Clara Luper's Behold the Walls remains the
    definitive account of the Oklahoma City sit-in movement that helped spark
    the modern civil rights movement. The editors' introduction explains
    the significance of what Luper, her allies in the state, and her students
    accomplished"—Provided by publisher.
Identifiers: LCCN 2023001535 | ISBN 978-0-8061-9279-6 (hardcover : acid-free
    paper)
Subjects: LCSH: Luper, Clara, 1923–2011. | African Americans—Civil rights—
    Oklahoma—History—20th century. | Civil rights demonstrations—
    Oklahoma—Oklahoma City—History—20th century. | Civil rights
    movements—Oklahoma—History—20th century. | Civil rights workers—
    Oklahoma—Biography. | Women civil rights workers—Oklahoma—
    Biography. | African American women—Oklahoma—Biography. | African
    Americans—Oklahoma—Biography.
Classification: LCC E185.93O4 L86 2023 | DDC 976.6/3800496073—dc23/
    eng/20230203
LC record available at https://lccn.loc.gov/2023001535

Behold the Walls: Commemorative Edition is Volume 3 in the Greenwood
Cultural Center Series in African Diaspora History and Culture.

The paper in this book meets the guidelines for permanence and durability of
the Committee on Production Guidelines for Book Longevity of the Council on
Library Resources, Inc. ∞

1 2 3 4 5 6 7 8 9 10

Special Dedication

The history of America is filled with the lives of great men and women who by their sacrificial lives have changed the course of history.

Men and women who explored the unknown, who plowed the fields, picked the cotton, mopped the floors, washed the dishes, cleaned the restrooms, and paved the way for my generation.

To those who lived with fear for their jobs and lives, yet donated their money, talents, time, food, and other meager means to "the cause."

To those who stood in the scorching heat of yesterday's sunshine and froze educationally, socially, and financially during the long snowy nights of segregation.

It is to those unsung and unknown heroes that this book is dedicated.

Many of these heroes sleep in yonder's soil; many are bent with misery, poverty, and frustration, and are victims of unpredictable circumstances and unknown diseases.

Many bear the scars of yesterday's battles and with renewed courage face the challenges of today's visible and invisible walls.

It is to these that this book is dedicated.

Behold the Walls!
By Clara Luper

Behold the walls!
Do you see what I see?
Visible walls, invisible walls
Separating you and me.
The visible walls are crumbling
As court decisions are handed down.
The invisible walls are still standing,
Making us go round and round.
Each of us must be a Joshua,
Blowing our trumpet of freedom's songs,
And the walls will come tumbling down,
And the world will right the wrong.

CONTENTS

FOREWORD

An important event in the Civil Rights Movement occurred in Oklahoma City on August 19, 1958, an event that has been overlooked by historians. Over a year before the Sit-In Movement started in Greensboro, North Carolina, the Oklahoma City NAACP Youth Council, led by Clara Luper, staged the first in a series of lunch counter sit-ins and other demonstrations that would last five years and eleven months.

These protests were important not only because they integrated eating places, but also because they were the first major demonstrations of the Sit-In Movement of the 1960s and the longest nonviolent concentrated movement in America's history. The sit-ins created a climate in which interracial progress could be made. They changed hiring practices and housing patterns, exposed hidden spots of segregation, and paved the way for unborn generations.

Rev. W. K. Jackson
Pastor, St. John Baptist Church
Oklahoma City

PREFACE TO THE
COMMEMORATIVE EDITION

Our mother was a schoolteacher who taught at several high schools in the Oklahoma City area during her career. She loved history, and every year she would write a play on Black history for the students to perform. Her 1957 play, titled *Brother President*, was about Martin Luther King Jr. and the 1955–56 bus boycott in Montgomery, Alabama. It was presented throughout Oklahoma, and at one of those performances the NAACP's national youth secretary, Herb Wright, happened to be in the audience. He liked *Brother President* so much that he invited our mother to come to New York City and present it at the NAACP National Convention. At first he was going to have her bring only one student, but in her typical way she said, "I can't do it with just one student. All of them have to go." Many of the students had never been out of Oklahoma before. Some had never even been to Oklahoma City. So this was a unique opportunity. Our group raised money by selling dinners, pickles, hot dogs, whatever it took.

We traveled to New York City by way of the northern route, and for the first time in our lives, we saw that there were places that were not like Oklahoma. We could go into restaurants and sit down and eat. We could drink out of the same water fountains as whites.

According to an old saying, "A little bit of freedom is a dangerous thing." When we came back to Oklahoma City, we were all fired up and ready to go, because we had had that taste of freedom. We started trying to negotiate with the restaurants here in Oklahoma City, but they told us that they didn't want to deal with us. White people did not want to sit next to Black people. We would put them out of business. So one Monday night during an NAACP Youth Council meeting at our house, we decided that we would go down to Katz Drug Store and just sit. We were going to sit there until they served us, as long as it took. And that's what we did.

We thought we were on a mission: this was something that we had to do. So we continued to go back, and we continued to sit in. We went from restaurant to restaurant to restaurant until the walls of segregation began to fall in Oklahoma City. *Behold the Walls* is our mother's memoir of the OKC movement, adding to the wider story of how the civil rights generation fought and overcame the walls of segregation. We hope all people, and especially the younger generations, will be inspired by her words.

Marilyn Luper Hildreth and Calvin Luper

EDITORS' ACKNOWLEDGMENTS

Clara Luper's *Behold the Walls* has been out of print for at least a decade. This new edition of Clara Luper's memoir of the Oklahoma sit-in movement has been made possible by the efforts of many people and organizations. Marilyn Luper Hildreth and Calvin Luper deserve special recognition for envisioning this Commemorative Edition as a way of marking and celebrating what would have been Clara Luper's one hundredth birthday, and what is the sixty-fifth anniversary of the iconic 1958 Katz Drug Store sit-in. In addition to Marilyn and Calvin, the Clara Luper Legacy Committee, a group devoted to telling the story of Clara Luper and the Oklahoma sit-ins, helped the editors understand and explain why Clara Luper's life and legacy continue to resonate today.

The Oklahoma Historical Society (OHS) deserves recognition, and particularly OHS Executive Director Trait Thompson and staff members Larry O'Dell, Dana Robinson, and Rachel Mosman for providing much-needed archival and reference support that helped bring the new edition to life. I would be remiss if I did not mention our research assistants, Danny Hurley and Kyla Lewis. During the three years it took to research and edit the new edition, Dani and Kyla always provided critical support when we needed it. Thank you. A special thank-you is owed to my friend and copyeditor Jane Lyle whose commitment, expertise, and attention to detail helped make this commemorative edition sparkle. Lastly, in the final stages of writing and revising the introduction, feedback from peer reviewers, especially Cheryl Wattley, was invaluable.

Thank you to all those not mentioned here but who nonetheless provided valuable contributions to this new and exciting edition of Clara Luper's *Behold the Walls*.

Dr. Karlos K. Hill and Dr. Bob Blackburn

BEHOLD THE WALLS

EDITORS' INTRODUCTION

In the summer of 1958, no one in America could have imagined that a small group of Black children, some just barely out of kindergarten, would be capable of launching a grassroots protest movement that would last six years and effectively end segregation in Oklahoma City. That is exactly what happened, however, after eleven-year-old Marilyn Luper suggested to her mother, Clara Luper, a high school history teacher and the advisor for the Youth Council of the Oklahoma City chapter of the National Association for the Advancement of Colored People (NAACP), that they should walk into a segregated Katz Drug Store, sit down in seats reserved for whites, and refuse to leave until they were served. On August 19, accompanied by Marilyn's brother Calvin and twelve other Youth Council members, they did just that. The resulting sit-in became the driving force behind the movement that eventually forced downtown Oklahoma City businesses to desegregate in June 1964, a month before the federal Civil Rights Act outlawed segregation in public accommodations nationwide. Over the course of those six years, Luper and the NAACP Youth Council used nonviolent direct action or nonviolent civil disobedience to demonstrate how Black people in this country were refused basic services that white Americans enjoyed. These young activists had decided that enough was enough: they were going to do what it took to shine a light on injustice.

In Oklahoma, Luper's story is emphasized in state-mandated learning lessons. Her portrait and a bronze bust are on display in the State Capitol, where her body also lay in repose in the rotunda after her death in 2011. The University of Oklahoma established the Clara Luper Department of African and African American Studies in 2018. Freedom Center, her base of operations, received millions in a city-wide infrastructure

3

package approved by a vote of the people in 2019. In 2021, the down-town post office in Oklahoma City was renamed in her honor. And a $3.6 million bronze monument depicting the sit-in will be erected in Clara Luper Sit-In Plaza, at the site of the former drug store, in 2024.[1]

Her influence, however, is not contained within Oklahoma's borders. As a teacher, she designed her lessons to teach her students about citizenship, what it meant to participate in a democracy, and most especially how injustice could be fought with nonviolence. The Oklahoma City Sit-In Movement was an extension of her classroom, and it offers a model for young people throughout the nation of how to strive for justice and equal rights.

When Clara Luper's name is invoked in public, Oklahomans instantly know what it means. Her story is a metaphor for personal courage, unflagging persistence, and the struggle for justice in an unjust world. Her status as a hero worthy of praise is a strong sign that the state has made huge strides in grappling with a legacy of racism. To appreciate Luper's historical significance more generally, we must understand the challenges she faced and the opportunities she seized. Those challenges and opportunities are deeply embedded in the history of both Oklahoma and the nation.

The stage of history on which Luper was a leading player was first set a century before she was born, when a few citizens of the Five Civilized Tribes brought slavery to the Indian Territory from their ancient homelands in the Deep South. One Choctaw entrepreneur, Robert M. Jones, used the labor of more than two hundred African slaves to amass a fortune that included seven plantations, two riverboats, warehouses in New Orleans, agents in England, and a palatial home not far from the convergence of the Verdigris and Red rivers near the present-day town of Hugo. Two slaves owned by another Choctaw planter, Uncle Wallace Willis and Aunt Minerva, are credited with writing the gospel song "Swing Low, Sweet Chariot," which was transcribed and made famous decades later by the Jubilee Singers of Fisk University.[2]

In 1861, when the issue of slavery's expansion into the territories brought the country to civil war, the mixed-blood leaders of the Five Civilized Tribes were pushed into a corner. They were surrounded by slave states on three sides, while cotton, the economic lifeblood of plantation owners, moved along rivers to the South and New Orleans. By education, cultural identification, and intermarriage, the economic and political elite of the tribes had a natural affinity with the Deep South. Although most tribal members wanted to be left alone in their neutrality, all five

Native governments signed treaties transferring their allegiance and fighting men to the Confederate States of America.[3]

Native people who remained loyal to the Union fled to Indian Territory and huddled in refugee camps in Kansas. They were joined there by thousands of runaway slaves from the Indian nations, who faced certain death if they were captured. The abolitionist leader of Kansas, Senator James Henry Lane, and his close associate James B. Blunt decided to give those refugees a chance to fight for their freedom. When President Abraham Lincoln authorized the enlistment of Black regiments in the U.S. military, the First Kansas Colored Infantry Regiment was the second all-Black unit organized in the entire country.[4]

The First Kansas Colored fought bravely in the future state of Oklahoma for the next three years. In July 1863, when the tide of war in the East turned at Gettysburg and the Confederacy was split in half after the fall of Vicksburg on the Mississippi River, the regiment's Black soldiers drew national attention when they were credited with winning the Battle of Honey Springs, the largest battle fought in the Indian nations. A day later, the all-Black 54th Massachusetts tragically stormed Fort Wagner in South Carolina with a devastating loss of life, later dramatized in the movie *Glory*. Both battles were celebrated across the North in 1863 as proof that Black soldiers could and would fight with ferocious valor, which should earn them freedom and hope for new opportunity. That legacy of courage would become part of the Oklahoma story.[5]

At the end of the Civil War, many of the veterans from the First Kansas Colored proudly reenlisted in the segregated all-Black Ninth and Tenth Cavalry regiments for duty on the expanding American frontier. Others returned to their homes and families in the Indian nations. For the civilians now free from bondage, hope for the future soared in 1866 when Congress forced the Five Civilized Tribes to end slavery and treat their former slaves as tribal members. Most importantly, according to the new treaties, if and when the tribes gave up communal ownership of land and accepted land allotments for individual Indians, the former slaves and their descendants would be included. The promise of forty acres and a mule, denied to most freed slaves in the Old South, was granted to the former slaves of the Five Civilized Tribes.[6]

From 1866 to 1907, Black people in the Indian nations were still treated as second-class citizens, but they had access to land, the primary means for generating wealth on the frontier and the best chance to break the cycle of poverty rooted in slavery. Notable among those who seized that opportunity was David Colbert Franklin, the son of a former

Choctaw slave who built two ranches in the Chickasaw Nation west of the Arbuckle Mountains. There he became a respected member of the Texas Cattlemen's Association, accumulated enough wealth to send his youngest son, B. C., to college in Nashville, and walked the streets of nearby Ardmore with dignity and status. B. C. Franklin became an attorney, and his own son, John Hope Franklin, was the first Black person to earn a PhD in history from Harvard.[7]

When Congress passed the Curtis Act in 1898, the countdown to statehood accelerated, and the Five Civilized Tribes were forced to allot their lands to individuals, both Indian and Black. The last to apportion their acreage were the Cherokees, who completed the process in 1904. With this legislation, suddenly thousands of freedmen and their descendants had clear title to land, from Kansas south to Texas, and many selected parcels for their homesteads that were adjacent to property owned by friends and family members. As a result, farming and ranching communities were created that soon needed a blacksmith, a teacher, a merchant, a post office, a church, and even a newspaper. Founded during what many historians call the "Golden Age of Farming" from 1898 to 1918, many of these prosperous villages grew into towns. By the 1920s, Oklahoma had more than thirty all-Black towns, including Clearview, Grayson, and Boley, which grew to more than five thousand people as Blacks from the Old South found new homes somewhat removed from terrorism, oppression, and exploitation.[8]

The all-Black towns were havens of hope for two generations of Black Oklahomans and instilled a sense of pride and communal identity that eventually would crystallize into what is now called the Civil Rights Movement. Adding to that growing sense of community were the urban Black neighborhoods of Greenwood in Tulsa and Deep Deuce in Oklahoma City. Isolated on the other side of the tracks by a racist majority of the white community and legally segregated by the U.S. Supreme Court's "separate but equal" ruling, Greenwood and Deep Deuce grew into vibrant cities within cities where talent and enterprise were rewarded with success, and a thriving middle class increasingly demanded more freedom in the larger community.[9]

Their demands for equal treatment were met with persistent and sometimes violent pushback. By the early 1920s, the Ku Klux Klan was a dominant force, both at the local community level, where beatings and lynchings were accepted by the legal community as necessary tools for maintaining social order, and at the state level, where segregation laws were passed by large majorities in the legislature. In May 1921, that culture of segregation and racial hatred erupted in Tulsa when a white mob defeated courageous Black defenders and destroyed Greenwood in a violent outburst of fury and fire. No one was prosecuted for the crimes, and insurance companies refused to pay for the properties lost. Resentment, hate, and fear smoldered like the ashes.[10]

John Hope Franklin, who grew up in Tulsa, later recalled another emotional reaction to the 1921 Tulsa Race Massacre, and that was pride. Around dinner tables, at picnics, and in the shops of Greenwood, people for decades would quietly remember the valiant defiance of a few young Black men who confronted the more than two thousand angry white men who had gathered in front of the courthouse, where they intended to lynch another Black brother. When guns were drawn and blood filled the streets, they set up a perimeter defense of Greenwood with tactics learned on the World War I battlefields of France and a sense of outrage learned through the harsh lessons of racial prejudice. The bricks and mortar of Greenwood may have been destroyed, but the spirit of defiance was undefeated.[11]

In Oklahoma City, where racism never flared into mass violence, the spirit of defiance grew equally strong decade by decade. With ink rather than bullets, Roscoe Dunjee fought back against racial injustice through the pages of his newspaper, the *Black Dispatch,* founded in 1915, the same year the Oklahoma City Council passed an ordinance that made it illegal for a Black person to move north of Northeast 8th Street on the east side of the tracks. When courageous Black homeowners were arrested for violating racist codes, both by ordinance and through deed restrictions, Dunjee raised funds to defend them in court. In 1920 he led the effort to organize the first branch of the NAACP in Oklahoma, a crucial step in channeling individual outrage into communal action.[12]

After World War II, Dunjee and his allies in the NAACP knew it was time to assault the walls of segregation brick by brick. With the legal assistance of Thurgood Marshall, a young Black attorney hired through the NAACP, they chose the University of Oklahoma School of Law as the best target for testing the legal doctrine of "separate but equal." At the time, Blacks were forbidden by state statute to enroll at any institution of higher education in Oklahoma other than Langston University, a historically Black school that had been founded in 1897 as the Colored Agricultural and Normal University. As a sign of the times, when women were just beginning to demand destruction of the glass ceiling over their gender, Dunjee and Marshall selected a young woman from Chickasha to lead the charge. Her name was Ada Lois Sipuel.[13]

As expected, she was denied admission to the law school. First the district court and then the Oklahoma Supreme Court said that no Black person could attend an all-white college. The case was accepted for review by the U.S. Supreme Court, where a new generation of justices appointed after the New Deal days of the 1930s were ready to test "separate but equal." When it appeared that the Court would side with Sipuel, the University of Oklahoma enrolled her, but she was required to sit separately from the other students in both her classrooms and the cafeteria.[14]

In other states, efforts to bring down the walls of segregation were being mounted with varying degrees of success. The most famous of these was *Brown v. Board of Education of Topeka* in Kansas, which worked its way through the federal courts until it got to the Supreme Court, where the legality of *Plessy v. Ferguson,* the cornerstone of "separate but equal," was finally struck down. In Oklahoma, to make sure the brick that had been removed in the Sipuel case was not replaced by a legal or illegal sleight of hand, Dunjee and his allies encouraged another group of Black students to test the enrollment prohibition at the University of Oklahoma. One of those students was accepted into the master's program in the OU Department of History. Her name was Clara Luper.[15]

Born in Grayson, Oklahoma, an all-Black town in Okfuskee County, deep in the heart of the Muscogee (Creek) Nation, Luper grew up in an area with a unique cultural identity, blending the Black and Native culture of descendants from former slaves in the Indian nations and the culture of Blacks who had recently arrived from the Old South states of Texas, Louisiana, Arkansas, Mississippi, Alabama, and Georgia. In many ways, Okfuskee County was a melting pot of the American melting pot, flavored by a rich blend of African and Indian influences, including defiance in the face of adversity, perseverance in the face of hardships, and pride in its African heritage.[16]

Luper attended the local schools, which ironically benefited from segregation because the best teachers rising from the Black community could not go elsewhere to earn a living. She also was surrounded by the cultural legacy of the all-Black towns, where self-reliant farm families and successful merchants and professionals were a daily reminder that anything was possible, even in an unjust world intent on rationing only a small dose of freedom to an entire community because of their skin color. After high school she enrolled at Langston University, a short drive to the west from her home. In 1944 she earned her bachelor's degree in history and launched her long career as an educator. Limited in her options due to legal segregation of schools at the time, she taught at the high school in Spencer, a mostly Black town east of Oklahoma City. As a foreshadowing of her coming exploits, the name of the school would eventually be changed to Dunjee High.[17]

In 1957, with the victory in *Brown v. Board of Education* offering hope, combined with the spirit of nonviolent resistance preached by Dr. Martin Luther King Jr. and the local leadership of Roscoe Dunjee, Luper volunteered to be the advisor for the Oklahoma City NAACP Youth Council. One year later, after fruitless months spent petitioning and pleading with segregated white businesses to integrate, she and a group of her Youth Council members decided it was time for action. On August 19, 1958, they walked into a Katz Drug Store in downtown Oklahoma City, sat down at the counter, and politely ordered soft drinks. When they were denied service, they sat quietly in their seats until closing time, despite being taunted and threatened by the store's white customers. They repeated their sit-in for several days, until the Katz Drug Company made the decision to end its segregation policy—a move that opened its lunch counters to Black customers not only in Oklahoma, but in Missouri, Kansas, and Iowa as well.

Luper continued to lead sit-ins and boycotts in Oklahoma over the next six years, as she and the Youth Council waged a broader campaign to achieve integration. She would be arrested more than twenty times and suffer abuses at the hands of those who did not share her dream of equality, but she was unswerving in her determination to rally others to the cause. Upon her death in 2011, she was widely lauded for her lifetime of service in the fight for civil rights. "In some way, she has touched every life in the state of Oklahoma, whether they know it or not, because of her contributions, her persistence, her dedication to her fellow man," said Mike Shelton, who at the time was a member of the Oklahoma House of Representatives. "There aren't many people you can say that about." As an influential leader and an inspirational advocate in the pursuit of racial justice, she left an indelible mark on the rest of the country, too.[18]

Clara Luper was a trailblazer who helped to usher in a new era of Black activism in which young people were at the center rather than the periphery of the story. Only thirteen brave youth took part in that initial sit-in at the Katz Drug Store; in the years to come, however, thousands more would join the movement. Believing that even children could play a transformational role in the betterment of society, Luper galvanized the students she worked with to not simply follow adult leadership, but rather become leaders themselves. She showed them that they could refuse to accept injustice, refuse to accept oppression, and refuse to accept that nothing could be done to change the situation. The love and admiration that her students have for her to this day is her most impressive legacy and her most enduring impact. She taught young people how to love one another and how to love the world—even when that world pushed, shoved, and spat on them for demanding equal treatment.

A shining exemplar of what makes America great, Clara Luper is an inspiration to everyone who learns her story. To that end, we offer this Commemorative Edition of *Behold the Walls*, Luper's own account of her and her students' struggle for equal rights in Oklahoma. It has something of a raw quality at times, having been written in the vernacular and rushed directly to print by a determined white supporter. Readers familiar with the original edition will note several changes in this one. The original photos have been replaced by a different selection. We learned to our dismay that the original photographic prints are long lost, so we could not have reproduced those images with anything but the poorest quality. The photos appearing in this edition come from the Oklahoma Historical Society. "Clara's Calendar," which appeared in the earlier edition's appendix, has been omitted. It is an extensive time line and list of historical events, personages, and ephemera related to the civil rights struggle in Oklahoma and to the contributions of Black people to state, national, and world history. The editors were unable to confidently verify the accuracy of its contents in time for publication. Also, in a number of instances, the contents of the original edition's chapters and appendixes have been reorganized in order to keep information about the individual protests together, with the events presented in as close to chronological order as we could get them, and with Luper's occasional asides moved out of the main text into boxes. And of course the typos have been corrected, along with most of the previously misspelled names. All of Clara Luper's text in the chapters of the first edition has been retained—only now readers can read it in proper sequence. We made these modifications to ensure that the widest possible audience of contemporary readers would find the contents of *Behold the Walls* appealing, accurate, and accessible.

The informality and directness of Luper's writing impart a sense of immediacy that helps to convey her strength of spirit, organization, and tenacity. *Behold the Walls* is a testament and a testimony to how a Black woman was able to inspire a generation of young people and show them that they were capable of changing the world. Clara Luper stands tall in the pantheon of both Oklahoma's and America's history. This is her story, in her own words, and we are proud to share it with a new and larger audience.

Notes

1. Jana Hayes, "'My Mother Would Be Joyous,' Says Clara Luper's Daughter at Sit-In Monument Announcement," *Oklahoman*, March 24, 2022.

2. Michael Bruce, "Our Best Men Are Fast Leaving Us: The Life and Times of Robert M. Jones," *Chronicles of Oklahoma* 66 (Fall 1988); Joseph B. Thoburn and Muriel Wright, *Oklahoma: A History of the State and Its People* (New York: Lewis Historical Publishing Co., 1929).

3. Kenny Franks, "Implementation of the Confederate Treaties with the Five Civilized Tribes," *Chronicles of Oklahoma* 51 (Spring 1973).

4. Lary Rampp, "Negro Troop Activity in Indian Territory, 1863–1865," *Chronicles of Oklahoma* 47 (Spring 1969).

5. Rampp, "Negro Troop Activity."

6. Annie H. Abel, *The American Indian under Reconstruction* (Cleveland: Arthur H. Clark Co., 1925).

7. B. C. Franklin, *My Life and an Era: The Autobiography of Buck C. Franklin* (Baton Rouge: Louisiana State University Press, 1997).

8. Norman Crockett, *The Black Towns* (Lawrence: University Press of Kansas, 1979).

9. Jimmie Franklin, *The Blacks in Oklahoma* (Norman: University of Oklahoma Press, 1980).

10. Scott Ellsworth, *Death in a Promised Land: The Tulsa Race Riot of 1921* (Baton Rouge: Louisiana State University Press, 1982).

11. Randy Krehbiel, *Tulsa, 1921: Reporting a Massacre* (Norman: University of Oklahoma Press, 2019).

12. Bob Burke and Angela Monson, *Roscoe Dunjee, Champion of Civil Rights* (Edmond: University of Central Oklahoma Press, 1998).

13. Ada Lois Sipuel Fisher, with Danney Goble, *A Matter of Black and White: The Autobiography of Ada Lois Sipuel Fisher* (Norman: University of Oklahoma Press, 1996).

14. Fisher, *A Matter of Black and White.*

15. Carl Graves, "The Right to Be Served: Oklahoma City's Lunch Counter Sit-Ins, 1958–1964," *Chronicles of Oklahoma* 59 (Summer 1981).

16. Graves, "The Right to Be Served."

17. Graves, "The Right to Be Served."

18. Graves, "The Right to Be Served"; "Oklahoma Civil Rights Icon Clara Luper Dies at 88," Associated Press, June 9, 2011.

PURPOSE

The purpose of this book is to present in a straightforward, challenging way the true story of America's longest individual sit-ins and the involvements that followed.

The book is a combination of original text and interpretations felt at the time of the incidents.

It is focused on nonviolence and on a movement that is inextricably interwoven into the history and development of Oklahoma.

This book is intended for those who are seeking firsthand information through the eyes of those who were on the scene when it happened.

Finally, it is intended to renew our faith in people and in the God of the Universe. It is only through the Grace of God that my life has been spared in order that I could write this story.

Clara Luper

INTRODUCTION TO
THE FIRST EDITION

Jim Crow eating and sleeping accommodations and restrooms have had a long history in America. Blacks had attacked these situations, which in some states were by law and others by custom and tradition. Into these practices were quilted the deep convictions of Black inferiority and white supremacy. There was also a smothering deep-seated fear that if the Black man got too close to the white man, his mere presence would upset the family structure, which had been based on color. Some people believed that the white man saw in the Black man a sexual threat, which would seep out occasionally, only to be wiped into his skin as a good lotion. Segregation often soothed sexual inhibitions.

Businessmen had stereotyped unfounded fears of business losses, riots, improper conduct, and improper odors. Segregation in public accommodations was "too hot" for politicians. "Why commit political suicide?" they asked. The silence of the churches neutralized any religious protest against segregation in public accommodations.

Traveling by Blacks was indeed a headache. If Blacks traveled, they'd have to carry their lunches, buy cold snacks at grocery stores, find all-Black restaurants, or eat in the back of a white restaurant if they could find one that would serve them. Many stories have been told to me about traveling experiences; however, I never shall forget the one that Reverend Earl Jennings Perry, the pastor of Tabernacle Baptist Church, told me. He said that one time J. W. Sanford (the president of Langston University), George Ragland, Bill Hazley, Roscoe Dunjee, and O. M. Simmons were going to Texas, and they decided to stop in the southern part of Oklahoma to eat. Mr. Simmons and Bill Hazley decided to pass for white; Roscoe Dunjee wrapped his head and passed as an Indian chief; and J. W. Sanford, the darkest one, posed as the chauffeur. Simmons went in and talked to the white restaurant owner and told him that they wanted steaks, but their chauffeur would have to eat, too. The restaurant owner said, "That's all right, we can arrange that." J. W. Sanford saw Simmons returning and jumped out to open the door for Mr. Simmons and Roscoe Dunjee. They went in and accepted all the courtesies that were reserved for whites.

When they were seated, the waitress handed the menu to Roscoe Dunjee, and Bill Hazley said, "Chief no speak English." Bill Hazley read the menu and ordered for the group. At the conclusion of the meal, the waitress handed the bill to Roscoe Dunjee. He turned the bill over to J. W. Sanford, who was posing as the chauffeur, and the chauffeur paid it.

Thomas Bridges said that when he was a kid, he took a lawn mower and went out looking for yards to cut in order to earn a dime to attend a segregated movie. He stopped at a drug store on Northeast Fourth and Lindsay Street in Oklahoma City when the weather was hot and ordered a small Coke. The waitress put a straw in it. He handed her a dime and sat down on the stool and started sipping his Coke. A white man appeared out of the back, snatched the Coke out of his hand, threw the cup in the wastebasket, and said, "Niggers can't sit in here. Niggers have to drink outside!" as he pushed Thomas out the door.

A Black couple traveling through Oklahoma in 1957 stopped in Chandler and asked to be locked up in jail in order that they could sleep during a stormy night.

There were only two restrooms in the downtown area in Oklahoma City that Blacks could use in 1957. Both were segregated. One was located at the Union Bus Station and the other in the basement of the county courthouse.

At Tinker Air Force Base, three Black airmen filed a complaint with the NAACP Youth Council in an effort to find "just any place where they could eat in Midwest City."

It was against the law in Oklahoma for Blacks and whites to use the same telephone booths if there was a demand for separate booths.

It was against the law for Blacks and whites to use the same bath-houses in coal mines.

These are just a few of the walls that Blacks had seen, and now the whole world would see the walls.

PROLOGUE
The Restaurant Story

Once upon a time, a big restaurant owner made a bargain with a man who needed a job. He said, "There are two big jobs to be done here Saturday. Somebody is going to have to attend to the money, and somebody is going to have to stay on the door, hold the chain, and keep this city from becoming a democratic city. I'll take care of the money and I'll stay in the office, so you get on that door and keep the Negroes out."

"Yes, sir," replied the worker.

The boss sat in the office and worried. He worried because he couldn't help but remember. He remembered his childhood, and how a Negro maid had taken care of him and ministered to his every need. He worried about democracy, which the Negro children believed in and which he had always thought he believed in. He found temporary consolation when he remembered that he had once helped a Negro and that some of his best friends were Negroes. He could no longer sit still. His worry continued, and now he called it "The Negro Problem."

The boss rushed to his guard and screamed, "You know you are superior to them! Stand on the door, guard the chain, the rope, and keep them out! That's the only way you can prove it, is to stand on the door and keep them out. They can read as well as you; they are college graduates and represent all classes and occupations. One of them represents us at the United Nations. That makes no difference. You are still superior to them. So stay on that door. The only way you can prove that the whites are superior is to stay on that door and keep the Negroes out!"

The worker looked at the boss and nervously spoke: "But the whites pass by and scream at me and—"

"And nothing!" the boss answered. "Listen! You hear me, the only way you can be superior is to stand on that door and keep these Negro children out."

"But, boss, there are some whites with them. What shall I do with them?"

"Oh, God! Why did they come? Oh! What shall I do?"

"But, boss, they are white!"

"I tell you, keep them out! Keep them out! Keep them out! They aren't white, they are demonstrators! We are superior! We are superior! I know it! I know it!"

"Who told you, boss?"

"Why, why, the members of the Restaurant Association! Why, these restaurants are our private businesses, yet we have public license. We advertise over the radio and in the newspapers. Negroes shouldn't listen to radios or read about our places. These are ours, and we are superior. I'm superior, you are superior! We won the wars, we built the bridges, we cleared the forests. We wrote the Constitution!

"Oh, you know, I believe I'm lying, but anyway, you stay on that door, and if you don't keep those Negroes and demonstrators out, YOU ARE FIRED!"

1

THE OKLAHOMA CITY
NAACP YOUTH COUNCIL

The NAACP Youth Council members had congregated at my house, located at 1819 Northeast Park Place in Oklahoma City, Oklahoma. It was August 19, 1958. The long, hot summer's heat seemed endurable in the small five-room white frame house, but the mosquitoes were in complete control outside, and the youngsters remained inside, where they, with sweat on their faces, held their weekly meetings. Gwendolyn Fuller, president of the council, was presiding. Ruth Tolliver and I were in the kitchen preparing grape Kool-Aid and lunchmeat sandwiches.

There was no advisor–Youth Council membership relationship then. It was a far deeper feeling that I had for the NAACP Youth Council members. I had watched them grow up from infancy. I had seen their minds develop and the values that they would carry through their lives change. I knew their parents and knew how much their parents loved them. I knew how unpopular it was to have your children involved in the Youth Council's activities. It was even more difficult to get adults involved in the council.

This was not the first NAACP Youth Council to operate in Oklahoma City. Mrs. Lucille McClendon had worked untiringly with a group some years before. Nonparticipation and nonsupport had spelled doom for the Youth Council then. Through the leadership of John B. White and the insistence of Mr. and Mrs. D. J. Diggs and others, I had decided to take over the responsibility of reorganizing the Oklahoma City NAACP Youth Council. The fact that I was teaching American history at Dunjee High School in Spencer, Oklahoma, and was a member of the Fifth Street Baptist Church furnished me with an ample number of young people who would become the nucleus of the Youth Council. William Miles, a student from Dunjee School, had been elected as the first president.

Each year at school, I would present plays during Negro History Week, as it was called then. In 1957 I presented *Brother President*, the story of Martin Luther King Jr. and the nonviolent techniques that were used to eliminate segregation in Montgomery, Alabama. The cast consisted of twenty-six students, who were all talented, ambitious, and dedicated. The leading characters were William Miles, Joseph Hill, and Maxine Dowdell. This play filled the auditorium at Dunjee High School and drew tremendous turnouts all over the state.

In 1957, it was presented at the East Sixth Street Christian Church, where Herbert Wright, the national youth director of the NAACP, was in attendance. He was so impressed with the play that he invited me to present it in New York City at a "Salute to Young Freedom Fighters" rally. He agreed to pay the main characters' expenses; however, I thoroughly understood the financial plight of the NAACP's national office, and we worked out a compromise. We would raise the money for transportation, and he would take care of our hotel and food bill in New York City.

Reverend J. S. Sykes, a very active CME minister; Mr. A. Willie James, the number-one NAACP membership writer; and Doc Williams, a well-known bondsman and real estate dealer, helped me raise $1,895 in order that we could make the trip. The Oklahoma City community responded rapidly and shared in our adventure.

The cast of *Brother President*, most of whom had never been out of Oklahoma City, stopped in St. Louis for dinner and experienced their first integrated lunch counter service. This they continued to enjoy and appreciate on the trip. Words are inadequate to describe the expressions and actions of young people who, by tradition and custom, had been separated by the strong visible walls of segregation.

The group stayed at the Henry Hudson Hotel in New York City, and the play was presented in both Manhattan and Harlem. The youth met freedom fighters from the South, and the excitement and adventure of such a trip had a permanent effect on their lives.

In planning the trip, we decided to go the northern route and return by the southern route. On our return trip, we stopped in Washington, D.C., and visited the top historical spots, including Arlington National Cemetery. As we stood in the cemetery and watched the changing of the guard, each youth had an opportunity to think about freedom. One asked, "What do you think would happen in this country if the Unknown Soldier's casket were opened and they found out that he was Black?" Joan Johnson said, "I don't know."

Barbara Posey, the secretary of the Youth Council, told the group that since all of these people had died for our freedom, "we need to really get busy and do something for our country. Yes, these people who are buried at Arlington Cemetery did all they could for freedom. I don't think the color of the Unknown Soldier's skin is important. I think it's what he did, and we have to do something."

Silently the group left Arlington Cemetery, after pledging that they would do something for their country, and loaded onto the Greyhound bus. As the bus headed southward, the walls of segregation became so visible. In Nashville, Tennessee, the bus driver admitted that he did not know of any place where Blacks could sit down and eat. So paper-sack lunches became the order of the day through Tennessee, Arkansas, and into Oklahoma.

John White's words "The Sooner State: the sooner we get rid of segregation, the better off we'll be" were repeated continuously by the group. "You know segregation just doesn't fit in with my personality," William Miles said with a quick smile that faded back to a face of solemnity. The group applauded with loud outbursts of "Freedom now! Freedom now!"

Back in Oklahoma City, the group decided to break down segregation in public accommodations for all time and pay any price for it. "That will be our project—to eliminate segregation in public accommodations," they said. A strategy was worked out, where the public accommodations' owners and managers would be approached directly by a small delegation. There was never to be over three in the delegation, and Mrs. Caroline Burks, a stately freedom-loving white woman, was to accompany the groups on all occasions. This she did with a dedication that was followed up with letters and personal visits. This campaign was followed by a direct private approach to the city manager and City Council, who told the group, "We are sorry, we do not have the power to interfere in private businesses. We don't tell the businessmen who to serve, and they don't tell us how to run our city government."

The campaign turned into a letter-writing campaign to churches, but the white church leaders turned a deaf ear, as their beautiful buildings stood as monuments to their dedication to Christianity. The Black churches did not want to get involved at this time and told us that we could meet in their churches. They would take up a collection for us and make announcements concerning our worthwhile activities.

The meeting continued with a warmup chanting rally. The group chanted:

We want to EAT—eat!
We want to EAT—eat!
NOW! NOW! NOW!
We don't want any more excuses!
We want to E-A-T—eat!
We want to E-A-T—eat!
NOW! NOW! NOW!

Gwendolyn Fuller leaned back in her chair and looked at the group as the singing and clapping grew louder and louder. Barbara Posey, the spokesman for the Public Accommodations Committee, made her report. "The owners of all public accommodations in Oklahoma City say they will not serve Blacks. Now what are we going to do?"

Marilyn Luper spoke out: "I'll tell you, Barbara. I move that we go down to Katz Drug Store and sit down and drink a Coke."

"I second the motion," said Areda Tolliver.

The motion was carried unanimously by the group.

"When shall we go?" the group asked as if in a choir.

"Gwen, let me tell you, you know that I made the motion to go, and I feel that I should have the privilege of deciding when we should go," said Marilyn.

A silence fell over the meeting, and after a few minutes, with Marilyn staring into the future, she said, "Tonight is the time, and as I read in Mr. Wisener's typing book, 'Now is the time for all good men to come to the aid of their party.'"

"That doesn't mean that we will have to go tonight!" shouted Calvin.

A brother-sister debate occurred, and in a high-toned voice Calvin said, "Don't you ever think that I'm afraid to go!"

Barbara Posey said, "We have waited for over fifteen months, and Oklahoma has waited fifty years. Let's go down and wait in front of the manager so that people can see our problem."

Portwood Williams Jr. said, "The men in the NAACP Youth Council are ready to go right now, and we are able to take care of any situation."

"We wouldn't doubt that," Gwendolyn said, and a bit of laughter sparkled in the air and echoed back into moments of silence.

Barbara Posey was recognized by the president, Gwendolyn Fuller, and she said, "We had better see what Mrs. Luper thinks. After all, she is the youth advisor."

I could feel the eyes of the members on me. I thought for a brief moment and traced the steps that we had taken. We had been *patient*, and I saw in the children's eyes reflections of my restless childhood, when I wanted to do something about a system that had paralyzed my movements and made me an outsider in my own country. Yet these were children whose ages ranged from seven to fifteen years old.

I thought about my father, who had died in 1957 in the Veterans' Hospital, and who had never been able to sit down and eat a meal in a decent restaurant. I remembered how he used to tell us that someday he would take us out to dinner and to parks and zoos. And when I asked him when was someday, he would always say, "Someday will be real soon" as tears ran down his cheeks. So my answer was, "Yes, tonight is the night. History compels us to go, and let history alone be our final judge."

We had another problem: we didn't have any transportation. Ruth Tolliver and I discussed the situation and decided to call three people who we knew wouldn't turn us down. Portwood Williams Sr., Lillian Oliver, and Mary Pogue were selected.

I called Portwood Williams first. He lived in the next block. Mr. Williams was a talkative man with a sharp tongue, a quick wit, and an adequate supply of words. He said, "I want to volunteer to drive car number one down to Katz Drug Store. My car is clean and ready. I don't blame you. I shined Mr. Charlie's shoes, and my mother washed Miss Ann's clothes. Now I'm an upholsterer, the best in town, and my car is ready. I'll be there."

My next call was to Mrs. Lillian Oliver, a tall, quiet, dignified schoolteacher, and one who had served as an assistant NAACP Youth Council advisor. I had known her since 1940, and through the years we had been very close friends. I told her that I needed another car to take the NAACP youth down to Katz Drug Store. She didn't ask any questions. She said, "I'll be there in a few minutes. If you all are crazy enough to go, I'm crazy enough to take you!"

Lillian Oliver's cousin, Mrs. Grace Daniels, had related some of her experiences in Phoenix, Arizona, to the group, and as I put the telephone down, I thought about Grace and how proud she would be of us. Lillian would have to call and tell her that we had started a direct-action campaign. I walked out on the porch, where the kids were singing "I want to be ready to sit for freedom, just like John."

I hurried back into the house and called Mary Pogue, the mother of two of the youth. I knew that she would make me explain everything to her in detail . . . and she did! After I had finished, she said, "I'll be there in a few minutes."

I put the telephone down and heard it ring again. I had a feeling that it was my mother, and I knew that it was not the proper time for me to tell her what we were going to do. I picked up the telephone and she said, "I just called to see if the NAACP youth meeting was over." I said, "No, Mother, it is not over. In fact, we are just beginning." She said, "Well, Clara, don't keep the kids up too late. You know, tomorrow . . ." I said, "Yes, Mother, I'm going to take you downtown to eat for your birthday," which was only two days away. She said, "Clara, you aren't going to take me anywhere tomorrow. I'm not thinking about those white folks. What day is tomorrow, anyway? Well, Clara, we won't worry about it, for tomorrow is just another day." I said, "Yes, Mama, tomorrow is just another day."

I rushed out of my house, and on the still, hot night of August 19, 1958, we headed to Katz Drug Store in the heart of Oklahoma City. I went to the three cars and called the following names: Richard Brown, Elmer Edwards, Linda Pogue, Lana Pogue, Areda Tolliver, Calvin Luper, Marilyn Luper, Portwood Williams Jr., Lynzetta Jones, Gwendolyn Fuller, Alma Faye Posey, Barbara Posey, Goldie Battle, and Betty Germany.

2

UNDERSTANDING
NONVIOLENCE

Are we ready to behold the walls, nonviolently?

All the way downtown, I wondered if we were really ready for a nonviolent war.

For eighteen months, the members of the NAACP Youth Council had been studying nonviolence as a way of overcoming injustices. Basically, the doctrine of nonviolence is rooted in the fundamental truth that whites are human. Being human, they will probably react with fear if they are threatened, but in the final analysis, they are likely to respond with goodwill. The white man's reaction may be one of surprise because we aren't answering injustices with injustices. He may then become angry because we are not. Then he may attempt to provoke us in a desperate attempt to incite us to violence.

He will become very suspicious and think that we are trying to make him do something that traditions and customs have taught him not to do. He recognizes that Blacks are in the minority and that our belief in nonviolence stems from weakness, and therefore he proceeds to take advantage of us. But gradually, if we have the tenacity to hold on to our nonviolent approach, the white man will gain respect for us. We aren't defeating him, we'll just be removing his hostility and insecurities, which will prepare him to function as a whole man in a democratic society.

Four basic rules had been used. First, we had defined our objective: to eliminate segregation in public accommodations. Second, we had to be honest: "Nonviolence is not an approach to be used by hypocrites—honesty pays!" Third, you must love your enemy: "A doctrine as old as time, but as newsworthy as this hour's news story. You are to remember that you aren't up against a deep-eyed monster, you are up against a man who has been handed an overdose of segregation and who knows that segregation is wrong, yet he practices it. You are not to ridicule, humiliate, nor vilify him at any time or in any way. Keep your goal in sight; you aren't out to defeat him, you are out to establish justice." Fourth, give the white man a way out. Nonviolence demonstrates a kind of strength that shows up the weakness of injustices. Recognize that he has weaknesses and can be embarrassed for mistreating his brother. Find a way to let him participate in victory when it comes.

For over a year, the four strategic steps in nonviolence had been used and had been reviewed over and over again. The steps were investigation, negotiation, education, and demonstration. Investigation: Get the facts. Make sure that an injustice has been done. A nonviolent approach will fail if it is based on false or shaky assumptions. Negotiation: Go to your opponent and put the case directly to him. It may be that a solution could be worked out and that there could be a grievance that we don't know about. Let the opponent know that you are going to stand firm in order that you'll be ready to negotiate anywhere and anytime. Education: Make sure that the group is well informed on the *issues*. Men have always hated change, yet change must come. Demonstration: This is the final step, only to be taken when all others have failed. Nonviolent demonstration calls for discipline that is firm. Every provocation must be answered with continued goodwill. You must be ready for self-sacrifice, which will leave no doubt as to your integrity, your dignity, and your self-respect. Suffering is part of the nonviolent approach. It is to be endured, never inflicted. This approach will give you the *moral* victory upon which the eternal struggle for freedom, justice, and equality can be won.

So nonviolently, we were on our way to Katz Drug Store.

Katz Drug Store was located on the southwest corner of Main Street and Robinson Avenue in downtown Oklahoma City. It was a center of activity, with its first-class pharmacy department, unique gifts, toys, and lunch counter. Blacks were permitted to shop freely in all parts of the store. They could order sandwiches and drinks to go. Orders were placed in a paper sack and were to be eaten in the streets.

This was the kind of wall that the older people should have taken on years earlier instead of financing this type of treatment. This was the kind of battle that the white Christians or the Jewish brothers should have fought. Maybe this was the kind of battle that the atheists should have fought. And now these thirteen little children could have been enjoying an evening at home with their parents.

As I was thinking about what should have been done, Lana Pogue, the six-year-old daughter of Mr. and Mrs. Louis J. Pogue, grabbed my hand, and we moved toward the counter. All my life, I had wanted to sit at those counters and drink a Coke or a Seven-Up—it really didn't matter which—but I had been taught that those seats were "for whites only." Blacks were to sweep around the seats and keep them clean so whites could sit down. It didn't make any difference what kind of white person it was—thief, rapist, murderer, uneducated; the only requirement was that he or she be white. Unbathed, unshaven—it just didn't make any difference. Nor did it make any difference what kind of Black you were: B.A. degree Black, Dr. Black, Attorney Black, Reverend Black, M.A. Black, Ph.D. Black, rich Black, poor Black, young Black, old Black, pretty Black, ugly Black; you were not to sit down at any lunch counter to eat. We were all seated now in the "for whites only" territory. The waitresses suffered a quick psychological stroke, and one said in a mean tone, "What do you all want?"

Barbara Posey spoke. "We'd like thirteen Cokes, please."

"You may have them to go," the waitress nervously said.

"We'll drink them here," Barbara said as she placed a five-dollar bill on the counter. The waitress nervously called for additional help.

Mr. Masoner, the red-faced, frightened-looking manager, rushed over to me as if he were going to slap me and said, "Mrs. Luper, you know better than this. You know we don't serve colored folks at the counter." I remained silent and looked him straight in the eyes as he nervously continued, "I don't see what's wrong with you colored folks. Mrs. Luper, you take these children out of here this moment! This moment, I say." He yelled, "Did you hear me?"

"Thirteen Cokes, please," I said.

"Mrs. Luper, if you don't move these colored children, what do you think my white customers will say? You know better, Clara. I don't blame the children! I blame you. You are just a troublemaker."

He turned and rushed to the telephone and called the police. In a matter of minutes, we were surrounded by policemen of all sizes, with all kinds of facial expressions. The sergeant and the manager had a conference; additional conferences were called as different ranks of policemen entered. Their faces portrayed their feelings of resentment. The press arrived, and I recognized Leonard Hanstein of channel 9 with his camera. I sat silently as they threw him out along with a whole crew of cameramen.

The whites who were seated at the counter got up, leaving their food unfinished, and emptied their hate terms into the air—things such as "Niggers go home!" "Who do they think they are?" "The nerve!" One man walked straight up to me and said, "Move, you black S.O.B." Others bent over to cough in my face and in the faces of the children. Linda Pogue was knocked off a seat. She smiled and sat back down on the stool. Profanity flowed evenly and forcefully from the crowd. One elderly lady rushed over to me as fast as she could with her walking cane in her hand and yelled, "The nerve of the niggers trying to eat in our places. Who does Clara Luper think she is? She is nothing but a damned fool, the black thing."

I started to walk over and tell her that I was one of God's children and He had made me in His own image, and if she didn't like how I looked, she was filing her complaint in the wrong department. She'd have to file it with the Creator. I'm the end product of His creation and not the maker. Then I realized her intellectual limitations and continued to watch the puzzled policemen and the frightened manager.

Tensions were building as racial slurs continued to be thrown at us. Hamburgers, Cokes, malts, etc., remained in place as pushing, cursing, and "nigger" became the "order of the day."

As the news media attempted to interview us, the hostile crowd increased in number. Never before had I seen so many hard, hate-filled white faces. Lana, the six-year-old, asked, "Why do they look so mean?"

I said, "Lana, their faces are as cold as Alaskan icicles."

As I sat quietly there that night, I prayed and remembered our nonviolent philosophy. I pulled out what we called Martin Luther King's Nonviolent Plans and read them over and over:

First, resist the evil of segregation in a passive, nonviolent way. We must refuse to cooperate with injustice; we shall not pay to be insulted. Segregation is an evil, it is contrary to the will of God, and when we support or submit to segregation, we are condoning an evil. Every man has a right and a personal responsibility to ignore certain local laws when they are contrary to the Constitution of the United States, no matter what the consequences are.

Second: Use the weapon of love in our everyday relations. Violence must be avoided at all costs. We must not fight back. We must resist peacefully and in a spirit of love. I mean the highest form of love—that love that seeketh nothing in return.

Third: We must mobilize for an all-out fight for first-class citizenship. We must have leaders who live first-class citizenship as a symbol. We must have slogans, for we will have to make these rights simple and understandable, so that they will filter into the hearts and minds of the people.

Fourth: We must get out the vote. The chief weapon of the Negro is the ballot. None of these other privileges will mean anything unless we also get the power of the ballot. We must vote and teach our children to vote.

Fifth: We must continue the legal and legislative fight. We must continue our struggles in the courts, and above all things, we must remember to support the National Association for the Advancement of Colored People. We must ever keep in mind that our major victories have come through the work of this great organization. At the same time, we must support other organizations that are molding public opinion.

Sixth: The Church must be awakened to its responsibility. Religion is the chief avenue to the minds and the souls of the masses. The masses go to church; they listen to the minister; they have a great deal of respect for him. The minister, more than anyone else, has the ear of the people. The ministers must be awakened to their responsibilities, for the individual Negro must hold on to the one thing that has made them great: their "spiritual genius." There is still hope; we must not give up, but we must push on.

Seventh: We must close the gap between the classes and the masses, for we are laboring to eliminate this existing evil. Therefore, it is imperative that the people—professionals, ministers, laborers, and all citizens—work together to achieve this freedom.

Last but not least, we must be prepared. We must prepare ourselves skillfully and intellectually to live in an integrated society. Whatever you as American citizens choose as your life's work, do it well. Do not be content with a job that is half done. Do your job so well that all the hosts of heaven and earth will say, "Here lived a man who did his job as though God Almighty had called him at this particular moment in history to do it." Be not afraid, for God being with us is more than all of the world against us.

As I folded the paper, I looked up and saw a big, burly policeman walking toward me. When he got within two feet of me, another officer called him to the telephone. I wondered why the policeman had to stand over us. We had no weapons, and the only thing we wanted was thirteen Cokes that we had the money to pay for.

Amid the cursing, I remembered the words of Professor Watkins, my elementary principal and teacher in Hoffman, Oklahoma. He had told us to "always consider the source."

There were some Blacks entering the drug store. I saw some of the cooks and janitors. I opened my purse and wrote,

When the time comes for cooking the food, Blacks are all right.
   When the time comes for washing the dishes, Blacks are all right.
   But when the time comes to sit down and eat, the Blacks are all wrong, and that's not neat.

My daughter, Marilyn, walked over and pointed out a big, fat, mean-looking white man, who walked over to me and said, "I can't understand it. You all didn't use to act this way; you all used to be so nice." We remained silent, and as he bumped into me, the police officers told him that he had to move on. An old white woman walked up to me and said, "If you don't get those poor little old ugly-looking children out of here, we are going to have a race riot. You just want to start some trouble." I remained silent. "Don't you know about the Tulsa race riots?" the woman asked.

I moved down to the south end of the counter, then back to the other end. This was repeated over and over. As I passed by Alma Faye Posey, she burst out laughing, and when I continued to look at her, she put her hands on the counter and pointed to a picture of a banana split.

It had been a long evening. Barbara, Gwen, and I had a quick conference, and we decided to leave without cracking a dent in the wall. Mr. Portwood Williams, Mrs. Lillian Oliver, and Mrs. Mary Pogue were waiting. We loaded in our cars and left the hecklers heckling.

We had passed our first test. They had pushed us, called us niggers, and did everything, the group said.

"Look at me, I'm really a nonviolent man," Richard Brown yelled. "Look at me. I can't believe it myself."

Small details of events were written out by Goldie Battle, and it was not easy to make plans for the next day because of the large number of obscene telephone calls and threats that I was receiving. The call that really caught me unexpectedly came from a Black man who would not tell me his name, but he did tell me how good the white folks had been to him and that I was disgracing my race by taking those poor innocent children downtown.

"Sir, do you have any recommendation on what we can do to eat downtown?" I asked.

He said, "No, I do not."

I said, "Then I have one for you, sir."

"Okay."

"I said, "Sir, since the white folks are so good to you, where do you urinate when you are dressed up in your fine suit downtown?"

He said, "I take my can with me."

"Then, sir, I feel that it is time for you to go and empty your can."

Another Black caller said she was so embarrassed that she could hardly hold her head up.

One Black lady said that she was working out in Nichols Hills, and the lady she was working for told her to look at what those people were doing and asked her, "Do you know them?" She said that she answered no. She continued to do her work, and when she got home she called me. I had never talked to my friend when she was in such a state of fright.

To my surprise, my mother and Mary Pogue came up to the house and explained to me all the dangers that I had gotten "all of us" in. Mary had taken us downtown, but she said, "Oh, it was awful. Those people mean business. You should have heard the things they were saying about you." The conversation continued until finally they went home.

As the crowd left my house, I hurried to bed and slept as soundly as a log.

The robins reminded me that it was another day. The telephone started ringing, mostly hate calls. Then Mary Pogue, my mother, Mrs. Pearl Chiles, and Ruth Tolliver called. They were all saying, "Be careful, Clara—please be careful."

As the calls continued to come in, I wondered if the kids would return. What were their parents saying? Would the parents be afraid of reprisals? Would there be violence today?

"Well," Reverend W. K. Jackson said in a sermon, "if you believe that you are right, go on and God will take care of you. Let His will be done."

I couldn't believe it: the kids were all back, along with new ones, including Edmund Atkins, Robert Lambeth, Elmer Smith, James Arthur Edwards, Carolyn Edwards, Henry Rolfe Jr., Leon Chandler, Willie Johnson, Arnetta Carmichael, Thomas Taylor, David Irving, and Theresa Scruggs. Cars were lining up in front of my house. I had calls from Rolfe Funeral Home, Temple Funeral Home, and McKay Funeral Home. They sent cars over to take the children downtown. Blanche, the owner of Blanche's Drive-In, called to say, "Clara, I'll send some food and anything you need."

We all started jumping up and down, for truly, "This was the beginning, oh no, it was not the beginning, it was the continuation of man's desperate struggle to be free, and Oklahoma City would never be the same." I joined the freedom band, and we all began to sing:

I want to be ready,
I want to be ready,
I want to be ready
To walk for freedom
Just like John!

In two days, the walls had fallen, and not only at Katz in Oklahoma City. Katz, billed as the world's leading cut-rate drug store, announced that all thirty-eight of its outlets in Missouri, Oklahoma, Kansas, and Iowa would serve all people regardless of race, creed, or color. No longer could anyone go to a Katz Drug Store and say, "Behold the walls!"

We had to talk about "our yesterday" at Katz Drug Store. Yesterday, when Gregory Pogue became the first Black to eat at Katz. (His order was delivered first. Some of the children had waited so long that they had forgotten what they wanted.)

"This is just great. It's not the food, it's the feeling. I just feel good inside," Theresa Scruggs said.

Mr. Leslie Brown, A. Willie James, Dr. E. C. Moon Jr., and a committee had collected the money to pay for our food. Willie James had been appointed as the NAACP youth financial advisor, and he took on the job with a witty smile and a strong determination.

Barbara reminded the group, "We have just begun; we must break down every wall that will keep Blacks from eating in Oklahoma City. As you all know, we selected five places—Katz, Veazey's, Kress, John A. Brown's, and Green's. I need three volunteers to go over to Veazey's." I agreed to be one of the three.

We walked across the street and were met at the door of Veazey's Drug Store by the manager.

"How are you today?"

"We're fine, sir."

"I'm happy that you all came over. We are very proud. Our management met yesterday and decided to change our policy. Our new policy states that the eating facilities at Veazey's Drug Store are open to all people."

We thanked him, sat down, ordered a soft drink, tipped the waitress twice as much as we were supposed to, and left. The rest of the group was still standing across the street, where they had been ready to move en masse to Veazey's to stage a demonstration.

Victory number two: Veazey's had opened its door. We must now go to target number three, S. H. Kress. Richard Brown yelled, "I can hardly wait to sit down in one of those fine soft-looking seats at Kress." As he spoke, he pointed to the part of his body that would occupy the seat and went through an imitation of how he'd sit.

"What are you going to order?" Calvin asked, with a burst of hearty laughter.

"French fries, a super hamburger, and some limeade," answered Richard in a proper imitationish manner.

"Shut up, Richard, you know colored folks don't drink limeade. Why don't you go on and order some red soda pop and a cold slice of watermelon," James Arthur Edwards said.

"Listen, boy," Richard shouted, "stop messing with me. I'm tired. You order what you want and I'll order what I want. Will you do me a special favor? Don't sit at my table when we get to Kress, you'll spoil my appetite."

Before James could answer, a signal was given by Barbara that meant silence, and we moved westward with a large number of uniformed officers into S. H. Kress.

As we entered, we were surprised because all of the chairs and tables had been removed. The manager came forward, grinning like a grinning champion. He spoke with a great deal of enthusiasm and said, "You all are welcome."

"Welcome to what?" I asked in a sharp voice.

"You are welcome to stand and be served like everyone else."

His face began to turn red as we looked at him. I felt as if I were looking clear through him. His head slowly began to turn toward the floor.

I turned to the children and said, "This is vertical integration, and from this day forward let's remember this store in a vertical manner. And since we are all standing, we cannot horizontally hand our money to any clerk for anything. Let's go to John A. Brown's."

Peggy Cosby, Doris Powell, Charles Reed, Larry Turner, and Carl Summers said, "We are ready," and the other youth followed Barbara Posey, Gwendolyn Fuller, and me into John A. Brown's Department Store.

3

JOHN A. BROWN'S

It was August 22, 1958, and we were on our way to the luncheonette in the basement of John A. Brown's. We had renewed hope and courage from the victories that we had already won. I knew that Brown's would welcome us with open arms. The John A. Brown Company was the largest department store in Oklahoma and had a large number of Black customers. A package from Brown's was a prestigious item.

A funny thing happened to me at the very moment that I walked into the store. Ninety-five percent of the times that I had gone downtown, I had gone to John A. Brown's, and yet now I felt as if I had never been there before. The clerks that I had known through the years stood as if they were frozen in their tracks. I felt as if I were behind an iron curtain and the clerks of yesterday had become my enemies. One clerk stuck out her tongue at me and made an ugly face. We continued to walk through the shoe department and took seats in the luncheonette.

We were immediately harassed by a white woman who had the strangest voice and mannerisms that I had ever encountered. "Who is she?" I asked. "Where did she come from? Am I in John A. Brown's or in the lion's den?"

Gwendolyn Fuller said, "Mrs. Luper, we aren't in the lion's den. I think that we are in hell."

This was not a sit-in. It was a wall. We were all scared inside. As fear began to crowd my thoughts, I started walking back and forth. Zella Hull started humming "Joshua fought the battle of Jericho, and the walls came tumbling down." Before we knew it, we were all singing the songs of our forefathers, songs that had come from the plantations and were now warming our souls.

This day it was not a matter of a few people having a great deal of courage, it was a matter of all of us having just a little courage.

The fact that I had thought it would be ludicrously easy, only to be met by a stone wall, meant it looked to me as if a coalition had been formed between the customers and the management. One white customer walked up to the lunch counter and sat down in the lap of Sallye Harris, a seven-year-old girl. A policeman made the woman leave the store. A white man entered the luncheonette and started preaching race hatred; the policeman made him leave.

Time has a way of passing, and now it was time for Brown's to close. We left quietly, surrounded by a number of police officers who followed us to our cars.

On August 23, at 10:30 a.m., we arrived again at John A. Brown's luncheonette. We went directly to the booths and counter and sat quietly. The waitresses ignored us completely. We deliberately divided up so that we could have one Black at each counter. A few whites came in, shared the booths, ordered food, and were served. Each child had a magazine; Barbara Posey had asked the children to use this time for reading. Someday the doors to new opportunities would open, and we should be ready.

Mr. Frank Wade came in and asked for a conference with Barbara Posey. The conference, according to Barbara, turned out to be an ultimatum when he ordered her to ask "permission" to share booths with whites, and if the whites did not want the Blacks to sit with them, they would have to move. Wade shrugged his shoulders, yelled, "That's the way it's going to be from now on," and walked back into the luncheonette.

"Things are getting worse. Yesterday there were no seats at all, and now we're going to have to ask permission to sit down. It's pretty hard to take, but we are going to do it. How about that, Mrs. Luper?" Barbara asked.

I said, "Barbara, we have to stay on the job. Remember, Joshua fought the battle of Jericho."

When we arrived at Brown's luncheonette on August 26, eight tables were missing. We stood in line and watched the white patrons as they were shuttled through the cashier's line. A middle-aged white man was making faces at us. Finally he blew up and ran to Lieutenant Williams and to the white girls in the dining area. He was raving like a wild animal and pointed at us as Lieutenant Williams took him out and carried him down to the police station.

Ruth Tolliver stopped by my house and picked up my mail, which consisted of about twenty hate letters. I had received about forty threatening calls. A police officer rushed over to tell me that they had just received a call in which a man stated that he was going to bomb my house. I looked at Ruth, and she was crying. She and Areda had gotten up early and had come down to be with us. They had stayed and helped us late that night. I stood and prayed: "Oh, Lord, what have I done? Why would they bomb my house? I love my home. It's not a fancy house, but it's mine. Why won't they leave me alone? Only last week, they deposited a sack of shotgun shells on my porch with a KKK note. Earlier in the week, someone went into my house and burned some of my furniture, including Calvin's dresser, and left a hate letter. I can replace some old furniture and clothes. I just don't have time to worry about it now. I'll put it in file number 13."

Then I thought about my father, a veteran of World War I, and that early morning in 1957 when I took him to the Veterans' Hospital. I was getting ready to go to New York City to present *Brother President*, a play that I had written, and he was proud of me and my work with the NAACP. He told me how difficult his life had been, how he'd had to "Uncle Tom" in order to feed his family, and every time he had said "Yes, sir, Mr. Lackey," he was thinking of his children and grandchildren and how he didn't want them to "Uncle Tom" to anyone. He said that he didn't know how long he'd be with us, but when he died, he wanted me to have the flag that the U.S. government would give to my mother. "This shall be my last wish," he said. Ninety days from that day, he died, and that flag was mine.

I felt as if he were standing before me and that I could hear his words. I started crying. "Ruth, we've got to go home this minute. My flag! My flag is in my house, and if anyone would burn the flag that was on my father's casket, I'd kill them." Ruth was crying, too, and we both cried all the way to my house. Mr. Ed McQuirter, Mr. Stewart, Mr. and Mrs. Loudermilk, Mrs. Abrams, Mrs. Benson, Mrs. Ethel Edmondson, and Mrs. Mary Watson were watching my house. Dr. A. L. Dowell and Dr. Charles Atkins arrived a few minutes later. It had been broadcast on the radio that someone had threatened to bomb my house and that I had left Brown's, rushing home after my U.S. flag. Both Ruth and I were relieved when we saw that everything was all right. My neighbors put their arms around me and told me that I could go on back to John A. Brown's. They would stay there and continue to watch my house.

When Ruth and I returned to Brown's, a group of men from the American Legion, Veterans of Foreign Wars, and John Witherspoon from the JFK Chapter of the American Legion had arrived. They offered their support and pledged to do everything they could to prevent bombings and violence in Oklahoma City.

An elderly white woman came over and demanded to speak to me. I asked Ruth to come with me. The lady felt a contemptuous pity for me. I had learned how to watch white people, how to observe their expressions, how to observe their fears, and how to read between the lines as they spoke.

The lady spoke slowly and painfully. "I came because I want to put the flag that your father left you in my safe deposit box." She leaned toward me and said, "I'm your friend, Clara, and you might not know it, but you have a lot of white friends. But we can't do nothing. We're so helpless. Let me do this little thing for you. It's a big thing to me. Please, Clara, let me keep that flag."

Without a word, I handed her the flag.

"Thanks," she said triumphantly. She hugged me and gave me her name, address, and telephone number.

"Thanks" was all that I could say. I turned and walked back to the group, where I was flooded with questions.

"You have never seen her before, and yet you gave her your flag? Why?" James Woods asked.

"Just because I trust her."

He frowned and said, "I'm glad you trust her, because I don't."

"You're young. Someday you'll learn that all white people aren't like these that we see here every day."

"Go home, you ugly niggers!"

Eat!! Yes!! Yes!!
Home? No!! No!!

We were cursed and spit on, and coffee was poured on us, but we stayed at Brown's. On August 27, eighty-five Black youths arrived at the luncheonette. We stood all day because the employees had removed the chairs. Everybody was tense that day. Richard James Adams, a twenty-three-year-old white man, was arrested on a charge of disorderly conduct after he walked up to Darryl May, a fifteen-year-old Black sit-inner, and slugged him. John A. Brown's—Oklahoma born, Oklahoma owned, and Oklahoma managed—would become the Bunker Hill of the Sit-In Movement.

On August 30, white youths occupied all the seats and would yield their places only to other white customers.

So we began to plan an all-out concentrated effort to break down the wall at Brown's. This would be a long, hard fight. It was John A. Brown's every day, in some form or another. We were there at all hours and continued to use different kinds of protests. We sat on the floor and blocked aisles, but we were never arrested.

The Blacks who worked there were proud of us. They would tell us about conditions and attitudes that were developing. Roberta Sledge was our key reporter. Finally we were able to solicit some white support in different departments, who said that we were right and they were going to help us. However, they could not let the management know about it.

Some days we returned to Brown's with a large crowd, then other days there were just a few. We always knew that Linda Pogue, Areda Tolliver, Calvin Luper, Michael Clayton, Arnetta Carmichael, Sallye Harris, Richard Brown, Lana Pogue, Marilyn Luper, and Zella Hull would be there. The crowd would always increase on Saturdays.

Brown's provided daily conversations for Oklahoma. I knew that "What happened at Brown's today?" was the first thing I'd hear when I answered my telephone.

One morning a handsome Black soldier who had just stepped off an airplane from Southeast Asia came directly to Brown's. His uniform was covered with medals, pins, etc., that he had earned in combat duty. He said, "Things haven't changed, have they, Mrs. Luper?"

"No, things are just the same," I said.

"I promised myself if God would let me live through the Korean War, I'd come back home and enjoy this democracy. If it's worth fighting for in Southeast Asia, it is worth fighting for in Oklahoma," the soldier stated as he stared at the children who were standing in line waiting to be served.

"Yes, everything is the same," I said. "Blacks are still segregated against. Things are just like they were when you left. We have been a victorious nation everywhere but at home. We are a re-enslaved people in a free country."

"I have to go to the Veterans' Hospital. I've got some bad health problems. But I want you to take this twenty-dollar bill and feed the children today."

As I looked into his dark eyes, I noticed that they were filled with tears. Then he broke down and cried.

Others came to talk. One Black couple talked to me. The man spoke first. He said that every time his wife went downtown, she would always go to John A. Brown's to shop. "Yes, Brown's has everything. I especially like the hats, and their clearance sales are terrific," the lady said. "Every month my charge account is sky high. Now look at us, and here's my seven-year-old grandchild standing down here in the one store where I have spent my salary as fast as Tinker Field could pay me."

A Black widow whose husband had died in Korea came down and told me how difficult it was for her to tell her son that his father had been killed in the war. "I told him about the day his father left to fight for his country. I was angry at him. I couldn't understand why any Black man would volunteer to fight for a country where Black people have no rights. When he went to volunteer, he had to ride downtown on the back seat of a bus. He couldn't get promoted on his job. He was on the dead-end street along with all the other Blacks. Our children had to be bused from one county to another to attend school. We couldn't go to any movies, restaurants, or anything, and he volunteered. I prayed that he'd change his mind. I cried, but it didn't do any good. The day he left, he said, 'Lucille, I know how you feel, but this is my country and I love it. I know things are not like we would like them to be, but if I go, things will be better for my children and their children.' Mrs. Luper, I never saw him again, and look where we are today," she said.

At John A. Brown's, the sit-ins continued, and we listened.

Some of the white students from Central High School came down after school for some hamburgers and Cokes just to show us that if we were white, we could eat and no one would question us. "Don't you wish you were white, so you could eat at Brown's?" they said.

"No," Lynzetta Jones said. "I don't want to be white, I just want to be free."

The sit-ins at John A. Brown's started out like a splash in a summer pool. They became like a tornado on a quiet, cloudy spring day. They were now bringing fear to the white community and a new kind of fear and respect to the Black community. This was becoming an organized community effort upsetting false assumptions and old traditions. It was a social revolution that was going to speak to the white community and say, in no uncertain terms, "We can no longer accept segregation as a practice or as a philosophy. We must take our place in the mainstream of American life."

• •

In September 1958, a citizens' group backed by the city's churches tried in vain to reach a settlement with restaurant owners. They presented a plan for integrating the city's eating places that had been drawn up by a citizens' group composed of representatives from educational groups and other agencies. Mrs. Vivian Reno of the Oklahoma City Council of Churches worked extremely hard with various committees, talking to restaurant officials who stated that they favored desegregation but feared a loss of white customers. The Reno plan called upon families to patronize eating places that served Blacks. The plan was submitted to the Oklahoma City Council of Churches, but the council gave it only an indirect endorsement. In a prepared statement, the Council of Churches attacked segregation.

• •

We may have been young, but we were old enough to know that we had had enough. In the basement at John A. Brown's, the whole essence of human dignity and respect was on trial.

One day, to my surprise, I looked up and saw Nancy R. Davis, the first Black student to enroll at Oklahoma State University in Stillwater, coming into John A. Brown's. As she entered, a skinny little white lady deliberately stepped on her feet and cursed her. Nancy lost her temper. I rushed over to tell Nancy to go home and start a prayer campaign for us. She could not be of any service to us down there in the lion's den. By this time, the mean-looking woman had moved over. I moved away from her, walked over to Nancy, and told her that I didn't want to see her at another sit-in demonstration. "You're just not ready for nonviolent demonstrations, Nancy. You're violent. You'll hurt us."

"Clara, you ought to stop. We don't have to go through all of this. Get the kids and let's go home. Why don't you quit?" Nancy said.

I said, "Goodbye, Nancy."

As I looked at the kids, I continued to hear Nancy's words "Why don't you quit?" That was a question that I had asked myself. I had thought this would be an easy struggle and a quick victory. But this was going to be a different "wall." There was no telling what would happen. I was frightened inside. I wanted to cry. I wanted to take my kids and run at that moment. Zella Hull started singing,

Freedom, freedom,
Everybody wants freedom,

Clara Luper wants freedom,
Theodosia Crawford wants freedom,
A. Willie James wants freedom,
Everybody wants freedom.

On the day before Halloween, the youth stayed up until 3:00 a.m. making white facial masks. They were finally finished and were given to the 150 protesters. The group arrived at Brown's, and when the store opened, they marched into the basement, saw the guard at the door, and said:

My face is white,
May I eat today?
I'm ready to pay,
My face is snow white,
May I eat today?
We aren't clowns,
But we're going to be around,
May we eat today?

. . . .

Halloween 1963 was our sixth Halloween, and the walls still stood. We rented a devil costume from the Colonial Costume Shop. We had at least twenty volunteers to wear it. The plan was that the devil would make two appearances downtown, one at John A. Brown's and the other at Anna Maude's, where the other half of the group was. We announced, "The devil's in." A large number of people came downtown just to see the devil.

At 11:30, a student in the devil's uniform came strolling calmly into John A. Brown's basement. He went straight to the guards and jumped up and down and said:

Tell Frank Wade
To keep up the work.
My disciples Mildred and Francis,
They are, and Frank too, always on duty,
Preparing themselves for an eternity with me in h e l l.

The devil would not demonstrate with the NAACP'ers. He rushed over to Anna Maude's Cafeteria and said:

Where is Quillan? Where is R. D. Cravens?
They are my angels.

So ended the devil's sit-in—another step in man's desperate effort to be free.

Once again Christmas had come to Oklahoma with its eternal message of love. This was our sixth Christmas that we had spent at John A. Brown's without being served. There were no Black shoppers in Brown's that day. We entered with shopping bags, which were left empty, and said:

All we want for Christmas
Is to eat at John A. Brown's.
Merry Christmas, Mr. Wade, may we eat today?
Aunt Francis, may we eat today?

We were completely ignored.

It was our sixth New Year at John A. Brown's. We would all say:

Happy New Year, Mr. Wade, may we eat today?

These words were falling on deaf ears.

. . . .

The NAACP Youth Council members were still talking about John A. Brown's as they staged their last sit-ins before leaving for the 1959 NAACP National Convention in New York City, where we would receive strength to continue the fight for first-class citizenship. Our council won the highest award in the nation there. This convention was filled with people from all over the South, who told stories of their struggles. Among those who related their struggles were Mrs. Vera Pigee, the NAACP youth advisor from Clarksdale, Mississippi, located in Coahoma County. Mrs. Pigee was well known in NAACP circles. Her vivid, dynamic personality mixed with her love for exotic hats, and her strong dedication to freedom was respected.

Mr. Charles Darden of Meridian, Mississippi, whose work in Meridian had made him a refugee in his own state, was also in attendance at the convention. He was a ring salesman who had to leave Mississippi in order to sell class rings. I had met him when the junior class I sponsored purchased rings from him at Dunjee High School. Although he was selling rings, he had gladly shared his experiences with the classes. His stories of what Blacks were experiencing in Mississippi were unbelievable.

We met Martin Luther King Jr. and heard him deliver a mammoth heart-warming freedom address, which furnished us with the freedom vitamins that we needed to continue.

The fact that we were congratulated by such outstanding NAACP freedom fighters as Roy Wilkins (executive director), Gloster Current (director of the Branches and Field Administration), Herbert Wright (national youth advisor), Lucille Black (membership secretary), and Kivie Kaplan (president) gave us new strength.

When the convention ended, we headed home. We stopped in Washington, D.C., and Senators Robert S. Kerr and Mike Monroney invited us to lunch in the Senate cafeteria, where, according to Senator Kerr, the same ice cream was served that was served at the White House. We had written our U.S. senators and had talked to them often about voting for a civil rights bill that would eliminate segregation in all public places. Senator Kerr and I agreed on many issues. I had respect for his love and devotion to Oklahoma, and his dedication to the industry that he had built and to the "water" that he loved. He told us that as far as the civil rights bill was concerned, he would not vote for it because he did not believe that the federal government had the right to control private businesses. He said that this country had grown on private enterprise.

I asked him about the Black votes that he always received and the large number of Black votes that he consistently got even when he was

• •

Samuel J. Cornelius and Barbara Posey represented Oklahoma City at the 1961 National Convention in Philadelphia, Pennsylvania. Samuel told a large crowd of freedom fighters that Blacks had sat and squatted for 761 days in order to get a cup of coffee. He said, "We will win because we have the determination and faith." In fact, he said that 171 restaurants had opened, and the answer to segregation and discrimination had been found. That answer consisted of two words: dedication and determination. Barbara Posey, president of the NAACP Youth Council, told the members that we had been sitting in for three years and would continue to do so.

• •

governor. He said, "The Blacks that worked for me were paid off. They worked for me, I paid them off, and I owe them nothing."

I looked at Helen Johnson, Lillian Oliver, and Willie James, and we were all shocked. The rest of the time was spent just talking.

We left Washington, D.C., and decided to go to Mount Vernon on the beautiful Potomac River. It was a bright summer day. We walked down to George Washington's grave, where we were greeted by a graying elderly Black man who spoke about General Washington with a flow of words that related the success story of the first president. As we left the grave, we found ourselves in a rainstorm. We rushed to our bus. Everyone wondered where the rain had come from. "We didn't even get a fair warning," some of the children complained.

"We must find satisfaction in knowing that we went to Mount Vernon because there are so many people who have never been there," Mrs. Helen Johnson said.

"You are right," said Mrs. Lillian Oliver.

As we headed homeward, it was decided that we would stop in Nashville, Tennessee, where we would eat. The students would visit Fisk University and Tennessee State, while I would find a beautician. "You can't just go back to Oklahoma City with your hair in such a mess," someone had said. I had agreed to go to the first beautician I could find in Nashville.

In the meantime, the bus driver stopped to inquire about a place where we could eat. After about a thirty-minute look, we found the Dunjee Drive Inn, a Black-owned restaurant. The food was delicious, the waitresses were beautiful, and the managers had the welcome mat out for us. The chicken was fried to a delicate brown and served with French fries, tomato salad, and hot rolls. After eating cold rolls in New York City for a week, we were happy to get back to the South with its hot rolls. This was evident from the way Willie James kept eating the rolls and talking and smiling.

We had a big sign on our bus that read "Oklahoma or bust!" As we looked up, a tall young student was running toward the bus telling his friends, "That bus is from Oklahoma. That's my home!"

Another student said, "Melvin Porter! Everybody knows that you are from Oklahoma. Do you know these people?"

With a wide smile showing a spark of gold mingled in with his white teeth, the young man threw his hands out and said, "Sure, I know them!" In order to impress his peers, he rushed over and said, "Welcome to Nashville. I'm Melvin Porter from Okmulgee, Oklahoma."

I said, "Oh, you are Victor Porter's son."

Porter was still smiling and acting as if he was going to pay for all of our lunches. "You all help yourselves and eat all you want. I don't want my home-staters to want for anything." When he had finished his formal welcome to each table of students, he came back and sat with Helen Johnson, Ruth Tolliver, Willie James, Lillian Oliver, and me.

I said, "Melvin, the children are thinking that you are going to pay for the extras that you told them to order."

He jumped up and said, "You see, I'm on a very limited budget. I'm a dishwasher here—I mean, I'm the night manager."

He took the floor, and with his right hand pointing at the kids, the cafeteria became a courtroom as he reinterpreted what he meant by helping themselves. "If I implied that I'd pay for your meals, I'm sorry. I'm a graduate of Tennessee State, and I'm getting ready to graduate from Vanderbilt University. I'm the first of my race to be accepted into the law school. My hospitality is verbal, not financial. I don't have but one dime in my pocket. If that will help you all, you can have it. I'm not the owner; I'm just the night manager."

As he sat down, the youth applauded, and Henry Rolfe Jr. said, "I like him."

I hurriedly finished my meal as we told Porter about our experiences in the sit-ins and what we were trying to accomplish. He wished us all the luck in the world. "I'll be praying for all of you, and since I don't have any money to give, I will give you all the South, with all of its outdated segregated Jim Crow Black-coded laws. I have been offered two jobs that pay the kind of money that I have prepared myself to make. One job is in Los Angeles, on the West Coast, and the other one is in Chicago. I'll be overlooking Lake Michigan. I can hardly wait for graduation."

When he had finished, I asked Porter if he would take me to the closest beautician. On the way, we continued to talk. I told him, "You must be awfully proud of yourself, going to the North or West where the walls of segregation aren't so visible. I want you to do me a favor. In the next two hours, we will be headed back to Oklahoma. Call it the South or the Southwest, I was born in Oklahoma and educated in its segregated schools. I love Oklahoma with a passion. I love the South. I know segregation is there, but I know there are people in the South, both Black and white, who are going to change the South. For over a year now, those little children that you saw in the restaurant have been spit on, cursed, pushed, called niggers, bitches, and bastards. They have stood in the rain, in the snow, in the heat, and one day there was even a hailstorm that they stood through. Not only have we had to fight the whites, but the apathetic Blacks. It's been tough. Maybe for the first time in my life, I understand how Robert E. Lee felt when he made up his mind to return and fight with the South over ninety years ago. But someday, I do believe that we shall overcome. When we do, I want you to bring your children to the South. Bring them to Oklahoma. Let them enjoy the hotels, cafeterias, amusement parks, and restaurants. Then you can feel proud of yourself, and you can tell them about your good-paying jobs in Chicago and Los Angeles, and how your own personal interest surpassed your racial national interest."

No other words were spoken. He took me on to the beauty shop, and in two hours we were loading onto the Greyhound bus.

In the midst of freedom songs and handclapping, we said goodbye to E. Melvin Porter, who was not smiling now, but was standing as if he were baking in the Tennessee sunshine. On the way back, the children talked about this young man who had such visible potential. "Gosh, we need him in Oklahoma," they said.

The March wind brought a "whirlwind of strength" to Oklahoma City in the form of E. Melvin Porter, the attorney from the state of Oklahoma whom we had met in Nashville. He had turned down offers in Chicago and Los Angeles and had set up a law practice on Second Street in Oklahoma City. Porter arrived in Oklahoma City in an old station wagon, which carried everything that he owned; his beautiful wife, Jewel; his son, Melvin Jr.; and a stack of law books. Amos Hall, a Tulsa attorney, helped him find an office and advanced him enough money for gas, groceries, office rent, and some spending change. His wife had a difficult time adjusting to the new standard of living since she came from an upper-middle-class family in Nashville.

Porter told us that he was so impressed with the NAACP Youth Council that he had decided to come to Oklahoma City and join them. "This was a financial sacrifice, but I guess it will be worth it," he said. He immediately began to work as an NAACP youth advisor. We nicknamed him "the Patrick Henry of the Sit-Ins." He was always at the churches, the YMCAs, and my house at 1819 Northeast Park Place, but he had been conspicuously absent from the "walls" at John A. Brown's. And yet he could out-articulate the articulator.

When he was questioned about his absence from the combat zone, as we called Brown's and the other restaurants, he delivered a speech that included his presidency of the student body in Nashville, Tennessee, the bar association at his school, and his work as a member of the Kappa Alpha Psi fraternity. When he finished, I said, "Sir, either you go today or send your money."

Porter looked around and said, "I don't have any money, but I can borrow some from Amos Hall." After a long pause he said, "At least I think I can," with a friendly smile.

"Oh, no, Melvin Porter. Come on and go with us to John A. Brown's," Barbara Posey said.

"I have a client first thing in the morning. As soon as I finish, I'll be there," Porter said.

"Just remember, Porter, this is a nonviolent protest, which means nonviolence in its truest sense."

We went on to Brown's. Francis, the mean waitress who cursed so profoundly well, greeted us with her usual salutation. This meant that she'd turn her nose up as if she smelled skunks, and then she'd make an ugly face that would make her gums quite annoying. We were forced to look at her frowning face—a face that was not easy to forget, and one that made minutes seem like hours.

• •

The NAACP'ers often related various experiences with Aunt Francis (the really ugly-acting white waitress), Aunt Mildred (another frowning waitress), and Uncle Frank (Frank Wade, the owner of the luncheonette), as the kids fondly called them.

On Christmas, we wanted to buy Frank Wade a pair of suspenders because during an hour-long sit-in he would pull his pants up sixty-two times. But we decided that watching him pull up his pants would make the minutes pass faster.

One day Francis got in a fuss with Harold Eugene Woodson, an eight-year-old Black NAACP member, and told him that she didn't want to marry him. This really made Harold angry. He came over and told me what Francis had said.

I said, "Harold, you're only eight years old. Why do you want to marry Francis?"

He said, "I don't. She's too ugly, too old, and too mean."

Lynzetta Jones said, "They say she is a miss. You mean Francis isn't married?"

"No, she isn't married, she's too mean," Harold said.

• •

After over an hour of quietness, to break the tenseness we started humming "We Shall Overcome." We were walking around and around to the rope that separated us and back to our original position. The singing gave us strength.

As Melvin Porter appeared in the basement, a white man pushed him, and he kept walking. He stepped out of line for a minute and then fell back. It appeared that he wanted to leave—to run—but he didn't like to be called a coward. He moved toward us. A huge, mean-looking man pushed Sallye Harris, who was only seven years old. Porter burst out, "Don't you push that child. Well, I mean don't you—"

He was interrupted by a detective who said, "Come with me."

Sweat popped out on Porter's face. Anger could be seen in his eyes as he spoke. "I'm not going anywhere with you. We might as well get that straight right here and now. You could be the grand dragon of the Ku Klux Klan or the president of the White Citizens' Council for all I know. I'm an attorney, and I am used to old tricks like that. You will have to show me something."

The detective pulled out his credentials and said, "You are under arrest. Come with me." Five or six policemen moved around Melvin Porter, and he spoke loudly, "Yes, sir!"

As they walked away, a conference was held, and in three minutes Porter was a free man. We asked him what had happened, but his answer was lost in a song that Harold Woodson was leading:

I want to be ready,
I want to be ready,
I want to be ready
To walk for freedom
Just like John.
John said the jail was just for squares.
I want to be ready,
I want to be ready,
I want to be ready
To walk for freedom
Just like John.
John, oh John, what do you say?
Walk for freedom
Just like John.
That there will be freedom
Some sweet day.

The singing continued, with Zella Hull leading. "Did you hear Barbara singing?" the group asked. "Reverend W. B. Parker praying? Calvin Luper pleading? The freedom songs? The freedom bells?"

In unison, they responded, "Yes, I heard. Yes, I heard. Yes, I heard."

"Did you see the paddy wagon? Brenda Wallace kicked? Arnetta Carmichael pushed? Old Francis frown?"

"Yes, I saw. Yes, I saw. Yes, I saw."

"Did you hear Eddie Stamps calling? Theodosia Crawford calling? Cecil Williams calling? Barbara Posey calling?"

"Yes, I did. Yes, I did."

"Will you stand? Will you stand?"

"Yes, I will. Yes, I will."

The clock on the wall said it was time to leave. Another day had ended at John A. Brown's. The walls of segregation still stood. I wrote:

Look at me, Mr. Wade.
I was born of America,
Born of her fertile soil.
I was born with a different color from yours.
I'm a proud American.
I was born with a heart.
I have blood, bones, and muscles.
I was born with a mind.
I'm a different color from you.
I'm a proud American.
If you are superior to me,
Perform a miracle—
Command your hamburgers to sing,
Turn your ice cream into diamonds.
Look at me, Mr. Wade,
I'm the same as you.
I'm a proud American.
I walk, I talk, I sing, and I'll die,
And you'll die, too, and will not be able to serve pie.
Segregation is a thing which cannot be hidden;
It is really a cancer in your space.
Someday history will record
That the color of skin determined
Whether you can drink black coffee.
Serve me coffee

Today
Completely integrated.
One half cream and
One half coffee.

As I sat in John A. Brown's waiting in 1961, I had plenty of time to think, to dream, and to remember. I constantly thanked God for memory, and I wrote and prayed for my people—some of them were Black and some were white.

While we were sitting, I was asked to tell the children about my school days. We started singing.

School days, school days,
Dear old golden rule days,
Reading 'n' writing 'n' 'rithmetic
Taught to the tune of the hickory stick

We sang that song with a lot of enthusiasm when I was in elementary school in Hoffman, Oklahoma. Professor Edgar Watkins was the principal, the janitor, and taught all grades. He was a professional disciplinarian, and how he did it, I still find difficult to believe. We called him "Professor Cleanliness." Racial pride was taught along with a key word that he called "Responsibility." The books he taught us from were books that had been mainly discarded by the white elementary school. We were separate, and we possessed, through Educational Calculated Manipulation, an overabundance of *promises* for better books, equipment, and supplies that never came. We were separate and unequal.

• •

In September 1961, Joyce Richardson wrote:

When I went to town, I went to John A. Brown's to pay my bills.
He said, "Thank you, Jill."
I went to the luncheonette to get a bite to eat.
He said, "No, Jill, you have to eat in the street."
I said, "No, John A. Brown, I believe I'll wait."

• •

I loved books, and the first day that Sister Baby Easley, Carrie Watkins, Oneita Shepard, and I peeped in through the windows of the all-white elementary school in Hoffman, I was shocked. I had never seen so many books. I wanted to read those books. I wanted to explore new ideas, but the walls separated us, and we were caught behind the walls.

We made the most of our situation and drank from Professor Watkins's "fountain of knowledge." I used to sit in my geography classes and dream of visiting every state in the Union. I dreamed of talking to some of the world's great thinkers. Yet the walls were always there.

My parents spent a great deal of time telling us how to survive in our environment. For example, our closest town was Henryetta, Oklahoma, and there was a sign that Blacks will always talk about. It read:

> NEGRO, READ AND RUN.
> IF YOU CAN'T READ,
> RUN ANYWAY.

There was a little train that came through Hoffman, called "the motor," and we were trained to sit in the back of it.

In Henryetta, we couldn't try on clothes in some stores. Our shoes were purchased from the back of the store, and sometimes we were not allowed to try them on. My father was called a "boy" and my mother a "good girl."

There were walls that separated us from entering theaters, restaurants, and libraries. In Okmulgee, there was one theater where we could use the balcony. It held about twenty or twenty-five people. When I first went in, I was seated behind the curtain in the balcony, where I could only hear the show.

The pecan orchards on the farms were divided. When we used to pick pecans, the Blacks picked pecans in one area and the whites in another.

My mother washed and ironed for Mrs. Lackey, and we had to carry her clothes to the back door. Blacks were educated not to use the front door. They knew their place.

When I finished elementary school, the children from Hoffman were bused five miles to Grayson High School, an all-Black school in Grayson, Oklahoma, where we received the old buses. So my busing experiences were 50 percent by foot, a fact that Gladys Caddy vividly described and never missed an opportunity to tell a joke about. My dad was the bus driver.

The walls separated us on the buses when we rode the MKO on special trips. We were in the back, where the smell of toilets and carbon dioxide formed another wall around us. However, whites were free to use the back seats, while Blacks were forbidden to use the front seats.

At Grayson High School, I finished in the top five of my class. As the list of graduates was called, I can still hear Professor F. D. West saying, "Hightower Byrd, James Arthur Edwards, Ella Mae Anderson, Clara Shepard, and Oneita Shepard." Being in the top five was not difficult for me because there were only five in my class!

There were "walls to behold" in my high school that are still difficult to understand. Lenses were missing from our first microscope that was sent to Grayson High School. Pages were missing from the history books that came from the white school. The outdated encyclopedias and the dictionaries were without the "r's." Our high school teachers, Mr. F. W. West, Miss Keyes, Mr. Phillips, Mr. Dean, Mr. House, and Mr. Garrett, must have been geniuses to have taught us under those circumstances.

At Langston University, I saw different kinds of walls. Walls of discrimination because we were "too poor" to live on campus. People like Mrs. Jones, Mrs. Sanders, Mrs. Cooper, and Reverend and Mrs. Ousley threw their doors open to me.

Walls of discrimination because I failed to pledge to a particular sorority.

Walls of discrimination because we asked why Oklahoma's only separate university didn't have the same equipment, books, and supplies as the white universities in Oklahoma.

These walls were discussed, and my classmate Ada Lois Sipuel broke down the educational wall at the University of Oklahoma and buried it in the annals of history as thousands of Black students entered formerly white universities all over the South.

After finishing at Langston University, I went to D. B. and O. [the Oklahoma School for the Deaf, Blind, and Orphaned], where I ran into another wall—a political wall. I was asked to give one-fourth of my first check to the Democratic Party. I resigned after "blowing my top."

At the University of Oklahoma, another wall—separate restrooms, separate sections in the cafeteria, bars separating us in the classrooms. In one class a professor told me that he had "never taught a nigger" and "never wanted to." I moved that wall by staying in his class and working so hard that at the end of the school term, he confessed his sins.

Jesse Tarver, a pharmacy student, and I were the first Blacks in the Social Science Department.

These are some of the stories that I told the children at John A. Brown's while we waited to be served.

Thousands of leaflets were passed out in downtown Oklahoma City and in churches calling the public's attention to the policy of discrimination and asking for additional help. Mrs. Buck, Mrs. Matthews, and Mrs. Kennedy planned an all-white sit-in at John A. Brown's. Approximately forty white women participated. All participants were pledged to nonviolence.

The whites had agreed to remain in their seats all day. Most of the white women went by twos, threes, and fours into the restaurant. They were, of course, seated without any trouble by Frank Wade, Francis, or Mildred. There was a whole new unit of white women ready to move in if any of the group had to leave. This was truly a confusing demonstration. The segregationists did not know what to do.

Some liberal whites who were not sitting in were writing letters and working on the telephone committees.

This demonstration was played down in the TV news; however, it made a great contribution to the cause. Much sympathy was aroused. Even some whites who were straddling the fence came and openly demonstrated with us. "Keep it up, we're all with you" could be heard constantly, and encouraging letters filled our mailboxes from both Blacks and whites.

These white women became an integral part of our movement. They worked on assignments that weakened the walls.

Sheldon Stirling, Oklahoma City's city manager, denied a parade permit to Gene Matthews, a white attorney who was a councilman from Village, Oklahoma. Matthews was not representing any group, but stated that he and several other families had decided to form a funeral procession to bury Jim Crow in downtown Oklahoma City. Students from the University of Oklahoma and Reverend Jim Shields wanted to join Gene in this mock procession. Stirling asked Mr. Matthews to wait several weeks, and he would give him a permit to parade.

"*Ne segregentur cives.*" Roughly translated, this means "Do not segregate our citizens." This attracted a lot of attention as three Black students and seventeen white University of Oklahoma students picketed John A. Brown's in Norman. Seven OU professors, three faculty wives, and a number of graduate assistants participated in the demonstration and carried signs with the other marchers. This was done in spite of a huge KKK sign that had been printed on the sidewalk. Clearance had been received from the proper school authorities, and at one o'clock, a group of pro-segregationists demonstrated across the street with signs that read "NAACP Unfair and Unfair to Fair Business."

A large number of students jammed the sidewalks near Brown's to watch the nonviolent demonstration. One OU student entered the store and purchased a small package of razor blades. A clerk placed the items in two large sacks, one inside the other. He went outside and picketed with the anti-segregationists in an attempt to get some negative reactions. He didn't.

Jack Nickson, a white student, continued to walk around and around all day in the same slow circle with a sign that read "Segregation Must End in America." It was not easy to organize a demonstration in Norman, but Jack Nickson was not the kind of person who looked for an easy job. For weeks he had been wrestling with his conscience. He had seen his wife participate in demonstrations against Brown's in Oklahoma City. Now he just had to get involved. He said, "I can no longer stand on the sidelines. I must get out in the arena and fight for freedom. I'm white, and I cannot be free until my Black brother is free also."

To organize this march, a list of sympathizers was found by a telephone committee. Then for two weeks, telephone calls were made and all kinds of meetings were held.

Mr. and Mrs. Jack Nickson, Robert Hendon, and Rod Miller of Norman were the leaders of the demonstrations. Lessons in nonviolence were taught. The fear of being arrested was wrestled with. If you should lose your temper, go get a cup of coffee.

It had been a long day for Norman's first demonstrators, and on February 1, 1961, they completed their first attack on segregation at John A. Brown's and went home with tired, sore feet. This gave additional strength and prestige to the Oklahoma City movement.

This demonstration came about three weeks after Mayor Norick, Police Chief Ed Rector, City Manager Sheldon Stirling, and Oklahoma City's segregated restaurants had received a petition from students at the University of Oklahoma. The students said that segregation was not in the best interests of either the business firms or the Oklahoma City community and served only to put the city's continuation of social inequality in the nation's spotlight and as a consequence cause national minds to look with scorn upon our state's lack of social progress. The petition was proudly signed by Henry James, a student and past senate president; Jed Johnson Jr.; George Hazeling; Charlotte Ester, president of the Association of Women Students; Ruth Sherwood, president of Cate Center; William Moore, president of the Inter-Religious Council; Gene Arnn, a student senator; and Larry Wade, editor of the *Oklahoma Daily* student newspaper. This petition demonstrated that the student body of the University of Oklahoma wanted the "walls of segregation" down in the state capital.

Who were these white folks who did not want to eat with Blacks? Where did they come from? Were these people whose children were raised by Black people? Were these white boys and girls whom Black maids used to feed and take care of? How long had Black maids been controlling white folks' homes and kitchens? How ungrateful! Why, I would much rather eat at a restaurant with a person than to let him in my house with all of my valuables.

Something was drastically wrong here. What were the Black people saying? Some were telling the whites that we were going "too fast" and that we did not represent the majority of Blacks. I knew that those Blacks who weren't participating in the movement would be the first ones to eat in the restaurants, the first ones to sleep in the hotels, and the first and only ones to be placed by their "good white folks" on boards, commissions, and in top-paying jobs, while those of us who were at John A. Brown's that day would continue to be isolated from the fruits of democracy.

I could not continue to think about what was happening. I had to make something happen. I knew what I would do: I would call John A. Brown's and talk to Mrs. Brown. She must be waiting for me to call her.

I called and received the same response that I had received in 1957, 1958, 1959, and 1960.

Okay, if Mrs. Brown didn't want to talk to me, I sure did not want to see her. We had nothing in common anyway. I still couldn't understand Mrs. Brown, however. She had never had us arrested in her store, and we had not discriminated against her with our sit-in techniques. Maybe—oh, I just couldn't understand her. There was only one thing that I was sure of: if she didn't want to see me, I did not want to see her. Mrs. Brown was the wall, and the sit-ins and boycott continued with John A. Brown's as the main target.

Then one day I received an emergency call from the John A. Brown Company asking if I would come down to the store immediately. "Why?" I asked.

"Because Mrs. Brown wants to talk to you," the voice on the telephone stated.

"Mrs. Brown wants to see me? I do not want to see her. After all that she has done to me, why, my feet are aching now, and Mrs. Brown wants to see me. She has nerve—the nerve of her telling me to come down immediately. No, I shall not talk to Mrs. Brown. Thank you for calling, but now I'm busy. How about tomorrow? I'm all filled up. I'm just too busy taking care of business."

This continued for several weeks.

I could hardly wait to tell my friends and relatives that Mrs. Brown wanted to see me. I called my mother first, and she told me that she thought that Mrs. Brown was a nice lady and that I should go and see her immediately. My mother called my aunt, Mrs. Alberta Felder, and they both talked and fussed at me. I invited them to come on and go down to John A. Brown's with me. They both laughed and told me that I must be the biggest fool in the world. I shouldn't have told them anyway.

I called Vera Pigee in Clarksdale, Mississippi, and she said, "Clara, I don't know how you sophisticated Blacks do in Oklahoma, but in Mississippi, when white folks want to talk, we put down everything we are doing and we go to them and talk. You see, when white folks stop shooting and start talking, we are happy to talk."

The sit-inners also contended that I should talk to Mrs. Brown.

I decided to call Charlie Bennett, the managing editor of the *Daily Oklahoman*, Oklahoma City's great newspaper. Mr. Bennett was one of the few white men I really trusted. I would indirectly get his advice on my seeing Mrs. Brown. Charlie and I talked about the problems that we were facing, and I casually mentioned the fact that Mrs. Brown had invited me in to have a conference and I had refused. He had no comment, and silence fell over the telephone. I said, "I don't understand. Can't you see my side of it? She refused to see me when I wanted to see her, and now that we're boycotting her store, she wants to talk. Frankly, I don't see what we have to talk about."

He said, "I'm surprised at you! If you want to keep the lines of communication open, you had better forget about minor problems and stick to the real issue. The lines of communication must be kept open at all times. Anyway, what do you have to lose?"

I didn't want to answer him and I tried to change the conversation, but he brought me right back to the question in his own way. He was the indisputable executive, and now he was compelling me to answer him.

I hesitated. He pressured me, and I finally answered. "No, I don't have anything to lose."

"Pure common sense, or any kind of statistical data, would show that you might have something to gain."

I hurriedly made up an excuse and terminated the telephone conversation. Why had I called him, anyway? I should have called Dr. Charles Atkins. I called him immediately. His advice had always been respected and carried out through the years he had been our family doctor. We had depended on both his medical and his recreational and educational advice. He had never missed an opportunity to support the sit-ins, mentally or financially. He checked on our welfare daily. His son, Edmund Atkins, was over to my house practically every day. His advice and encouragement had been appreciated. His wife had been helpful in supplying us with new information and materials. Dr. Atkins said, "You had better see her. This is part of being a winner. Never miss the opportunity to do right."

I wrestled with my conscience. After talking with about ten more people, and since I was convinced that I was not going to get any support for my way of thinking, I decided that I would see Mrs. Brown. Her secretary called, and I told her I was so busy that I could not see Mrs. Brown until the next Tuesday, a week later.

In the meantime, the sit-ins continued at John A. Brown's. Every day I was wondering what my conference with Mrs. Brown would be like. During the years we had been at Brown's, we had never seen her. However, the week was so full of activities that I did not have time to think.

On the next Tuesday, the telephone rang. Mrs. Brown asked if I wanted her chauffeur to pick me up for the meeting. "No," I said, "I shall have my chauffeur drive me down." (I was my own chauffeur.) I got into my car and headed for Brown's Department Store.

It was common information at John A. Brown's that Mrs. Brown and I were going to meet. I could feel the tension as I walked into the store alone and toward her office. I was graciously welcomed by her attractive secretary. She talked to me briefly and told me to go into Mrs. Brown's office, and she would be with me in a few minutes.

That day I was ready for Mrs. Brown. All of the frustrations that had been building within me for the last four years were going to come out "right in her white face."

When the secretary opened the door, I walked into an office. I was overcome with history because that office was Mr. Brown's former office.

The furniture, the pictures, the papers—in spite of the improvements and refurnishing that had happened at John A. Brown's, that office was just as it had been when Mr. Brown died years earlier. My frustration began to diminish. When Mrs. Brown opened the door, we both stood there speechless, and with tears in our eyes we embraced each other as if we had been friends for years. Oh, I know that couldn't be, but it was, and now we were talking. Two women, one Black and one white. One rich and one poor.

Historical circumstances had brought us together. We talked about our families and some of the problems that we had faced as we both tried to compete in a man's business world. We both cried again as I told her how I had tried to make it. How I was working at three jobs trying to educate my children and to provide them with the necessities of life. She told me about her husband and how he had died. We talked about how much we had loved and how much we had lost.

Finally she said, "I have been told that you hate me. Is that true?"

I said, "No, Mrs. Brown, I do not hate you. I respect you. You have challenged the male-oriented business world. You shall always have my respect. I have been told that *you* hate *me*."

"Oh, no, Clara, I've heard that, but it is not true. I admire your courage. I have stood here and wondered, day in and day out, what you and your children were saying about me. Clara, tell me, please tell me, what do the children think about me? What do they say, Clara?"

As I looked at her, I knew that I had to tell her the truth. Her penetrating eyes stared directly into mine.

"Mrs. Brown, they say that they wish you had died in place of Mr. Brown. They say that if he were living, they believe they would be able to eat here," I said.

For a few minutes there was complete silence, and then she spoke. "Clara, day in and day out, I have worried about this thing. I just don't know how to deal with it. You see, Frank Wade has leased space in my store to operate the luncheonette, and under his lease he has the sole right to run it his own way. You see, my hands have been completely tied."

"Yes, Mrs. Brown, but we don't know anything about Mr. Wade and could care less. But John A. Brown's, that's different. This is the store where we have spent our money, and we can't see how we can be discriminated against under the roof of a John A. Brown store. Even the name reminds us of the martyr John Brown who died for our cause."

We talked for nearly an hour. Mr. Anderson came in and brought us some lemonade. He offered her the first glass, and she said, "Serve Clara first."

Finally she said, "Take this message back to the children: segregation will end at John A. Brown's."

I was so proud of her. She admitted to me that the first time I was arrested, she had called and offered to pay my bond. She had never missed calling to see if I was all right, she said.

She asked me to do her a favor—to come and meet with all of the executives of the John A. Brown's store and tell them why we had selected Brown's. I followed her to a spacious conference room, where I told my story. I liked everybody there immediately, except Attorney Lyle. He continued to harass me about insignificant things. I had already been warned about him. I started to raise my voice at him, but I looked at Mrs. Brown and she smiled at me. Then I knew everything was going to be all right.

When I left John A. Brown's that day, I had respect for Miss Ambrosia and Mr. Hardwick, and I knew that I had a lifetime friend in Mrs. Brown.

An agreement was made that day that John A. Brown's segregation walls would fall. And in less than a week, Blacks were eating at Brown's.

Mrs. Brown and I continued to talk to each other by telephone. She invited me to go to Europe with her. I turned it down because of other commitments. Before she went into the hospital for the last time, she called me and told me that she was going into the hospital under a different name, and she probably would never see me again, but she wanted me to know that she appreciated what we had done for this city, a city that she loved so well.

Mrs. Brown acquainted me with loneliness in a way that I had never known before. When she died, I couldn't control my emotions. I went to her funeral and followed the procession to her final resting place.

A white executive of the store said, "I'm glad you came."

She was my friend. I loved her, and I had to come.

. . . .

WE SIT-IN—
    After 246 Years of Slavery
       And
        96 Years of Segregation—
          —After Other Methods Failed
    Our Reasons:

1. Segregation has no place in a democracy.
2. Segregation violates all religious and moral principles.
3. Segregation destroys our prestige among the people of the world.
4. Segregation rates one-tenth of our American citizens as second-class citizens.
5. Segregation makes us a hypocritical nation.
6. Segregation hinders our nation's internal progress and growth.
7. Segregation makes our city the laughingstock of the world.
8. Segregation stops conventions and tourists from coming to our city.
9. Segregation puts an inferior tag on Negroes, and God has not made an inferior people.
10. Segregation insults foreign visitors and embarrasses God-fearing people.
11. Segregation is wrong: we are tired of it, and, we've got to wipe it out.

Join us Saturday, January 21, 1961, at Calvary Baptist Church, 2nd and Walnut Streets, at 9:30 a.m.

NAACP YOUTH COUNCIL,
Calvin Luper, President
Areda Tolliver, Secretary

. . . .

4

ANNA MAUDE'S CAFETERIA

"Where are we going today?" Mike Clayton asked.

"To Anna Maude's Cafeteria," I said.

Mike Clayton usually bombarded us with questions so that we would be forced to explain things in detail.

Larry Collier sank down into a seat at Calvary. Samuel Craig eased his tall figure into a seat near the front. The rest of the children gathered at the front of the church, and the group began to yell, "We want freedom! Everybody wants freedom! Oklahoma wants freedom! We want freedom!"

The children's heads were bowed reverently in prayer. Reverend W. B. Parker asked the group to pray silently as he prayed aloud. The Twenty-Third Psalm was read; the American flag was proudly saluted. Freedom songs continued. The song leaders began to march around the aisle. For months, this had been a common scene at Calvary Baptist Church, located at Second and Walnut Streets. It was the oldest Black Baptist church in Oklahoma City. However, the membership was very small, and a small number participated in the sit-ins. This was A. Willie James's church. Happiness to him was to see that the heat was at the proper temperature and that the sound system worked. The young people knew better than to drop paper or do anything that would mess up the church. Willie told the children, "This is God's house."

"All right, Uncle Willie," as the children so fondly called him.

As the singing continued, I watched him check and recheck to make sure everything was all right. It seemed that he was quite nervous that day. When I asked him why, he hastily told me that was his business and I had better take care of the children.

Dr. A. L. Dowell, Oklahoma's only Black optometrist, was there. He and his wife's office building on North Durland Avenue served as an information headquarters. They would coordinate and sift information, giving it to their clients. They were working, and because of the nature of their work, they hired people to stand in for them when they couldn't come, and they supported the movement financially daily.

Theodosia Crawford, Cecil L. Williams, Reverend Macon, and Bobby Moon were swaying back and forth to the rhythm of the music.

Go down, Moses,
Way down in Egypt's land,
Tell old Pharaoh
To let us eat today.

Cecil, who had arrived late, was singing, and his voice came out as a sort of froggish croak. Maybe we had expected too much out of his voice because he constantly reminded us that he sang in the Church of the Redeemer's choir on North Eastern Avenue.

A rainy morning was a welcome relief. It gave us more time—time for additional youth to come.

Willie R. James, the president of the NAACP, was calling for me to come and give some directions. Al Kavanaugh's son John had called the night before and said that he represented a social action group from the Catholic Church, and they wanted to help. I said, "If your group wants to help, be sure to meet us at Calvary at nine o'clock in the morning."

I couldn't believe my eyes when I saw a redheaded priest and a few whites enter. A welcome committee greeted them. A spark of hope could be seen through the audience. Now Blacks and whites were together— Oklahoma City whites. The first whites had previously come from Oklahoma City University and from Norman, under the leadership of Reverend Jim Shields and Reverend John Heidbrink.

I went over the rules of nonviolence. If anyone should hit you on one cheek, turn the other one. If anyone should spit on you, wipe it off. Love your enemy. If you aren't a nonviolent person, we have other places where you can work.

I saw the priest, who had introduced himself as Father Robert McDole, take out a folded white handkerchief. He wiped his face and neck. That priest looked as if he were scared stiff.

Cecil Williams, who was in charge of searching for weapons, yelled out, "Give me your weapons. This minute, this minute!" He took up five knives. He moved to the front and said, "These knives will get you in trouble. And if you go to jail because of a knife, you are going to stay there. You are in the wrong place. This is a nonviolent movement." He brought the knives over and presented them to me, saying, "This is what your precious little children had." I immediately gave them to A. Willie James. I knew the young men personally and knew the humiliations that they had been through the day before.

The sign committee was now giving out signs that read:

FREEDOM NOW!
SEGREGATION MUST GO!

Cecil and Reverend Macon continued to walk up and down. Cecil was wearing a big straw hat, which became his trademark during the movement. He gave me the count for the day—201.

The final instructions: We were to walk in twos and go directly to Anna Maude's. This was to be a silent march. Footsteps. Footsteps on the sidewalks of Oklahoma City.

Someone once referred to Anna Maude's Cafeteria as "the cafeteria of cafeterias," where every person was "fed like a king." The food was always fresh, delicious, and artistically arranged. It was a cafeteria whose clients were old and young, male and female, married and single—and all white. You could enjoy eating and meeting at Anna Maude's. Owned by A. Cooper Lyon and Robert N. Smith, it was located in the basement of the Cravens Building in downtown Oklahoma City. Now the Oklahoma City NAACP Youth Council had decided to open the cafeteria to all people, regardless of race, creed, or color, and we were on our way.

In 1958, Mr. Lyon had met with our delegation and told us that he would not serve Blacks. We'd had an understanding in 1958, but because of the demonstrations since that time, he had hired guards to watch the entrance to the cafeteria, to advise Blacks that they could not eat at Anna Maude's, and that any person accompanied by Blacks could not be served. "We reserve the right to refuse service to anyone," Mr. Smith said. "There are many whites that we have refused, too. We decide, and not the Cravens Building—our own policy. These people are only here to cause a disturbance." Dr. Louis J. West, head of the Department of

Psychiatry at the University of Oklahoma Medical Center, was accused of acting in concert with the NAACP.

When we arrived at the cafeteria on January 14, 1961, they were prepared for us. Guards were stationed at the top of the steps. When we turned to enter the cafeteria, I felt something unusually smashing in the segregated atmosphere. I was learning rapidly how to watch people, how to observe their every move, every fleeting expression, and how to interpret what was said and what was unsaid.

"Do you want to get killed?" a guard asked.

"No," I said.

"Then for God's sake, get these children and go home!"

"Why can't I go downstairs and eat?" I asked.

At that moment a white man stepped in front of me and started yelling. "Mrs. Luper, this is not your building. Take these children out of here this minute! This is my building. This is not your building; it is mine. I own this building!"

I hated to interrupt him, but I was afraid that he would burst with anger. So I introduced myself to him formally and said, "I didn't get your name." He started to shake hands with me. For one brief moment he lost his composure. In spite of his verbal, sweaty outburst, I found him to be a challenge.

"My name is R. D. Cravens. I'm the owner of this building," he said as he pointed his finger in my face.

"I'm so happy to meet you, Mr. Cravens. How have you been?" I asked.

"It's none of your business how I've been. You just get those children out of my building. This is the worst I have ever seen. What about my clients? You don't care, do you? Why don't you say something? I'm talking to you, Clara Luper!"

People had started gathering around us. "I don't want to create a scene. Let's go up to my office and talk," he said.

"What are we going to talk about, sir?" I asked.

"My legal rights!" he shouted.

"Mr. Cravens, if you want to discuss the legal aspects of my being here, I will not be able to discuss that with you. You will have to discuss that with my lawyer."

"Who is your lawyer?" he asked.

"Do you mean my head lawyer, Thurgood Marshall? I will give you his number and you can call him!" I said.

He dropped his pen. "I don't want to talk to Thurgood Marshall," he said. "Come on, Clara Luper, we need to talk."

I said, "If you want to talk about what I would like to eat, I shall be happy to talk and then eat."

"Come on, Clara!" he screamed.

"I'll have to wait on one of my local lawyers. Cecil has gone to call E. Melvin Porter," I explained.

He replied, "All right, I'll wait right here."

R. D. Cravens and I stood there eyeballing each other. He was wearing a brown suit with a matching brown hat that I felt covered a bald spot. Standing beside him were his attorney, Carmon C. Harris, and J. W. Quillan. They stood as if they were guarding Mr. Cravens.

Who in the world was Mr. Quillan? Who did he think was afraid of him? I had heard that he was the manager of the building and was related to R. D. Cravens by marriage. Just one look at Quillan and I felt as if we were getting ready to fight the devil. After listening to him, I felt that we would be dealing with a bold, ill-mannered segregationist.

My attorney, E. Melvin Porter, arrived, and we went up to Cravens's office. When I walked into the office, I was immediately caught up in its exquisite beauty. Porter called to me, asking me to stop looking at the office and come on so we could talk.

They talked about rights. I kept my mouth shut. When they finished, R. D. Cravens asked me what I was going to do. I said, "I'm going to eat at Anna Maude's today and Huckins tomorrow."

"Oh, no you aren't!" Cravens said.

"Oh, yes I am!" I said. "I am perfectly disgusted with you, R. D. Cravens. I can understand these little parasitical individuals that you're surrounded with. Here you are with money and power. That's all you've got going for you. You don't have enough courage to do what's right. You might be Mr. R. D. Cravens to them, but you are Mr. C. to me, and that means Mr. Coward." I slammed the door and joined the young people who were waiting to go into Anna Maude's.

A few minutes later, I was in a police car on my way to the city jail along with Theodosia Crawford, Cecil Williams, Father McDole, Dr. Donald Yates, and some others.

On January 26, Municipal Judge Hillis Sanford agreed with Carmon Harris, attorney for the Cravens Building, to postpone our trial for two weeks. After the hearing, we marched on City Hall and demanded to see Mayor Norick. Ed Stone, a white sit-inner, was told that the mayor had gone to his printing company. We went to his company, but he was not there.*

On March 11, 1961, far from the cafeteria where the demonstrations were taking place, a child suddenly stopped at Tabernacle Baptist Church and said, "Come on, Mrs. Luper, we've got to go."

A well-dressed man stumbled against me on the steps as he hurried inside. James said, "Can't you be more careful?"

Then we walked inside the church. Father McDole, now feeling sure of himself, said nothing. Six months ago, he would have been shaking. He might even have smiled indulgently. But today tension was rising in small, subtle ways among people who had long prided themselves as conservative, tolerant, and patient. They were tired of waiting.

Anna Maude's Cafeteria, Bishop's, and John A. Brown's were the battlegrounds, despite the property rights, the cries of the hecklers who continued to throw out obscenities, and the ropes that were used as barricades to keep Blacks out. People asked anxiously about the latest number of places that had opened their doors to Blacks. "Are the sit-ins working?" "Is the boycott working?" "When do you think the walls of Anna Maude's will fall?"

The mood of the city had changed. Apprehension, anger, frustration, soul-searching, and shame were the order of the day. As I sat in Tabernacle Baptist Church that day, I remembered something that had happened the day before. I wrote it down.

"The niggers are going too far," a bitter white passerby had said.

"It's too quiet," a grim detective had said, looking over a busy street. "I'm afraid there could be real trouble."

"I'm all for segregation, but I'm tired of demonstrations," a white businessman had said.

City officials, businessmen, and civic leaders were worried about the city's reputation and the effect on business. Many of them deplored the newspaper, television, and radio reports that were covering it. They overemphasized the sit-ins, which only represented a tiny minority in the Black community. Only a few churches had deplored the behavior of the restaurant and hotel owners or the fact that citizens were being denied

---

*Editors' note: The trial was held on February 8. Judge Sanford found them guilty of disorderly conduct and ordered them to pay fines. The charges against Father McDole had already been dismissed.

Dr. Paul Brinker, University of Oklahoma economics professor, offered a resolution that the members of the Trinity Lutheran Church in Norman would boycott all racially segregated eating and other business establishments in Norman and in Oklahoma City. It was approved by the governing body of the church. The resolution called for the congregation's minister to write letters of protest to all firms that were known to practice segregation. "Such practice of discrimination is contrary to Christian beliefs," the resolution stated. Similar resolutions had been passed by the Oklahoma City Chapter of the Lutheran Human Relations Association in May and had been adopted by the Lutheran Church, Missouri Synod, in St. Paul, Minnesota, in 1956 and at San Francisco in 1959.

Dr. Kenneth Feaver, minister of the First Presbyterian Church in Norman, opposed possible boycott action there. Dr. Feaver urged negotiations with merchants rather than picket lines.

eating rights only because of race. However, a small number of white leaders and a very few organizations openly supported the sit-ins.

The number of demonstrators varied; some days there were two hundred, some days one hundred, some days fifty, but there was always Sallye Harris, Linda Pogue, Lana Pogue, Calvin Luper, Marilyn Luper, and Areda Tolliver. At every demonstration, you could always count on these adults: A. Willie James, Lillian Oliver, Mary Pogue, Ruth Tolliver, Theodosia Crawford, Cecil Williams, Father McDole, Reverend Macon, and Dr. Yates.

At times we felt as if the Black community had forsaken us, but this day was different. A large crowd had gathered at Tabernacle, and we had the votes to carry out a "squat-in."

LaMar Clark, a student from Jarvis Christian College in Hawkins, Texas, had arrived in Oklahoma City. His Black face sparkled as he told us how much he believed in the cause of freedom, justice, and equality. He stated that his religious beliefs were wholly wrapped up in what we were doing. He had written me a week before and asked if we needed him, saying that he wanted to offer himself "for freedom." Now we were sitting side by side, ready to die for freedom.

On that day, we sang "Amazing Grace," a hymn that was really touching. Reverend West, the proud pastor of Bethlehem Star Baptist Church, had suggested it. He had related some of the trials and tribulations that he had experienced, and now we were all singing, and it was a heavenly feeling. Prayers and music were what we needed that day. Reverend Earl

Jennings Perry, the pastor of Tabernacle Baptist Church, called for me to come to the front of the group and give the directions for the day.

As I stood there in front of the crowd, I recalled how Reverend Perry's father, Reverend E. W. Perry, had paved the streets of opportunity for us and how he used to come out to Langston University to preach about real freedom and real love. I said, "This is the day that we're going to offer our bodies in sacrifice for the cause of freedom. It has been nearly three years of continuous demonstrations, and we have not eaten or gotten into Anna Maude's Cafeteria. We've been kept out of Anna Maude's by mean, evil, impolite, and ugly guards who are posted at the doors with chains in their hands, and there is a grilled gate across the entrance.

"In light of that, the planning committee has recommended that today we'll have a 'squat-in.' It is not a new technique; it was used by land seekers in the past, and since freedom is more valuable than land, we feel that it will be quite appropriate. To participate, you will have to be completely committed to nonviolence. This is the way the 'squat-in' will work. First, when we leave the church, we're going directly to Anna Maude's Cafeteria. Second, we cannot look back under any condition. (Just remember, Lot's wife looked back and turned into a pillar of salt.) Third, go as far as you can and sit down on the floor. Fourth, there will be complete silence. Fifth, don't move; let them do whatever is necessary to move you. That means complete self-control. Whatever happens, you are to remain silent. Don't say anything. If they beat you, take it. If they kick you, take it. If they lift you up and drag you to jail, take it. If they spit on you, take it."

I was interrupted by Reverend Perry. He smiled and said, "Clara, I'm not ready for that today." Reverend W. K. Jackson, the pastor of St. John Baptist Church, said in a deep, loud, sincere voice, "Amen, brother!"

I looked at Nancy Davis, Dorothy Stewart, Oneita Brown, and Lillian Oliver, and I knew that they could not participate in a "squat-in." A "fight-in" would be more in keeping with the way they were thinking. I said, "Those are the directions. Our cars are waiting."

The final prayer was completed, and we were on our way to a new experience. Mr. Leslie Brown, the inquisitive secretary of the Senior Branch of the NAACP, weighed over two hundred pounds, and I was wondering how many policemen would be needed to take him out. And just who was behind me? I didn't have any more time to think, because we were at the Cravens Building. Ruthie Lythcott, Steve Lythcott, Linda Pogue, and all were close to me. They were the pioneer sit-inners. I walked straight to the entrance and sat down. I heard the following expressions:

"Oh my God! I've never seen anything like this."

"Just look at the niggers! Oh, no, it can't be!"

"Oh, just look at the black flies!"

Old white women were cursing as they stepped on our toes and hands as they went downstairs to Anna Maude's Cafeteria.

I heard the familiar voices of Sergeant M. M. Maulding and Traffic Lieutenant I. G. Purser. Purser was known as the smiling officer. He would smile as he arrested you. Now they were commanding us to leave immediately or we would all be arrested. Finally, they called my name and asked me to remove these people from the Cravens Building. I kept my mouth shut and my eyes straight ahead. Two officers grabbed me and dragged me out of the building onto the sidewalk and threw me in the paddy wagon. I felt something on my legs and looked down at the blood that was soaking through my stockings. I pulled my stockings off and tried to wipe the blood from my scarred legs. There was not enough time for me to think about myself because the police officers had LaMar Clark by one arm and were dragging him out the door. God was truly with Theodosia Crawford that day, because as they were dragging her out of the building, she was silent. Poor Freddie Lee Edwards was being dragged, but the white female demonstrators were being carried out and gently placed in the police car. Lieutenant Purser and another police officer picked Father McDole up and placed him in the patrol wagon. Purser told Father McDole, "It is below your dignity to be carried out of here." Father McDole said nothing.

When we arrived at the police station, I found that the following Blacks had been arrested with me: Jimmy Carr, LaMar Clark, Ella Louise Floyd, and Freddie Edwards. The whites arrested were Father McDole, William Roy Kirkwood (an OU student), Benny Paul VanMeter, Bill James Clifford, Ross Joseph Williams, Thomas William Brozden, Nellie Ruth Zoeller, and Doris Marie Manning. We were booked into city jail on a complaint signed by J. W. Quillan Jr. for blocking the entrance to Anna Maude's Cafeteria.

We stayed in jail until we were forcibly put out. When I saw LaMar Clark, he was laughing. I said, "What's funny?" He said when they got to their cell, there was a white drunk in there. When the drunk saw Father McDole with his priest's collar and black suit, he asked him what he was doing in jail. Father McDole didn't say anything. LaMar took the top bunk and continued to watch as the drunk looked Father McDole over from head to toe.

The drunk got up and walked over again and said, "Father, what are you doing in here?"

"I'm a prisoner, just like you," Father McDole answered.

"Do you think that God is going to come down here and unlock the jail and let you out?" the drunk asked.

Before Father McDole could answer, the drunk moved closer and with bloodshot eyes stared into his face, saying, "Father, I know one thing. If God comes in here and opens the jail door for you, I'm going right out the door with you."

LaMar said he fell off the bunk and just couldn't keep from laughing.

• •

I had never seen a group of Black children so sad as the NAACP'ers were on June 7, 1961, the day I told them that Father Robert McDole had been transferred from Corpus Christi Catholic Church in Oklahoma City to a new parish in Ponca City. "Why?" the children asked as tears flowed freely down their cheeks.

Father McDole arrived at Calvary Baptist Church. His eyes, too, were filled with tears. The children started chanting:

We love Father McDole.
We love Father McDole.
We love Father McDole.

He moved slowly to the front of the church as tears rolled down his cheeks. He spoke slowly and sincerely, telling the children that he loved them as if they were his own. "I'm leaving now, but I want you to know that I'm leaving a piece of my heart with each of you. And though we'll be separated, I will always be with you. Not even time itself can separate us from the experiences that we have had together. You will always have my heart."

He left, and we all cried.

Joe Hill said, "We must carry on now, because Father McDole is depending on us and we can't let him down." We left Calvary and marched downtown as if time itself had turned against us. We chanted:

Let freedom ring.
From the basement of John A. Brown's
To the top of the Skirvin Hotel,
Let freedom ring.

Father McDole had given us faith when we needed it. He had strengthened our faith when it was flagging, and we had made use of his musical talent and his training. We had listened to his sermons, which were sober, intelligent, well-constructed, and harmoniously illustrated, designed to make people think, to make them mad because of their own hypocrisy. His sermons were not designed to make you shout; nor were his jokes designed to make you laugh. He admitted his weaknesses, and we proudly recognized his strong points.

Recognizing his permanent absence, we clung to the memorable hours that he had walked with us. After he left the Sit-In Movement, he would continue to fight the walls of misunderstanding, which were higher than the highest mountaintop. He left a few of his loyal followers with us, such as Ross Williams, Nellie Zoeller, Mary Kennedy, and John Kennedy.

. . . .

The big question in Oklahoma was, what would the Most Reverend Bishop Victor J. Reed say about Father McDole being arrested? The answer came quickly. The head of the Oklahoma City–Tulsa Diocese, Bishop Reed became involved in the sit-ins because it was thrust upon him. He used his voice and the power of his position to speak out against segregation, and he permitted and encouraged his priests and laymen to become involved. He called for an end to "a policy of silence by Christians in the matter of racial segregation."

When Father McDole was carried out of the Cravens Building by the police, Bishop Reed said, "It was not a very dignified sight, but it is the man who appreciates the importance of personal dignity who properly reacts to the deplorable indignities suffered by so many of the Negro race in their own communities. If a priest must occasionally suffer indignity to call a reluctant public's attention to the indignity of racial discrimination, then I feel that the breach of decorum is justified."

Bishop Reed spoke at a Civil Rights Mass, which he celebrated during the closing session of the four-day National Catholic Conference for Interracial Justice. He said that he wanted to be a real moderate, as defined by Father John LaFarge. In Father LaFarge's definition, a real moderate was one who had recognized the many steps that ordinarily are needed to attain a given end. In the question of race relations, a real moderate was alive to the need for creating a new and more favorable climate of public opinion and was deeply convinced of the need for personal integrity and consistency.

Bishop Reed grew up in a segregated society and had not had any association with Blacks in school, social affairs, or local travel. He often related the difficulties that were faced by whites who had grown up in similar circumstances, "where long-prevailing custom is at loggerheads with law and principle." He was extremely concerned about Oklahoma, and he often talked about his beloved country, which stands as a world leader, and explained how her internal failures affect other nations. America's public image was being disturbed by her enemies as a result of racial segregation difficulties. The day had dawned when the problem of segregation must be squarely faced.

As E. Melvin Porter listened to the reports of the sit-inners and viewed the television coverage of the thirteen arrests, he was furious. He called for a march on City Hall and launched a drive for seven thousand new NAACP memberships. He also called for a renewed effort in the boycott of downtown Oklahoma City. Only the merchants could demand that restaurant owners begin serving Blacks. There would be no more asking on our part. We were going to demand.

Porter had been asking Mayor Norick to issue a city policy favoring the integration of public accommodations. Mayor Norick pointed out that he could not issue a policy in favor of only 11 percent of Oklahoma City's total population. But what difference did the population percentage make? Did Mayor Norick judge citizens on numerical strength, equal wealth, or education? The day of acceptance of any American citizen comes with birth.

Following the arrests of March 11, R. D. Cooper of the Cravens Building Corporation brought a suit against the NAACP, local NAACP officials, and individual sit-in demonstrators. Toward the end of March, an injunction was filed to prevent further demonstrations at the Cravens Building. The opening statement by B. H. Carey, chief counsel for the Cravens Building, was quite lengthy. The short and stocky attorney was really fired up. Emotional epithets rang in the air. He described our actions at City Hall as "unbelievable, terrible lie-ins, lay-ins, white sympathizers, and Negroes. They sat on their butts down on the floor, where they formed a human chain and blocked all entrances." He called Melvin Porter to the witness stand and shouted: "Didn't you see Clara Luper

Opposition to the "squat-in" came from all directions. Attorney U. Simpson Tate, an ardent NAACP worker, explained the association's stance: "The policy of the NAACP is to scrupulously observe and obey the constituted law, including municipal ordinances and state and national laws. We will remain with the sit-ins until their purpose has been achieved, but we will maintain our position with the same dignity and respect for the rights of others that we have demonstrated for the past fifty-two years of our operation. Notwithstanding some notorious utterances to the contrary, it can be said that there has not been any difference in practice or opinion on this point between Porter and Clara Luper." Although Tate vigorously disagreed with the "squat-ins," he was one of the greatest NAACP leaders that this nation has produced. His knowledge of constitutional law and his years of dedicated service will never be forgotten.

sitting on her butt on the floor in the Cravens Building in front of Anna Maude's Cafeteria?" and he stated the date.

Senator Porter raised his heavy eyebrows, frowned, rolled his big brown eyes at attorney Carey, and said, "Sitting on her butt? I don't know what you mean. You show me your butt, and then I can answer your question. I say, you point at your butt, and I'll tell you if she was sitting on her butt." The crowd burst out in uncontrollable laughter. I looked up at Porter, and he looked as if he wanted to go over and hit Carey and attorney Carmon Harris, who was with Carey.

The judge called for order in the court and then called for a recess.

The case went on for days: arguments on the constitutionality of the case, human rights versus property rights. In November, Judge Kenneth Shilling, from the southern part of Oklahoma, ruled in favor of the Cravens Building.

Our next move was to continue to protest without disobeying the injunction. We found legal loopholes, and the sit-ins continued, along with additional arrests and injunctions. Other tactics, like walking through the building and looking, were used. The Cravens Building took on the semblance of a war buffer zone, and we were prepared to die for our freedom every day. Judge Shilling had ruled that the group would have legal standing if a store offered services in one of its departments but refused them in another. Reverend B. G. Macon, an Oklahoma City minister who pastored in Wellston, purchased a Holy Bible in Brown's and then asked to be served at the luncheonette; he was refused. Harvey Gordon purchased a book at Green's and was refused service at the lunch counter there. This was proof that Judge Shilling's ruling was not an answer to the problem.

"You'll never get a Black person into Anna Maude's Cafeteria," stated a lawyer who had been a constant observer of our protests.

"Oh, yes, we'll get a Black person into Anna Maude's Cafeteria today," I said.

"I'll bet you five dollars that you'll not get a Black into Anna Maude's today!" he said with a quick victorious smile.

"Oh, yes I will," I replied.

"Oh, no you won't," he said.

"I need a couple of hours," I said.

"Okay, I'll be around," he stated.

We exchanged handshakes and he walked away.

I walked to the nearest telephone booth. Cecil and I held a quick conference. I called Carolyn Nixon, a white worker, and asked her to come up immediately and bring her little girl. She lived in Norman and had been participating in demonstrations along with her husband. While I was calling Carolyn, Cecil was also making telephone calls. We were having problems finding a black-skinned baby. We finally found one. The mother dressed him in his Sunday clothes and proceeded to get him downtown.

We walked down to the corner of Second and Broadway, where Carolyn and the baby were scheduled to meet us. We went over the final instructions. The baby, who was a little over seven months old, was to be wrapped from head to foot. Carolyn was to take her own little four-year-old girl into the cafeteria and was to ignore us as she passed.

Now Carolyn was on her way to Anna Maude's for lunch, and we were on our way to Anna Maude's to stand, sing, wait, and wonder. There were so many questions. What would happen if the guard took the baby? Suppose the baby started crying the moment that Carolyn got in line?

We waited. Someone ran out and said, "Oh! There's a nigger eating in Anna Maude's. Oh my God, they've gotten one in." No one asked for a description of the Black person. Rumors began to spread. One man said he had stepped in as a dishwasher; someone else said she must be a light-skinned Black who had slipped by the guard. Others were talking about how the guards should be fired because they were not efficient.

It was now on radio and TV that a Black person was eating in Anna Maude's Cafeteria in downtown Oklahoma City.

We continued to march and sing out in the lobby. I wondered if someone would attempt to beat Carolyn up. The lawyer who had bet me came downstairs, handed me five dollars, and said, "You think you're smart, don't you, Clara?"

"It all depends on how you look at it. Don't ever underestimate a woman's ability to outsmart men. Just remember, if women had been in power, we would not be standing out here," I said. He walked away and joined the crowd that was waiting to see this Black person come out of Anna Maude's Cafeteria.

Amid bright camera lights, Carolyn Nixon proudly walked out of Anna Maude's with a Black baby in her arms and her own white daughter beside her. She walked over and hugged me, saying, "Oh, it was a beautiful experience. This truly is the happiest day of my life. The baby didn't cry. Everything went just perfectly." She added, "As I continue to work with the NAACP in Norman, I'm ready to face the criticism and every other kind of harassment that I'll have to experience. I'm ready for any kind of assignment, I don't care how dangerous. I see the walls and I want to help remove them. I hope you all understand."

We all understood, and a big burst of applause went out as she left Oklahoma City for Norman. The next morning, the *Daily Oklahoman* carried the story, headlined "Baby Breaks Race Barrier, Thurs. 6-8-61."

Carolyn continued to work in the sit-ins. She was a professional engineer, and from that day on, she was harassed on her job and was finally fired.

On June 15, 1961, Ella Louise Floyd, Richard Odell Brown, Freddie Lee Edwards, and Edmund Earl Atkins were arrested at Anna Maude's Cafeteria and charged with violating other citizens' rights. Assistant City Attorney Herb Standeven prosecuted the case. J. W. Quillan testified that the sit-inners were blocking the building lobby and that tenants couldn't leave or enter from Robinson Avenue. Officer Jack Thorne said, "I saw thirty-two persons who had to walk out in the street in order to get around the demonstrators. One woman had to push her baby carriage into the street." We had dramatized anew the searing conflict over public accommodations.

Go down, Moses,
Way down at Anna Maude's.
Tell old Frank Wade
To let my people go.

It was the last Monday in August 1961, and a discouraged group of NAACP'ers sat on my front porch debating what we should do now that school was starting. Not only did the children have to go back to school, I had to go back. I had received hundreds of letters. They were mainly from members of the Ku Klux Klan and the White Citizens' Council. They sent me all kinds of materials—materials that were meant to prove my inferiority and why I should resign as a teacher in a public school. We went over a large number of the letters and agreed to give a box of them to the Quakers, who were collecting hate letters and sending them all over the world. Mr. Byerling, a devout Quaker, and his wife worked closely with us.

Our work started each day after school and on Saturdays. I felt as if we were hitting our heads against an iron wall. Yet we continued to hammer and hammer.

Earl Temple was an unusual man in many respects—a successful businessman and a community worker. He was a man whom Mr. and Mrs. D. J. Diggs spoke of with "pride and affection." He was a Black man by choice, not by color. He maintained his Black identity in spite of his white features.

Temple played the same kind of role for the NAACP Youth Council that Walter White had played for the NAACP. He was able to get inside hotels, restaurants, theaters, and parks. Therefore, we were able to get some "feedback" as to what the whites inside were saying. One morning we called him and told him that we needed to put a Black person in Anna Maude's Cafeteria. Temple, a freedom lover, stated, "I will do whatever you need."

"Earl, let's confuse 'the man.' Go to Anna Maude's and eat today." So it was that Earl Temple walked into Anna Maude's.

Fifteen minutes later, I walked up to a guard. He promptly stopped me. I asked why. "Clara, you know that we don't serve you colored folks," he said.

I said, "You do serve Black people. In fact, I just saw a Black person walk into the restaurant."

The guard turned red and called another guard, and to add to the confusion, the two guards moved from person to person. Finally one of them decided to check the backs of their customers' heads for Black features. I said, "I don't believe the 'head check' will work because there are thousands of Blacks who have the same hair texture and appearance as whites. Don't you know that Blacks come in all colors? There are Black Blacks, Black Browns, Brown Blacks, and Black Whites."

So Earl Temple had an opportunity to talk to many whites. One told him, "I wish that they would let those poor colored people eat."

"There is a Black person eating in here now," Earl told the white man.

The white man said, "Where? Where?" But before Earl could answer, the man jumped up. He said, "I'm going to get out of here, because there might be some trouble down here."

Dr. Donald Yates was a resident ophthalmologist at the Veterans' Hospital and an ordained minister in the Christian Church. He talked often of his plans to work in the foreign medical field. He started right here in Oklahoma City when he became involved in the sit-ins. His commitment was one of soul, mind, and body.

On May 20, 1961, he was booked at police headquarters on a complaint signed by Carmon C. Harris, the Cravens Building attorney, on a charge of loitering and disorderly conduct. Dr. Yates, a white man, and a Black youth had been denied admission to Anna Maude's Cafeteria and refused to leave the Cravens Building lobby, which was an entry to the cafeteria.

Dr. Yates said that instead of talking like a lawyer, Harris reminded him of a country psychiatrist when he said Yates wanted the publicity. This was the last thing that Dr. Yates wanted. Carmon Harris reminded me of a man who could easily become a dictator if conditions afforded. He stood and looked at his watch and in a Hitler-type voice ordered Dr. Yates to move in three minutes. Then he changed it to three seconds. Still showing his inherent powers, he said, "If you don't leave by the time that I count to three, I'm going to sign a complaint and have you arrested."

Yates said, "You can yell 'froggy' all you want to, but I'm not going to jump. I'm white, too, and I have some rights." Dr. Yates was taken to jail and refused to pay his fine. After a couple of hours, he was released on his own recognizance, pending a trial.

On May 21, Dr. Yates called me and said, "Clara, guess who just called?"

"Who?" I asked.

"Dr. Ray M. Balyeat Jr.," he said.

"I know he congratulated you for participating in the sit-ins. I bet they all are proud of you," I said.

"No, he did not congratulate me. He told me that my residency at the University of Oklahoma Medical School has been terminated," Yates stated.

I told Yates, "The first day that you came to the church, I told you that whites were tough on whites who helped or attempted to help Blacks. I told you and explained to you how the system worked. You are in for it, and I'm sorry. I didn't know that Dr. Balyeat was like that. What connection does he have with the medical school, anyway?" I asked.

"He is on the eye department faculty, and he has a part-time teaching appointment at the medical school," he said.

Dr. Yates explained in detail how he had had an appointment to be the second-year resident in a combined medical program. The programs were to be combined on July 1, 1961. He said that he was not permitted to appear before the doctors or members of the policy-making boards to tell his side of the story.

Attorney John E. Green explained that Dr. Yates had not violated any laws, and even if he had or were found guilty, municipal courts are not courts of record, and any conviction in municipal court could not be used to smear his record. Yates told us that he met with Dr. Mark Everett, the dean of the medical school, and three other medical officials. He continued to demonstrate at Anna Maude's Cafeteria and all over town.

• •

I had a whole crew of attorneys. In addition to John E. Green and my NAACP attorney from New York City, Robert Carter, there were a large number of other attorneys who had volunteered to represent the sit-inners, including Gene Matthews, Jay Bond, Archibald Hill, Melvin Porter, U. Simpson Tate of Wewoka, James Barrett, and Pat Parker.

Looking at all my attorneys, I was reminded of the two retired vaudevillians in Neil Simon's *The Sunshine Boys*, whose relationship was compounded by mutual irritation, conflicting vanities, differing personalities, and possibly an underlying respect and affection. All of my attorneys were ebullient and outgoing. They were enthusiastically and unashamedly involved in civil rights. My lawyers were full of life, vim, vitality, and dedication. I was constantly astounded by the eloquence of their arguments. Details, details, details, and they would always give me an alternative: "Tell us the minute details or pay us." They made me sit though long hours of constitutional arguments. Melvin Porter and John Green complained frequently about representing me, but they were always there.

• •

5

SIT-INS AND PROTESTS

Adair's Cafeteria

Louise Morrison was such a sweet person that I was not afraid to ask her to go to Adair's Cafeteria and bring me a slice of chess pie. This she'd willingly do. She was a light-skinned Black and could move freely in either the Black or white society. She decided to remain Black and use her life in helping people. She did not pretend to be white; no one asked her if she was Black or white as she ate in restaurants and cafés all over town, and especially at Adair's. Because of the lightness of her skin, they knew that she was white.

In 1959, we added Adair's Cafeteria on Lincoln Boulevard to our list. In February, four members of the Youth Council went to Adair's and were refused service. Ironically, Ralph Adair had operated an ice docket on Northeast Eighth Street and had been very closely associated with the Black community. He was county commissioner of a district that contained 90 percent of the county's Black population. He had voted to integrate eating facilities at the county courthouse, but he refused to serve Blacks at his cafeteria. He said, "I cannot make money serving Negroes because I will lose my white customers."

I shall never forget the day that we decided to go out to Adair's to eat. There were about fifty of us. The sun was shining brightly. We walked right in and made it up to the trays. We were stopped. "Oh, no! You cannot be served here. We're sorry." We stood there and waited, all in vain. Mrs. Ralph Adair and the waitress were extremely nervous. Our line extended to the outside of the building. We stood there and were not served. Leaving Adair's, we vowed to return and continue to return until the walls would fall.

Bishop's Restaurant

Until two centuries ago, the idea of freedom was only a dream. Human importance was only an idea. Tyranny and slavery were the realities of man's experiences. Then suddenly, the dream, the idea, grew into a bold and beautiful political system called "democracy." Men said, "Never hereafter will human beings be satisfied with anything less. When they hear of this, they will demand it as their right." History has taught us that America became the headquarters of this new freedom, and people came from all over the world seeking this freedom and the right to enjoy it. History has also taught us that this country was founded upon two principles: the Fatherhood of God and the Brotherhood of Man.

Wars have been fought all over the world for freedom—but a close look at America will convince anyone that freedom is still in its embryonic stage. An idea, yet someway, somehow, this idea must become a reality. This idea would take us to Bishop's, and we would say *Behold the walls!* So we went to Bishop's searching for freedom, and it was going to be a long, hard fight.

The management at Bishop's had decided on their own firm policy, which was to keep Blacks out at any cost. This was done by placing two strong men at the door. These two men evidently loved their jobs so well that they would not talk. We would go up to ask for permission to enter, and they would remain silent and hold the door with strong hands.

• •

In July 1962, Anna Marie Weems, director of human rights for the AFL-CIO in Waterloo, Iowa, was invited to a Human Relations Seminar at the University of Oklahoma in Norman. "The Human Relations workshop was one of the best that I have ever attended," she said. While in Oklahoma City she went to Bishop's Restaurant, where she was immediately refused while her white friend was offered service. The manager asked Weems to leave. She told him that she was an American citizen, and she would not cooperate with segregation and she was not going to leave. The manager called the police, and she was physically taken to jail for trespassing. She called me, and Doc Williams and I went downtown to get her out of jail. She was released on a twenty-dollar bond. Since her job called for her to travel all over the United States, she always related her horrible experiences in Oklahoma.

• •

"I was a paratrooper in the U.S. Army: I know how to land in enemy territory," Cecil Williams, the Youth Council's clean-shaven advisor, stated to the sit-in advisory group. "I am going to get into Bishop's today." Ryan Caldwell, an eighteen-year-old white student from Central State University in Edmond, Oklahoma, agreed with Cecil. They were part of a group of thirty who had joined entrance into Bishop's. The children left at 4:00 p.m., and I stayed until 6:00 p.m. Cecil and Ryan decided to stay all night.

A group from off Reno Street came in to say, "We are going to hang a nigger."

"I'm too afraid to leave and too afraid to stay," Cecil said.

They were paratroopers. Ryan didn't budge. He didn't eat or drink or go to the restroom. He stayed in front.

"Hey, nigger lover," they continued to harass Ryan. They told Cecil that he didn't belong. They stood over them and cursed them continuously.

Dr. Donald Yates took them some food; they continued to sit. The NAACP youth picketed outside from 11:30 p.m. to 12:00 a.m. and left Cecil and Ryan still sitting. We all returned at 8:00 a.m. with Mr. and Mrs. Leford Williams, Cecil's wife, Martha, and a large number of friends.

When Cecil and Ryan walked out, their faces looked as if they had not shaved for two weeks. Cecil said he was tired, stiff, scared, and thankful. Ryan solemnly added, "Me, too."

We were back at my home at 1819 Northeast Park Place, making plans. We were all sitting on the floor.

"We must change our strategy," Jimmie Stewart Jr. said.

Mickey Anderson said, "We must do something different."

"What?" said Edmund Atkins. "This is a war, and we must now resort to some guerrilla tactics."

"What do you mean?"

Jimmie said, "The Minutemen have a plan all worked out; we have been working on it for weeks.* We have everything planned down to the last detail. We need to meet at a church at 4:30 a.m. for a brief prayer and singing service." Robert Lambeth, Elmer Smith, Mickey Anderson, Gerald Wright, Tommy Barnett, and all of the other Minutemen had been working hard every day—from John A. Brown's to Bishop's.

---

*Editors' note: The Minutemen Commandos provided protection for the Youth Council members during the sit-ins and other demonstrations.

"You all may go to Fifth Street Baptist Church," I said. "Reverend Bratton said we could use the church at any time. We'll divide into groups. We'll go downtown and unload at Main and Robinson. Both groups will move in at five minutes to five; we'll be at the door and we will all rush in. Our main problem at Bishop's has been that we have not been able to get inside. Once we get in, we'll stay until we're served. If we can break down Bishop's, it will all be over, and all the walls will fall."

The group voted unanimously to follow the Minutemen's plans. The young men stayed up all night and kept a continuous eye on Bishop's. They knew the exact moment that the guards were pulled off the door. They saw them leave the building. They reported to Freedom's Headquarters, as they called 1819 Northeast Park Place.

It was 3:30 a.m. on May 31, 1963, and we were still on the telephone trying to be sure that we would have fifty people for the "Countdown" at Bishop's. Three hundred other youths were to meet at Calvary Baptist Church; they were to wait and come down to Bishop's as they were needed.

I was in the second group that arrived at Bishop's. I walked in, and the waitresses were in a rage.

In the midst of raving waitresses and angry customers, and with the manager at home asleep, we got into Bishop's Restaurant.

One waitress said, "Lord have mercy, what are we going to do?"

"Serve us," Tommy Barnett replied.

"We can't do that; we don't serve colored people here."

"You work them here, for nothing, don't you?"

Our quiet signal was given, and silence fell over the room. We sat and watched the operation. The waitresses were on the telephone talking to the manager. A middle-aged white man, who I thought was the assistant night manager, rushed to the front door and locked it.

A new situation had developed. We were locked inside the restaurant with several white people who could not get out. After a few minutes, we heard arguments between the man with the door keys and the white customers who were locked in. One well-dressed white man said, "I'm tired of this damn mess. Why don't you go on and serve those people?"

The waitress smiled and walked away.

"We've got to get to work, and you haven't seen no hell if I lose my job because of this ignorance. Once I get out, I'll never come back in here," one white man said.

It might have been by the providence of God that we were inside Bishop's on May 31, because it intensified the drive to eliminate segregation in public places. It demonstrated the utter fallacy of discrimination as both Blacks and whites were turned away. The door was locked, so no one, regardless of his color, could get into Bishop's that day. Many of them had been eating at Bishop's for years and were very angry because they couldn't get inside. A well-dressed white woman tried to enter and was turned away. She said to Harvey Gordon, "You stay with it. You're right, and I'm with you." She looked in the window and walked away.

Bishop's was indeed a battleground. A ten-year-old freedom fighter moved back and forth with an American flag on his shoulder. Well-dressed white men stood around and talked. Some wanted to serve us, and others said "No!" The wall was so strong that the cashier refused to give Kay Dyer, a reporter for the *Daily Oklahoman*, change for a one-dollar bill. One man outside yelled, "This is the old story of the sheep-men and the cowmen. Both sides are right, and neither will give in."

We remained quiet and watched the clock. Each second brought the knowledge that we had won a great victory. We had done what the management said would "never be done." We had got into Bishop's Restaurant en masse. Now that we were locked in, the customers were locked out, and Bishop's was suffering a financial stroke. The only question was, how long could she stand?

Martin Luther King had explained in one of his addresses how time was neutral and it could be used to benefit us or to discredit us. The decision was ours, and we had to make use of this day. The group consisted of college, high school, and elementary students. Wayne Lee James, a bright-eyed eight-year-old boy, came over and asked me, "When are we going to eat breakfast?"

I put my arms around him and said, "Wayne, it won't be long now."

He went back to his seat. In a few minutes, he was back with the same question.

"Wayne, it won't be long."

I looked up as Assistant Chief of Police Bill Williams came in. I didn't know what was going to happen. "I guess we are on our way to jail again," Reginald Johnson said.

Wayne James came back over, grinning, and said, "Mrs. Luper, are we fixing to go to jail? I see all the policemen have come. Did they come after us? Oh, goody! I'm ready to go to jail just like John."

Bill Williams walked over and spoke politely to me. In a few minutes, representatives from the fire department arrived. The assistant chief made it plain that he was only concerned with the safety factor that was involved. He kept asking the manager what would happen if a fire should break out.

Big Bud walked over to Calvin and said, "I'll tell you what will happen: Bishop's could serve fried nigger stew."

"Yes, mixed with boiled cream of waitress soup. One thing, all ashes look alike."

Morning was slowly fading away. We corresponded with the group outside by writing notes and holding them up to the window.

It was interesting to watch the fire inspector, Fred Rucker, and Bill Williams reading the city ordinances and conversing. I heard Rucker say that the city ordinance required at least one entrance and one exit to be open at all times. Rucker told me that he was not there to take sides; he was just there to see to it that the city ordinances would not be disobeyed. The fire chief, Haskell Grave, and inspector John Anderson were engaged in a deep conversation.

Ruth Lythcott walked over to tell me that the white customers were leaving through the back door. Things were beginning to happen.

What was going to happen now? What should we do? "There are too many white firemen and policemen down here for me to worry about," I whispered. "I'm just going to sit here and leave it to God. I sure don't know what to do. They are getting paid to do this; I'll let them do it."

Wayne James had made his round again. Edmund brought him over to my table and told me that Wayne was asking too many questions and I should keep him with me. I said, "Edmund, just remember that he is only eight years old."

We had gone over eight hours without any food or drink, and only three children out of the fifty had eaten breakfast. Not only were we suffering from hunger, but guards were standing at the door of the restaurant and would not allow us to use the restrooms. This was especially hard for the younger children.

At 11:15 a.m., I called all the people together and told them how proud I was of them. They had conducted themselves in such a manner that the whole country would be proud of them. As I looked at these young people, I was overcome with gratitude because they believed in me and trusted me so much. It was nothing for one to walk up to me and say "Thanks." So I began to really think about what I could say to them.

Suddenly, it became clear. I could tell them about the founders of our country and the price they had to pay for freedom. I went into detail about General George Washington and his brave troops who suffered at Valley Forge enduring cold and hunger. They had fought against all odds. Can you imagine thirteen small, unorganized colonies fighting a colonial giant like England?

I told them about my father, Ezell Shepard, who had gone into a Jim Crow army and fought, and had been wounded in France. He had suffered all kinds of humiliations just because he was a fourth-class citizen at home. When I finished, I told those tired, hungry children who needed to go to the restroom that in the final analysis, this whole operation at Bishop's depended upon each one of us. "Do you feel that we should go or stay? I want to have you think about it and make up your own minds as to what you individually want to do. This must be your decision."

The waitresses, managers, policemen, and firemen had stopped and were watching the youth. My heart was pounding, and my eyes were heavy since we had been working on Operation Bishop's all night. "Let's vote," I said. "All in favor of leaving, say aye." Not one voice was heard. "All in favor of staying, say aye." Ayes rang out all over the place.

"Why are you staying?" They answered in song. Because:

We shall overcome, we shall overcome,
We shall overcome someday.
Oh, deep in my heart, I do believe
That we shall overcome someday.
God is on our side, God is on our side,
God is on our side today.
Oh, deep in my heart, I do believe
That we shall overcome someday.

Zella Hull, Marilyn Luper, Carolyn House, Arnetta Carmichael, and Linda Pogue started saying together:

If you want your freedom,
Clap your hands.
If you want your freedom,
Shake your head.
If you want your freedom,
Say Amen!

The next song was by special request. Zella Hull was to sing "Joshua fought the Battle of Jericho, and the walls came tumbling down." When Zella would open her mouth, a kind of relief would pass over the crowd, bringing with it a strange feeling. We just knew the walls would fall.

As the group headed back to the tables, I reminded them why we were there. "We are here to build a better Oklahoma City and a better

America. I don't want you to destroy anything in here. I'm not convinced today that the manager and the owners hate us; however, I am convinced that they are victims of a system that's designed by the disciples of white supremacy, which must be destroyed now. No matter what happens, we've got to love. We've got to love those who would deny us."

The group sat silently. Willie Johnson demonstrated a rhythm exercise that could be done with spoons. "Mrs. Luper, just listen to this rhythm," he said as he shrugged his oversized shoulders from side to side. He stopped and went over to use a pay telephone.

The manager or assistant manager yelled, "You can't use that telephone!!"

Willie smiled and said, "Thanks, sir."

The man walked over to me and said, "I don't want any of these children to use the telephone. Do you understand?"

I said, "No! I don't understand."

I took a dime out of my pocket and walked over to the telephone. The strong man at the door rushed over and attempted to take the receiver from me. I held on to it with my left hand while he twisted my right hand trying to take it from me. I took my right hand and dropped the dime in and called Mary Pogue. I tried to convince her that we were all right.

She asked, "How long will you stay down there?"

I told her that we would stay until we were served.

She said, "You'll be down there the rest of your life."

We both laughed, and I hung up the receiver, looked at the man at the door straight in his eyes, and went back to the table.

In a few minutes, I saw the manager of Bishop's, the policeman, Dr. M. L. Peters from the Oklahoma County Health Department, and two other people engaged in a heated discussion. The manager and waitresses continued pointing at us. We didn't know what was happening. Finally, a policeman came over very politely and asked if they could speak to me for a minute. I replied, "Yes," and followed the officer.

When I arrived, I was formally introduced to Dr. Peters, who said, "I'm here because a health problem has arisen, not to take sides."

"Like what, sir?"

He went on to explain that there was an unusual health problem occurring there. I didn't understand and continued to ask him to be more specific. Finally, he told me that the workers had reported that the demonstrators were using the drinking glasses to urinate in rather than the locked restrooms.

"I just want to know if this is true. Is it true, Mrs. Luper?"

I said, "Sir, urine and tea or lemonade could look alike, and I don't feel that I have enough information to affirm or deny your statement. I know that we have been denied the use of the restrooms. We have been here since five a.m., and it's now nearly four o'clock."

"I only want to know."

"I know you want to be fair."

Dr. Peters repeated, "I'm only interested in the health part of this thing. I'm not here to take sides."

I said, "You said that you want to be fair with all of us. Based on that premise, I have a recommendation."

The doctor smiled and said, "Yes, Mrs. Luper?"

I continued, "Since the NAACP Youth Council members, the waitresses, the manager, the policemen, and I have been in here all day, the only way that the urine could be properly identified and classified would be by taking a specimen from each of us to match it with the urine in question. Then the proper urine identification could determine who is guilty. I don't mind going to jail, but I'd sure hate to go to jail for some urine that was not mine or my children's. If I'm going to jail for urine, I want to be sure that it is Black people's urine. I'm ready for my test. I refuse to go to jail for white folks' urine."

No one said anything else. We all just stood there. After a few minutes, I turned and went back to my table. Dr. Peters and his staff left, and we did not see them again.

I walked over to the window, where we communicated with the people outside. A crowd was gathering. A white man had just given A. Willie James twenty dollars to feed the children. He was all smiles. We exchanged victory signs, and I went back to the table.

Newspaper, radio, and television reporters were also outside. Jim Standard and Bob Lee mingled with the others.

Wayne James and Jimmie Stewart Jr. were busy talking. Wayne was telling Jimmie that he was hungry; he wanted some candy. Jimmie was telling him to leave. He said, "I don't want to leave, I've got to stay here and take care of Mrs. Luper."

So we stayed at Bishop's. When we finally left, the restaurant was closed for the day.

Monday, June 2, 1963, was the fourth straight day of Operation Bishop's. The restaurant had been closed on Friday and part of Saturday and

Sunday. Our numbers had increased and our drive was being felt. When we arrived at Bishop's, the door was locked. This was a visible sign of progress and a relief, because I didn't want to look at the two strong men who I felt would soon be unemployed. They saw us and rushed to the door. They were there to admit whites and to keep the Blacks out.

The Minutemen, with Wayne Chandler, Mickey Anderson, Jimmie Stewart Jr., James Woods, and others, were in complete control. We were marching in a circle. We were carrying signs that said:

FREEDOM NOW!

THE TIME IS NOW!

WAKE UP, AMERICA!

We continued to march. I heard a growl, and when I looked up, I saw a chimpanzee. It was growling and snapping at the children. The sockless white man threw it toward me. "He'll bite niggers. He has been trained to bite them," he said. Tommy Barnett completely lost his temper and started after him. A white man who had not participated in the sit-ins but had always watched them yelled as he jumped between the chimpanzee and me, "You damn fool!!"

Tommy jerked the door open and went after the man. Calvin said, "Oh, no you won't!" The man and his chimpanzee were warmly welcomed, and they went inside Bishop's Restaurant.

The Minutemen were angry, and they headed for the door. The strong men at the door were trembling, and one of them said, "No violence! No violence! No violence!" The Minutemen continued trying to pull the door open while the employees were holding it. I rushed up and got Big Bud. The group continued to rush up and to push against the door with their shoulders. Elmer Smith, Curley Sloss, and Harvey Gordon went around to the back door and attempted to force their way in. They came back and joined the high-tempered crowd. A large crowd was gathering, and we began to sing:

> I'm not going to let nobody turn me around,
> I'm moving on to victory.
> I'm not going to let no chimpanzee turn me around,
> No white men.
> I'm not going to let no chimpanzee turn me around,
> No Black men.

I was walking around saying to each group leader, "We're too close now! For five years. We are too close to victory to fail."

The group continued to sing as the man with the chimpanzee walked back out. By this time the place was completely filled with police officers, and we found out that this man had come to Oklahoma City from Stillwater.

"Thank God there was no violence today," Willie James said as we left Bishop's Restaurant. "Just remember, tomorrow is another day."

When Bishop's reopened the next day, we returned for "another day." And on June 4, 1963, the *Oklahoman* carried a newspaper article relating an agreement to meet and work for integration of the downtown eating establishments.

Perhaps Wana McNeil is unknown to most people. Perhaps she does not possess tact, skill, and concern for people's feelings. She said what she thought. But no one could match her ferocious tenacity on project opinions—she possessed a true individualistic personality. She was stubborn, but consistent. She constantly reminded me that she was white and I should stop and listen to reason. "Clara, I don't know why in the hell I keep calling and talking to you. I guess I do it because you aren't perfect. I want you to eat anywhere, but I just don't like sit-ins; but I'm happy that Bishop's Restaurant is opened."

The Bouldin Café

One day we sat silently in the Bouldin Café, at 408 North Broadway, and watched white waitresses serve other customers. "I will not serve you under any circumstance," Raymond Bouldin told us. We waited from 3:30 p.m. to 10:30 p.m. We left when Bouldin shut off the lights and angrily announced that the café was closed.

The Civic Center Grill

It was the end of a long day. We had tried to eat at the Huckins Hotel, Anna Maude's Cafeteria, and John A. Brown's and had failed. As we passed by a little eating place called the Civic Center Grill, at the back of the courthouse, the children suggested that we should stop in for a snack.

There were twenty-one members in our group. When we walked in, we were greeted by a pleasant-looking lady named Frances Adamson,

who told us to leave "this minute." It was 2:30 p.m., and she said that
they were closed. We knew that the place never closed until 6:00. A
white man walked in behind us and ordered twenty-two Cokes. He was
referred to as a "nigger lover" by Mrs. Adamson and Mr. McLean as they
refused to serve him.

Mr. McLean rushed over to the door to lock it. He went to the grill and
poured something that smelled like Clorox, Ajax, and lye. He heated a
skillet with hot grease and began to play a game with us. He'd bring the
skillet over and pretend that he was going to pour the grease on us. He'd
put it back on the stove to heat it until the smoke would come bursting
out to fill the room, and then he would walk over and pretend that he
was going to pour it on us. He put a sheet of paper in front of us and
said, "Sign your name, address, and telephone number." We signed our
names because we were proud of what we were doing for our country.
When we decided to leave, we went to the door only to find that he had
locked it and we couldn't get out.

"Nobody told you that you could come in here. Now I'm not going to
let you out of here until morning."

With the door locked and smoke filling the room, the children were
coughing and tears filled their eyes.

We started singing. I went to the telephone to call Dr. E. C. Moon,
John E. Green, Leslie Brown, and E. Melvin Porter. I had never seen
Attorney Green so upset. I didn't know what kind of discussions were
going on outside. All I knew was that they had called for additional help
and the doors were unlocked by the police. The twenty-one children ran
out and hugged the men responsible for their freedom.

We left the Civic Center Grill after telling Mr. McLean that we would
be back. We continued to go back on a "popcorn" basis. However, it was
not until three years later that we were able to eat there freely. A year
later, Mr. McLean sent each sit-inner a silver dollar.

The Forum Cafeteria

When we first heard that the Forum Cafeteria was going to open on
Main Street in Oklahoma City, we were happy. We believed that if we
could get a large nationally owned firm like the Forum to open its doors
to Blacks, the rest of the cafeterias would follow. Several conferences
with the management convinced us that the Forum Cafeteria was just
another wall to behold. It seemed as if the management felt a sort of
contemptuous pity for us. But who needed pity?

Eleven-year-old Areda Tolliver told of her experiences in the Forum: "I remember the day before we were to go to the Forum. Mrs. Luper took us over the things that we had to do. We only had one leader, and that was Barbara Posey. We were to watch her and remain quiet. Zella Hull was the song leader, and she was the one who was supposed to start the songs. The fact that we were going into the Forum—the brand-new cafeteria—was really exciting. I got up early the next morning. My mother turned on the TV, and we looked at yesterday's sit-ins. My mother was walking back and forth from room to room with a sad expression. She wanted me to take a sandwich and some LifeSavers. Before Mrs. Luper picked me up, Mother called me into the bedroom. She said, 'Remember that God will take care of you.' Then I walked out on the porch. In a few minutes, Mrs. Luper, Calvin, and Marilyn picked me up.

"From Calvary Baptist Church, we rode down to Halliburton's store and then walked up to Forum's. A big guard was at the door with a big chain in his hand. He was letting the whites in and keeping the Blacks out. Barbara Posey told us that we were to get into the cafeteria. As we marched around in a circle, the 'out' door opened, and I walked into the Forum by way of the 'out' door. I kept walking. I walked in line and saw a lot of pretty salads and pies. I walked on by, seeing all kinds of meat. I said to myself, 'That ham looks good. I wonder how it tastes.' It looked like everybody was staring at me. I turned my head, and the braid that was hanging down my back brushed against me, and I thought that someone from our group had touched me. I thought that meant for me to go and sit down. I saw an empty table and felt like running to it, but I knew that the group was behind me, so I couldn't afford to run. I saw an empty table and went over to sit down. I waited, and none of the other kids came. I felt all alone, and I looked at all the people. I thought, 'Maybe the waitress will help me' as I sat there conscious of the crowd.

"I was nervous and afraid—then one of my knees started to shake. I began to wonder if I could make it back out the door. I was inside looking out, and the rest of the NAACP'ers were outside looking in. I sat there for two hours before I could get enough strength to move outside. In order to get out, I had to go through the inside door. When I walked outside, Mrs. Luper put her arms around me, and I was no longer nervous or scared."

As the weeks went by, we continued to test the Forum Cafeteria. One day one of our inspectors noticed that the guards were off the door. We immediately moved thirty of our sit-inners into the cafeteria. We went through the line and picked up salads before we were stopped. A. Willie

James, our financial director, was with us, and he pulled out the money to pay for the salads. I told the people to go ahead and eat them: "Maybe we'll integrate the salads today, the meat department tomorrow, the vegetables the next day, then the desserts, and finally the drinks."

We tried to talk to the manager and his assistant, but they refused to talk and refused to take the money for the salads, for if they'd taken it, they would have been accepting us as human beings, which they refused to do. We spent two hours inside and finally left with our stomachs full of salad and our money still in our pockets.

Frye's Restaurant

While diligently engaged in the preparations for an entirely new sit-in, we did not neglect to test new places of public accommodation. The exigencies of sit-ins permitted no cloistered calm days, and opportunities to test new policies were ever imminent.

We had achieved some resounding successes, and one victory called for another. So twenty-five of us were walking the cold, hard streets on Oklahoma City looking for freedom. I was walking in front of the group, and I started to open the door to Frye's Restaurant. Jack Frye stood in the door as if to block it, and I said, "Merry Christmas, Mr. Frye. May we eat today?"

He said, "No, but you may have this." And he spit in my face. That spit hit me like a thunderbolt, but I wiped it off.

My children's lacerated pride had suffered the ultimate agony. The soothing words of the Christ of the Ages, "Forgive him," comforted me. This was an indignity that I must take, and I must push it into a recess of my mind because I had mountains to climb.

I'm not going to let no spit turn me around,
Turn me around, turn me around,
I'm headed for the Promised Land.

We stayed at Jack Frye's restaurant for three more hours. He locked the door, and every once in a while he'd stick his head out the door and yell at us.

Green's

On August 10, 1960, eighty-five youths entered S. H. Green's luncheonette in the 200 block of West Main Street in downtown Oklahoma City.

We had our groups divided between John A. Brown's, Huckins, Anna Maude's Cafeteria, Bishop's, and Green's. Mrs. Helen Grimmett, one of the adult demonstrators, came over to Brown's and recommended to me that we should move all of our people over to Green's.

I said, "Helen, we have already integrated Green's."

She said, "No, Clara, you have only integrated one-half of Green's. The eating facilities on the east side serve Blacks, but they will not serve Blacks on the west side."

After a lengthy conversation on the advantages and disadvantages of the plan, I agreed to go over to the west-side luncheonette with her. We went in and were refused service. We left immediately and walked down to Bishop's Restaurant, where the NAACP'ers were conducting a silent demonstration, and moved the entire group to Green's west-side luncheonette.

This mass entrance came as a shock to Mr. R. N. Henson, the manager, and he immediately closed the lunchroom, locked the front door, and placed a black umbrella stand across the door. He said, "I'm sorry, we're closed for the day." He turned the lights out, and we started singing spontaneously and quoting the Twenty-Third Psalm over and over.

We sat patiently in the dark as Mr. Henson and the employees paced nervously up and down the aisles. We stayed until the store closed and felt as if we had exposed another wall within Green's Variety Store.

By June 1961, security had been tightened at Green's, and for months we could not get in. One day, thirteen-year-old Deborah Morrow slipped past a guard and sat for four hours. She was not served, but when she came out she said, "Those hamburgers sure do smell good."

During the sit-ins, the Holy Bible was our constant companion. While Zella Hull sang "Joshua Fought the Battle of Jericho," we decided to enact that biblical passage. We were going to walk seven times past the entrances of Green's, Bishop's, the Huckins Hotel, Anna Maude's Cafeteria, and John A. Brown's. This we did, but the walls remained.

The Huckins Hotel

On June 21, 1961, C. Clifford Kerns, a seventy-seven-year-old Oklahoma City doorman at the Huckins Hotel, refused to allow two Blacks to come inside. They told Mr. Kerns that they wanted to buy some coffee. He stood in the center of the doorway, and while one of them argued with him, the other grabbed the cuff of his trousers and pulled his feet out from under him. He was hospitalized with a broken left wrist. The Blacks left the scene and were never heard from or apprehended.

John Frain had eaten at the Huckins Hotel for ten years. He had undergone three recent spinal operations and decided to observe the sit-in at the hotel. He and Dr. Yates entered the coffee shop, where they both had coffee and talked about the day when no person would be discriminated against because of race. As they were leaving, according to Dr. Yates, "Don Kent Bell, a thirty-five-year-old guard who had been stationed there to keep out Blacks, shocked [Frain] and called him a 'nigger lover.'" Bell started hitting Frain, who had to be rushed to the doctor afterward. Bell said he had asked Yates and Frain to leave the hotel, and when they refused, he threw them out.

O'Mealey's Cafeteria

In January 1962, a white lady wrote this letter:

> 2325 Westlawn Place
> Oklahoma City 12, Okla.
> January 22, 1962
> Mrs. O'Mealey
> Manager of O'Mealey's Cafeteria
> 3132 N. May
> Oklahoma City, Oklahoma
>
> Dear Mrs. O'Mealey:
>
> It was I who called you asking why your cafeteria was not open for service around noon Saturday, January 20th.
> You said to me, "You tend to your business and I will tend to mine." Dear Mrs. O'Mealey, that is exactly what I was doing. It is the business of every good citizen to work for the high moral and ethical standing of his state and country. I had hoped to get you to see that it was not your thought that you would lose money by serving Negroes, but your prejudice and hate which you had stimulated and let grow through the years which was activating you. For you would not lose a cent by admitting Negroes, but gain.
> John A. Brown Company had the same idea as you—that they would lose trade if they served Negroes. But they found out

later that they lost trade because they did not serve Negroes. The Youth Council put on a boycott. The Negroes withdrew their trade with Brown's, and many, many decent white people did the same. Finally trade became so bad that Mrs. Brown called in the leader of the Youth Council and made the statement that they were losing money, not only by the withdrawal of Negroes, but also by white people, and if they (Brown's) would serve Negroes, would they call off the boycott? The Negroes agreed. The boycott was called off, and the Browns served Negroes and took down their segregated toilet signs.

I am one of the white people who did not buy at Brown's for three years, or until they treated Negroes as human beings. I encouraged white people to boycott Brown's, and many did. I could do the same with you, but I won't, for I have been informed by some of the people who eat with you that you have a good heart but that we will have to give you time to eradicate the prejudice and hate that has been growing in you for years. Many of the white people who patronize your cafeteria disapprove of your actions.

Mrs. O'Mealey, cultured people do not have such prejudices. It is largely the illiterates who are jealous of the achievements of the Negro. Can you name any white person in America who can top Dr. Ralph Bunche? Thurgood Marshall, the greatest constitutional lawyer in the country, and who won every case for the NAACP that he carried to the U.S. Supreme Court, is now a federal judge. Why was he appointed? Because he is the best qualified for said position in the U.S.A.

President Kennedy has Negroes in other administrative positions. Judge William Hastie has been a federal judge for years, and so highly respected.

You will have to get into step, Mrs. O'Mealey, with progress and humanity or be classified with the horse and buggy era and illiterates. You have to make the choice. If you make it for humanity you will be most happy.

I beg of you to join the human race and be human.

I love my Negro friends as well as I do my white friends, and am always happy when I can have them dine with me. I am glad to be associated with a Negro family in my church.

Get acquainted with Negroes and you will love them.

My very best wishes,

Caroline E. M. Burks, Retired Educator

In December 1962, we carried out Operation O'Mealey's. Mrs. O'Mealey refused service to ten Blacks, and told me that President Kennedy was trying to destroy the white people's rights.

The Pink Kitchen

On the west corner of Northeast Twenty-Third and Lottie Streets stood a railroad car–shaped eating place called the Pink Kitchen. It was located in an area that was rapidly changing from a predominantly white neighborhood to a Black one. One day Calvin, Marilyn, and I decided to stop by and eat a good old hamburger with French fries. We were greeted at the door by Merl G. Walker, the owner, who started fussing and yelling at me. "You know better, Clara Luper. I wouldn't serve you folks under any condition. I'm just a poor small businessman, and I don't like being picked on," he said.

"Thank you, sir, but in the words of one of our great generals, 'We shall return,'" I said. We went home and called an emergency meeting of the NAACP Youth Council. The group agreed to pay a visit to the Pink Kitchen the next day. The technique would change, in that we would use adults, because one look at Merl Walker and I knew that he was a tough man and would do anything to perpetuate segregation at the Pink Kitchen.

It was near noon the next day when we arrived at the Pink Kitchen. Dr. James Cox, Dr. Donald Yates, Cecil Williams, Reverend Macon, and I walked anxiously toward the door. Merl Walker saw us coming and immediately called the police. His customers represented an uncouth segregated group, who booed and jeered us that day. We had become used to people calling us niggers and giving the whites a hard time.

Dr. Cox, Oklahoma City's only Black psychiatrist, was not wholly or even partially committed to nonviolence, and he put aside his medical terms and systematically laid before them a multitude of curse words, which came out of his mouth so rapidly that Merl Walker stood silently as if in a state of shock. The policemen arrived with extra scout cars and held a quick conference with Mr. Walker. One of the policemen walked over to me and said, "Mrs. Luper, you all must leave the Pink Kitchen, or I'll have to take you all down and you'll be in jail again."

A crowd was gathering, and the people in the Pink Kitchen were silent and were now staring at us.

I looked at Cecil, who was watching Dr. Cox. At any minute I expected Mr. Williams to burst out in his usual hysterical rhetoric. But, to my surprise, he put on his militaristic paratrooper's manners and saluted the police officer, then proceeded to the police car.

The policeman walked over to Dr. Cox, who yelled, "Man, don't you put your hands on me. I say, don't you put your hands on me! I mean that! Don't you touch me!"

I walked over to Dr. Cox, and he told me that he was not thinking about that nonviolence stuff. "This is no Sunday school class, this is hell!!"

I said, "You're right, Doc. Come on, let's go."

Dr. Cox told the officer that he always had respected me. Because of the respect that he had for me, he'd go on downtown, nonviolently. "Why, we're out here on the sidewalk," he said as we walked to the police car. He asked the officer if he could ride downtown with his wife, who was sitting across the street.

"No, you may not," the police office said.

Dr. Cox entered the back seat with Cecil. As the policeman drove toward the city jail, Dr. Cox talked. "You know, you must be awfully dumb. Don't you know that you are wasting the taxpayers' money by taking us to jail? How much is the fine?"

Cecil said, "Twenty dollars for standing on the sidewalk, one hundred dollars for being Black, fifty dollars for being Negro, and thirty dollars for being colored. A grand total of two hundred dollars. Oh, Professor F. D. Moon must be proud of my math today."

We all laughed. The police officer was swelling and tried to look tough.

"I don't care how much the fine is. I could get out," Dr. Cox said. "Don't you know I get paid to look through people's heads. Look, that's my wife who is driving behind us. She has enough money to get all of us out."

When we arrived at the police station, somebody said, "Here they come again." We went through the same old shakedown procedures and were finally placed in cells.

While we were in jail, Merl Walker, owner of the Pink Kitchen, filed a suit in district court against us. District judge William Wallace Jr. issued a temporary restraining order against further demonstrations. The injunctions named E. Melvin Porter, president of the NAACP; Clara Luper, NAACP youth advisor; and Dr. Donald L. Yates, city optometrist, among others.

Merl Walker alleged that we had stirred up trouble and unrest around the Pink Kitchen and created disturbances that had not existed before. He stated that we had deliberately and unlawfully blocked mass occupancy of the front entrance of the restaurant, destroying ingress and egress; and because of the demonstrations, we had created and maintained an atmosphere of danger, unrest, tension, and fear that was wholly incompatible and inconsistent with the orderly operation and maintenance of the Pink Kitchen.

Melvin Porter filed a $50,000 suit for false arrest on behalf of Cecil Williams, A. Willie James, and Reverend Macon, which alleged that they were arrested and forced to spend time in jail, and that the Pink Kitchen maliciously, unlawfully, and without cause was responsible for their arrests and being charged in open court. The suit sought $150 for expenses in hiring attorneys, $4,850 for mental suffering, and $45,000 for injury to health and reputation. It was never brought to court.

Ralph's Drug Store

On November 19, 1963, twenty-five of us went into Ralph's Drug Store at Northwest Fourth and Broadway. Ralph Wooten announced that the store was closed, and anyone inside was going to jail. We left and told him that we would return. We did return, and on January 28, 1964, Ralph's filed an injunction suit against the NAACP and CORE.

Melvin Porter, Cecil Williams, Theodosia Crawford, and I led a demonstration there. It was Porter's turn to teach the lesson on nonviolence. He taught it at Calvary, but when we got to Ralph's, the manager called me a black bitch, and Porter swung at the manager's head. The Minutemen, led by Ronnie Spivey, grabbed Porter, and a fight was avoided.

James D. Giles, the attorney for Ralph's Drug Store, said that the injunction request filed against the Congress of Racial Equality would be dropped, because CORE demonstrators had acted within the law. The case against the NAACP would be heard before Judge W. P. Keene on February 10, 1964. At that time a permanent injunction was issued against us.

The Skirvin Hotel

It was raining in Oklahoma City on June 6, 1961, and we prayed to God that the doors of the Skirvin Hotel would be open. We had been demonstrating outside at Bishop's. The door was open, and we walked into the hotel at 10:00 a.m. Ronnie Spivey led the group out around 2:00 p.m. after being refused service.

Inside the Skirvin, a young white man stood and discussed the shouting and the abuses that were coming from the hecklers who had been yelling at us. He asked if he could talk to me for a minute. I said, "Yes, I have plenty of time. It doesn't look as if we will be served today."

He shook his head in bitter sadness as he watched the Black children standing in line "waiting and waiting" to be served. "I completely deplore what's happening here," he said. "This makes me ashamed of my town; it makes me ashamed of myself and my own convictions about segregation."

He talked faster, as if only momentum could get his words out. He told me that his roots were deep in the South, and the southern traditions had been instilled into every cell of his white-skinned body. His forefathers were slave owners, and one of his relatives had served on the personal staff of Jefferson Davis. "I think about it, analyze it, and I can't justify my feelings on any grounds intellectually, morally, socially, or religiously. I have great sympathy for you all as products of God's creation. I am religious. I'm a Baptist and I never miss church. I work in my church and believe the Bible. But I just can't get ready for integration in hotels and restaurants. I don't say that easily.

"I ask myself, just what do I fear in public accommodations? Integration? I'm not afraid of you people. Some of my best friends are good colored people. I'm not afraid of what other people will say. I know deep in my heart that I don't fear intermarriage because I'm confident that none of my children will ever marry a colored boy.

"I don't fear you people, economically or educationally. I'm financially and educationally secure. You people threaten me in no way. Why? Why? Why? I keep asking myself, why do I oppose integration here at the Skirvin, and the emotional answers come back fast. Colored folks aren't as clean, as healthy, or as intelligent as whites," he yelled.

"Say something, Clara," he said as he cast his blue eyes toward the floor.

"No, you go on and talk," I said.

"Oh, Clara, you could talk me out of those arguments. I hear you all the time on Abram Ross's show, and I have heard you on *Sunday Forum* on KOMA. Go on, strip me of my rationalization. You can, but I'll still be against it. Why? Why? Why? Because I know I'm better than you all are. I just know it." He stopped as if he had reached a sudden stop sign.

"Go on," I said. "You couldn't be through. I have plenty of time, and it doesn't look like we're going to be served today."

He went on slowly as his eyes flashed from the Black children who were standing in line back toward me.

"The colored people were the slaves. We brought them here from Africa; we auctioned them off like cattle at what my grandfather called

'African Square' or 'Jungle Avenue.' Slaves were like animals, no brains. If they looked good, we bought them; and if they were sick, we left their diseased and infected bodies in the stables. I can't defend this, but it is here in my blood, deep, deep in my bloodstream. Sure, colored folks cooked for us. But that was different. It was in the grand manner of the 'Old South.' They were always so happy, laughing and showing their big white teeth. They always stayed in their place. I used to ride horseback with a clean little colored boy in Texas. He didn't mind riding behind me. Colored folks always addressed us as 'Massa' or 'Mister.' They were always helping us, and we remember that. I can't get away from the spirit of those days. It's ingrained in me, and I just can't shake it out of me. I can't endure the thought of colored people checking into this hotel, the same as me and my people. Look, Clara, I sure have enjoyed talking to you."

He moved to the side for a moment, then said very sadly, "I may as well complete the worst of the confession. About a month ago, I went to the manager here and told him to keep you all out, and if he let you all eat and sleep here, I wouldn't come back. Not only that, I got my friends to do the same."

He stood and waited for me to respond.

"Thank you," I said.

"Is that all you have to say? 'Thank you'? Do you know this is the first time in my life that I've ever told a colored person just how I have felt, and you just say 'Thank you.' I'll be darned. What are you going to do now that you know?"

I said, "I'm going to do what I've been doing."

"And what is that?" he asked.

"I'm just going to continue to love you," I said.

"Why?" he asked.

"Somewhere I read that the religious specifications state plainly and distinctly that 'You must love your enemy,' and Reverend J. B. Bratton Jr., my pastor, told us last Sunday that there is no other way."

He pulled out his handkerchief and walked off abruptly. As he passed, Theodosia Crawford said, "White trash, white trash. That's all he is."

Theodosia Crawford, a hardworking NAACP member and advisor, never missed a sit-in. Sometimes when she had a hair appointment, she would tell us that she would be late. She was a rare individual who was nonviolent in physical action but violent with her tongue. She could rip white and Black folks with hard, cold, provoking words. She always carried several magazines and newspapers and never missed anything in a paper that related to any kind of human rights. She could be reading and some white person would step on her, and she would violently and verbally attack the person and turn politely back to her reading material. If the person would react violently, she would challenge him in any manner and as viciously as she could with words and the movement of her eyes. She was a very detailed person and well organized. The children loved her at times and fondly called her Aunt Theodosia. She believed in discipline, and when she would tell the children to shut up, they would. She developed an eye technique that I called "eye in." She used it frequently, and it was now visible as she faced the small hostess at the Skirvin.

The Skirvin Hotel was located on Broadway and First in downtown Oklahoma City and possessed the dignity and tradition of being Oklahoma City's top hotel. A large number of Blacks were employed there in the traditional positions. The moment that I saw Dan James, the owner, I knew that we were not going to get along, and we didn't. We fussed at each other with the ferociousness of dogs and cats.

I told him that he would make an elephant in any zoo sick. He told me that I made him sick, and this town was all right until I started all this mess. "I didn't start it; you started it!" This led to another one of our verbal arguments. In further conferences, we accomplished nothing, and we would deliberately avoid speaking to each other during the sit-ins. He would always peep at us and rush on to his office.

When we arrived at the Skirvin one day, the hostess had gone to the back of the room, and about seventy of us got into the Sooner Room and took seats at those beautifully arranged tables. The white customers ran out as if the world were on fire. This brought a burst of laughter from all of us, including Father Robert McDole and the other whites who were with us. In a few minutes, I was greeted by Dan James. He spoke to me and used harsh words that meant "Take these people out of my place, right now!"

I said, "We need menus so that we can order."

He said, "You'll never get them. Who do you think you are, Clara Luper?"

Father McDole spoke: "She is a very intelligent lady." Dan James asked him to shut up, and those two white men then engaged in a bitter dispute that drew the attention of everyone in the building. Father McDole told him that he was tired of bigots and tired of segregation, and these people were humans and should be treated just like everybody else. The argument continued with the usual human rights versus property rights arguments. We stayed in the Sooner Room for about six hours as the waitress stood with folded arms and watched us.

After this entrance into the Sooner Room, additional staff was mobilized in such a way that someone was always at the door. So we would proceed to ask for service and leave. We would often talk about Ira Hall Jr., the brilliant son of Mr. and Mrs. Ira Hall, and how he was the first one to get into the Sooner Room plaza. How he got by the hostess is still one of the mysteries of the Sit-In Movement. All I know is that Ira Hall Jr. was sitting in the Sooner Room with the dignity of a British prince. It gave us a sense of pride just to see him sitting there. As we watched him, we'd quote from a Langston Hughes poem:

I, too, sing America.

I am the darker brother.
They send me to eat in the kitchen
When company comes,
But I laugh,
And eat well,
And grow strong.

Tomorrow,
I'll sit at the table
When company comes.
Nobody'll dare
Say to me,
"Eat in the kitchen,"
Then.

Besides,
They'll see how beautiful I am
And be ashamed—

I, too, am America.

"Ira sure is handsome," Doris Powell said. All the other girls quickly agreed. He had come from a long line of freedom fighters. His parents had been put out of their home on Northeast Seventh Street because they were Black, and Black people were not supposed to live across Seventh

Street. So the sheriff had their furnishings thrown out into the street. At that time Mrs. Hall was pregnant, but no one cared. Mrs. Hall was a Hibler, a family that believed in education, and Mr. Hall had fought for freedom for years. Now their small son was inside, taking all the humiliations that were thrown at him. As I looked at him, I said, "Thanks be to God."

The other children went wild with applause when Ira finally decided to leave. He told them how he felt and how the food smelled. The egg custard and everything looked so delicious. "We've got to get back in there and eat," he said. "Someday I'll have the type of job where I can afford everything that I want to eat, and no one will deny me anything because of my color."

Demonstrations continued at the Skirvin Hotel. After a state NAACP convention, a group of adults decided to demonstrate at the Skirvin with us. We went over the rules and asked the adults to cooperate with us, if they could only remember that it was a nonviolent demonstration. They agreed. We left Calvary Baptist Church and marched silently to the Skirvin. As we stood in line, a big, burly white man came and pushed J. J. Simmons Jr., the president of the state NAACP and a successful oilman from Muskogee. That white man made a mistake, and for a few minutes I thought the "J" in Simmons's name stood for "Joe Louis," because Jake Simmons started boxing that man with heated words. Although he is an African Methodist Episcopal layman, he mixed spoonfuls of profanity with his words. Sweat was popping out of his delicate brown skin like popcorn and dripping to the floor. I walked over as he was putting his hat on. He said, "Here's twenty-five dollars. Buy the children's lunch. I'm not cut out for this kind of thing. I'll kill that man. I have to leave."

I started laughing and said, "You are excused from all further sit-ins. You've just flunked your first test in sit-in-ology." So Jake Simmons left, as we sang "We Shall Overcome."

The battle against the walls of the Skirvin continued. One day, I led about fifty children into the hotel and walked up to the hostess. She said very angrily, "What do you want, Clara Luper?"

I said, "I want you to move out of that doorway and let me eat!!"

She said, "Oh, no, I'm not going to do that. You've been coming down here all these years; you ought to take your black self home and stay!!"

I raised my voice: "If you don't open that door, I'm going to . . ." At that moment, she called her assistant manager and the manager. They held a quick conference and called the police. When the police arrived, they had another conference. Evidently, they were trying to decide what charges to file against me. Finally, the manager, the hostess, and a policeman walked up to me. The police officer asked if I would step away from the crowd and follow them. I did. We stopped at the northwest end of the lobby.

The police officer told me that I had threatened the hostess. I said, "I beg your pardon, sir. I have not threatened the hostess. Please ask her to tell you what I said."

He asked her to tell him. She said, "Mrs. Luper rolled her eyes at me and said in a loud, mean voice, 'If you don't open that door I'm going to . . .'"

The officer had the situation clearly in hand, and representing the arm of the law, he was ready to hear the rest of my words. "What did she say that she was going to do to you?" the officer asked.

"She, she, she said—," the hostess began.

"Go on; it could be embarrassing. I mean, the profanity she probably used. Go on and tell us."

The officers looked at me when she couldn't find words to say it. They asked in an authoritative manner, "What did you say, Clara?"

"I told her that if she didn't open that—and before I could finish, she left. If I could've finished, I would have said, 'If you don't open that door, I'm going to walk away.'"

The manager was embarrassed. The hostess started crying. The officer said, "I can't arrest her for that."

"Thanks," I said as I joined my group in singing "Joshua Fought the Battle of Jericho."

The sit-ins continued at the Skirvin Hotel until 1964.

Another day
Without any food.
That's not good,
So we'll eat today.

On Sunday, July 9, 1961, Ruth Lythcott, the fifteen-year-old daughter of Dr. and Mrs. George Lythcott, led a group to the Sooner Room at the Skirvin Hotel. When Ruth attempted to walk in, two tall white men pushed her out the door and forced her back into the street.

Also on Sunday, July 9, 1961, Dr. Donald Yates, the white ophthalmologist, entered the Sooner Room at the Skirvin Hotel. The hostess asked him, "How many?"

"Six," he answered.

She said, "If they are white, they can come in. But if they are Black, they cannot come into the hotel. Is that clear?"

The Sooner Inn

On August 27, 1960, we went into the Sooner Inn and asked for Cokes. The waitress told me that we would have to take them and leave. I sat down and said, "I don't mind waiting." The waitress called the police. We waited and waited. The police came, but did not arrest us.

The Split-T

In early May 1964, we decided to change our strategy. This time, we would go out to the Split-T Restaurant, located in Nichols Hills at 5701 North Western Avenue. This area was home to the so-called upper crust of the city. It was an area that had not been touched by any kind of demonstration. These were people whose children had been reared by Black people. Black people cleaned their homes and nursed them during their illnesses.

I thought it would be better to go on a Sunday night. I knew that those who had gone to church would have an opportunity to practice their Christianity.

When we arrived, profanity came from all directions. Teenagers started cursing us. They cursed and cursed. The manager jumped up and told us that we had to leave right that moment. We started singing "We Shall Overcome." The song was blending with curse words, which continued to come from teenagers who had been sitting in fine cars. We didn't come to fight, we came to eat.

As I listened to those young people, I began to wonder, who were their parents? Who were their grandparents? Why, those were the craziest-acting kids I had ever seen. It was like all hell had broken loose.

"Go home, niggers, we don't want you here," they said.

"Go back to Africa, you damned niggers," they said.

The teenagers said that they were mainly from John Marshall High School, and frowns were glued to their young faces as profanity continued to come out of their mouths. They started throwing sacks, paper cups, ice, and rocks at us.

Eight police officers and one K-9 unit came out and stood between forty-two of us and about ninety white teenagers. Major Wayne Lawson came over and said, "Mrs. Luper, this is really a touchy situation. I sure don't want any violence."

I got angry with Major Lawson and said, "Why don't you go over and tell the white teenagers what you are telling us. We are not cursing or threatening anyone. We are not telling those kids whose parents come from Ireland, France, England, Germany, or another country to go back to the countries where their forefathers came from. This is Indian Territory, anyway. I could yell back 'Give the Indians their land,' but these young people believe they are right, and we aren't saying anything." So we continued to stand.

Melvin Porter arrived on the scene, and he was puffing, sweating, and fussing. "Clara, what in the hell are you doing out here causing all this hell? You all had better get your Black asses back over to the east side, or else you'll all be dead and you won't get to eat anywhere." I didn't say anything, and this really made him mad. He yelled, "Clara, it's no use for you all to act like damn fools. Those people mean business. Oh my lord! What's going to happen next? We had better go somewhere and pray." He stood there, erect like a British soldier, and in a few minutes he started praying.

In his prayer, I noticed that he was using a single "I" when he asked the Lord for protection. I said, "Porter, since you are praying, why don't you ask God to care of all of us." He told me to shut up. I walked over and continued talking with the youth. After over an hour, we were on our way to jail.

Porter called for a halt to the demonstrations and for a week of prayer and meditation. This was necessary, he said, "in order to try to resolve the problems." He tried to get me to agree with him.

An open fuss developed between Melvin Porter and Archibald Hill, the president of CORE. Hill told Porter in no uncertain terms, "We have prayed enough. We must now put some legs on our prayers and some common sense in our heads, because these white folks aren't going to give us anything."

David Haynes, the manager of the Split-T, signed a complaint against Calvin Luper, Edward Maurice Willie, and Wayne Shannon, and we were booked at the Oklahoma City police headquarters for disorderly conduct. We spent about an hour in jail and were released on twenty-dollar bonds that were put up by Doc E. Williams.

The next day we went back to the Split-T and were again arrested. We were then served with a restraining order.

The 3300 Restaurant

On September 5, 1960, we arrived at the 3300 Restaurant and were refused service. Mrs. Los Angeles Joseph wrote her husband, "Today's experience in singing, praying, and waiting to be served is one that I shall always cherish."

Val Gene's

One day when we arrived for a sit-in at Val Gene's, a waitress said: "Here they come, the niggers are here again!"

The manager walked up and spoke very kindly. "How are you today?"

"I'm fine today, and I'm ready to eat," I said.

"Mrs. Luper, we have decided to serve you all today."

I was caught by surprise. I counted the children: there were sixteen. We had an agreement that whenever we would get into a place, we'd eat a dollar's worth of food. The children were happy, and they rushed to the various tables. I had a minor problem, which had become a major problem: I didn't have any money.

I took a seat at a table. The waitress continued to ask me to order. Here I was with a one-hundred-year appetite, and for four years I had been trying to break down segregation in restaurants—and now I had the privilege but no money.

Dr. Atkins, Ruth Tolliver, Mary Pogue, A. Willie James, and others had reminded me that this could happen. I started to go to the telephone, but I didn't have a dime to make a call. The children were so happy. I ordered very slowly: "A hamburger and a glass of water, please!" As the waitress walked away, I started praying. I pulled out my day-to-day book and wrote:

> Dear God,
>
> Here we are. Only a miracle can save us from this dilemma. You delivered the children of Israel out of Egypt. Deliver us from this penniless situation. Just provide enough money to take care of this bill, and we need some tip money. I'll eat the hamburger and wait. Thank you, God, in advance. I'll sign.
>
> Heavenly yours,
>
> Clara Luper

Whites continue to congratulate us, and one blonde lady stopped, put her arms around me, placed a twenty-dollar bill in my lap, and rushed out.

The children asked me what had happened. God was on His throne, and He had just sent a blonde angel to answer my prayer. I have never seen that lady since; I just wish that I knew her name and could see her again.

The YMCA

The YMCA was founded in 1884, and one of its purposes was to spread Christianity. It was in its thirty-ninth annual membership drive. Its Christian doctrine was part of America's history. Its bulletins, newsletters, etc., told the story of the Y's program. The story that was not told was the story of its segregation policy, a policy that we had tried to change through negotiations and had failed.

In May 1961, Melvin Porter, Edmund Atkins, and Calvin Luper went to the YMCA and requested rooms in order to rest their tired bodies. This was done after some white members of the NAACP Youth Council had gone in and asked for rooms. The clerk told the white members that there were vacancies and how happy they were to have them at the YMCA. The same clerk told Melvin, Edmund, and Calvin that there were no vacancies.

Porter came out to give the signal, and we started picketing outside. Ten of our experienced sit-inners walked into the YMCA with their pillows and lay down on the floor in the front lobby.

Claude Monnet, president of the YMCA, stated that it was the position of the board that Negroes were not to stay in the YMCA dormitory. He went into his personal love and respect for Blacks and concluded by telling us all about the YMCA that had been built for Blacks, and how he had stuck his neck out time and time again to assist the director and the board of directors with their program. When I finished listening to all that, I said, "Bull corn," and joined the first organized "lay-in–sit-in" in Oklahoma City.

Samuel Cornelius was the key man on the negotiation team for the YMCA's board. They asked him to hold a conference with us. He did a professional job in presenting the issues. When he finished, I said, "Bull corn," and lay back down on my pillow.

Samuel went back to tell them that it was his recommendation that the YMCA change its segregation patterns immediately. After several meetings, the board accepted his recommendations, and we could no longer say "behold the walls" at the YMCA.

After the "lay-in" at the YMCA, the walls also fell at the YWCA, where Blacks had been permitted to eat in a segregated place upstairs that had been "reserved for colored."

The Police Department

Since the Oklahoma City Police Department was used by restaurant owners to perpetuate segregation, we took a look at it. The police department had been segregated for years. Black policemen were rarely hired and never promoted. They could only patrol in the Black part of town. Blacks were discouraged from taking the police examination for promotions. Police brutality on the east side of town was a "way of life." The police department was used as an effective weapon to "keep the niggers in their place." For years, committees led by Roscoe Dunjee, Jimmie Stewart, and others had held conferences with different police chiefs concerning these inequities.

Tensions continued to build against the Jim Crow police department, and on April 4, 1965, Linda Pogue (president of the NAACP Youth Council), E. Melvin Porter (president of the Senior Branch of the NAACP, and by this time a state senator), and I led a march against the police chief, Hilton Geer. In addition to Linda Pogue and Senator Porter, our delegation consisted of Reverend T. J. Houston, the pastor of Mt. Carmel Baptist Church; Dr. F. D. Moon, a nationally known educator; and Susan Dooley, the secretary of the NAACP. We marched to the police station and stood on the north side of the building. We said, "We have come here on this beautiful day because we have a message for the chief of police. We did not come here asking for any special privileges; we came here asking for an integrated police force and an end to police brutality in Oklahoma City. We don't like what happened to Mrs. Walter Davis last week, when she was arrested on several traffic violations and beaten so badly that one of her eyes was completely closed. That's why we are here, and we're on our way to see the chief."

When we walked into the office, Chief Geer's face reminded me of an iron wall, and I knew it would take "fire hotter than hell" to melt it. I asked him, "Why are Black officers assigned to Black areas?"

He said in a slow, southern manner, "This is the best for the officers and for the people of the city. The Black officers on the force are not dissatisfied. They are well pleased with the operation, and I don't see why you all are down here complaining. You all should be sending us some more Black applicants."

"For what?" I asked. "To be discriminated against, Chief? You have underestimated our ability as free Americans. We wouldn't send you one applicant for these segregated positions. I just wanted to know if you are going to integrate the police department."

He said, "No." I got up and left the room.

For years, we continued to fight segregation in the police department and the attitude of the policemen toward minorities.

Even Blacks who were not demonstrating felt the prejudices of the police. On June 1, 1961, Abram Ross, the first Black radio and television personality in Oklahoma City, went to the scene of an accident in the 600 block of North Central, along with white reporters from radio, newspapers, and television stations. When he arrived, officer A. F. Blackshere was using harsh, offensive language as he demanded that spectators move out of the street. Officer Blackshere went over to Ross and yelled, "Move, damn it to hell, move!" When Ross refused to move and explained that he had a police pass just as the officer did, Blackshere commanded that he get out of the street. Ross looked at him and said, "Why is it that you are allowing the white reporters to stay and commanding me to move?" Ross was arrested and charged with interfering with a police officer. The case was dismissed in municipal court by Judge Hillis Sanford. Ross received over one hundred calls concerning his arrest.

The Housing Ordinance

December 11, 1967, was a cold day. About 350 Blacks and whites met at Freedom Center, at 2609 North Eastern Avenue, for final instructions. We left Freedom Center in a car caravan and proceeded to Hillcrest Shopping Center at Southwest 59th Street and Pennsylvania Avenue. We were greeted by about twenty-five hecklers. We marched down the three-mile route through freezing wind and light snow. The march was led by State Representative Archibald Hill, who carried a large American flag, and Senator E. Melvin Porter, who carried a Bible.

We marched by Councilman John Smith's house, and he invited us in for hot coffee and doughnuts. Smith spoke briefly to the group and told them that he wanted them to know that everybody was welcome on Capitol Hill. "I'm glad you are here," he said. "Now you know you are welcome and that Capitol Hill has *no* problems." Henry Floyd, president of the Senior Branch of the NAACP, presented Smith with the first copy of a proposed amended ordinance. He was asked to read it carefully and vote for it. Senator Porter and Representative Hill joined Floyd in asking Councilman Smith to vote for a city fair housing ordinance.

Councilman Smith and I had our usual arguments, and I left to join the marchers, who were about 25 percent white. Sudie Treppett, a member of Students for a Democratic Society at the University of Oklahoma, and a large number of priests and ministers were part of the march.

On December 23, Representative Archibald Hill led a group of three hundred people into northwest Oklahoma City. The group met at North May Avenue and Wilshire Boulevard, then marched west on Wilshire to Lakehurst Drive, where they turned north and proceeded to Elmhurst Avenue. The group then traveled east on Elmhurst to Greystone Avenue and south on Wilshire back to May.

The purpose of this march was to point out to the citizens of Oklahoma City the need for open housing. The white people in Oklahoma City were not aware of how great the need was, so we were going to white town and take the message.

Mayor Norick lived at 2909 Elmhurst, and as we marched by his house, Archibald Hill said, "We hope the mayor will take the leadership and get something done. Because now we are without leadership at City Hall. This is 1967, and we still don't have an ordinance outlawing segregation in the capital city of Oklahoma."

I was really proud of Hill and all of the people who marched with us that night. When we had concluded the march, everybody was asking me to say something. I said, "I have a recommendation. I hereby recommend that the time of the marches be changed to twelve o'clock midnight, and that we form four groups that will all march at the same time. One group will march at midnight in Nichols Hills, one group in the Village, one in Capitol Hill, and one downtown. We will march to the break of day." The crowd, mainly youth, went wild with applause, and the freedom songs of our forefathers rang out in the air.

Dr. A. L. Dowell worked for the open housing program, and when the City Council refused to pass a city housing ordinance, he staged a one man stand-in. He stood through City Council meetings for weeks. It was the first time in the history of Oklahoma that a council member had stood to protest the inaction of the body.

The March on Washington, August 1963

The Oklahoma City NAACP Youth Council chartered two buses to Washington, D.C., for the 1963 March on Washington. Mr. Victor Porter was unanimously elected as the marshal of the trip. Reverend J. S. Sykes was the praying minister.

Selma, Alabama, 1965

I left Oklahoma City for Selma, Alabama, with the deep realization that I was a very fortunate person. Blacks, whites, and Jews had marched together from Calvary Baptist Church to the downtown Federal Building. We were marching in memory of Reverend James Reeb, a Unitarian minister who had been killed in Selma, and in support of the Fifteenth Amendment, which guaranteed to each American citizen the right to vote.

I was fortunate that I had just left Langston University, where Dr. William Hale, the president, had given me an award, the highest award that a graduate could receive. To be honored by one's own university is truly great. The students and teachers presented me with a sack of money to take to Selma. For a moment, I wanted to stay out at Langston and enjoy the warmth of people who truly loved me. There were so many memories that I had of Langston University, where I saw my first football game and where teachers understood my problems and actually became an integral part of my life. For a few moments, I remembered Alberta Farmer, Willola Butler, Rosie Dell Goodlow, and Isabell Masters. I remembered how on my birthday Rosie Dell Goodlow had baked a bread pudding for me. I wrote these words in my diary: "Today, I've known love and I have experienced the satisfaction of being loved and respected. Now I must go to a strange land where hate and brutality, to some, is a way, the only way, of life. Of all the things in the world, I just wanted to thank God, for *memories*."

Mrs. Mary Clanton, a white woman I had never seen, had purchased an airplane ticket for me. Senator Porter called and, because of an unexpected headache, said that he could not go to Selma, but he would be praying for us.

I rushed out to the airport, and as we were getting ready to leave, I looked up. To my surprise, John R. Kennedy was standing there with a little green bag and was boarding the plane. He was a young radical white man who had tried to convince me not to go to Selma. He had notified me that he was with us, but the lines had been drawn, and he said that he would not make the trip. Now he looked at me and said, "I guess I'm just a fool for freedom."

C. R. Anthony had called and given me five good reasons why I should not go. After he found that he could not stop me, he said in his Arkansas dialect, "If you are so hardheaded, just go on, and if you get into trouble, you know you can always call on me. Now, you call me (after a long pause)—if you need me."

Betty Gallaghan, Margaret Phiffer, Miriam Logue, Eddie Stamps, John R. Kennedy, and I left Oklahoma City for Selma. As the jet turned southward, I thought about Father Edward Kelly, Father Vrana, Henry Floyd, Reverend Wade Watts, Sister Hermanna, Sister Heldegrade, Sister Pauline, Father James McGlinchey, Father Allen, Father Gallaton, Father Rath, and Cecil Williams, who were already in Selma. I started wondering if Frank Cooney, Richard Cotton, and David Noah were safe. They had volunteered to take food that the people in Oklahoma had sent to the marchers in Selma.

Arriving in Selma, we joined others in one of the most dangerous marches in the history of this country. True hatred can be understood through this experience.

Betty Gallaghan, Margaret Phiffer, and Miriam Logue were white young ladies, and they were standing in the front line. I stepped up to the front of the line. They yelled, "No, Mother, don't do that." (The Blacks up to the front of the line were hit by the possemen, but the whites were lectured to.)

When the possemen heard them calling me "Mother," they stepped back and said, "Why, she couldn't be their mother." Then one asked them, "Is that nigger woman your mother?"

They said, "Yes."

Then they yelled at me and asked, "Who is their father?!"

I said, "*God.*"

And one old posseman said, "I just don't know what will happen next. God has no business screwing niggers."

This was the kind of wall that we faced in Selma. I returned to Oklahoma City with a deep cut on my knee and the memory of some dark days in American history.

Charlton Heston

It was the last Saturday in May 1961, and Charlton Heston, Hollywood's Oscar-winning biblical actor, was on his way to Oklahoma City, where he, the nationally known psychiatrist Dr. Jolly West, and Dr. Chester M. Pierce, a Black scientist on the staff of the Veterans' Administration Hospital, were scheduled to lead a protest march against segregation in public accommodations in Oklahoma City. The news had spread like wildfire, and large crowds had assembled on Main Street to get a quick glimpse of the star.

Heston was met by the NAACP youth officers, led by the president, and about one hundred Black and white demonstrators, six policemen, a number of newsmen, and Trudy, the black dog that took part in all the marches. I was stationed with a large crowd of NAACP workers, friends, well-wishers, and people of all ages, creeds, and colors.

I have never seen anything more dramatic, more historical, than those three handsome, dignified, successful men walking down the streets carrying signs that they had prepared themselves. The blue and black sign that Charlton Heston carried said "All men are created equal—Jefferson" on the front and "Radical discrimination is un-American" on the back. Dr. Pierce's sign was green. The front said "Radical discrimination is un-Christian," and the back read "Love thy neighbor—Jesus Christ." Dr. West's sign was pink and read "Bias here helps communism everywhere." The back side had the quotation "We will bury you—Khrushchev" and "Fight communism by fighting racialism."

The crowd was caught up in the unbelievable reality of the moment, and when the trio reached our group, wild applause went up in the air. Oklahomans sounded like they do when the Big Red football team scores against Texas or Nebraska. We waved flags and sang songs, and in a military-sounding voice, Dr. West issued a command. The trio marched, with the crowd following. Heston stopped, shook hands, talked, and marched.

A few hecklers yelled, "Go back to Hollywood, you Jew!!" "West, you are no psychiatrist, you're a damn fool!!" But the march continued. We marched slowly by John A. Brown's Department Store, Anna Maude's Cafeteria, and Bishop's Restaurant—the three strongholds of segregation. There was no violence.

Elliott Tyler, Jerry Nutt, and John Fast carried anti-Heston signs that read, "Is Beverly Hills integrated?"

Charlton Heston's face was lighted with love and understanding for an oppressed people. He told the group that he sincerely believed that most Americans agreed with Thomas Jefferson. This was his first demonstration. He said, "A great many of us have only paid lip service to the equality of man, and this is a very bitter thing for me to do."

Every step that Heston, West, and Pierce took was adding tons of freedom vitamins to our tired bodies that had been protesting for three years.

Heston took pictures with NAACP'ers and carhops, and the three men got into a waiting automobile after the hour's march and went to Calvary Baptist Church, where a large crowd was waiting. There he told the crowd, "I was very pleased with the march, and I was prepared for some hostility at the start of it. I'm used to taking part in marches and chariot races only when they're fixed, but today I didn't have a script!" he said, smiling.

Heston explained that as far as he knew, Beverly Hills was integrated; however, he had been in Spain making a movie in which he would play an eleventh-century heroic knight fighting the Moors and kings. The audience went wild, and Heston looked to be enjoying every moment.

Heston, his wife, and photographers stopped by my house at 1819 Northeast Park Place, and Mrs. Heston forgot one of her expensive cameras there. We were very relieved when we delivered it to her. Charlton Heston, Dr. Chester Pierce, and Dr. Jolly West saw the walls, and their actions said to the world, "Behold the walls."

6

LETTERS TO AMERICA, 1961

July 1961

Dear America,

We are now at John A. Brown's waiting for freedom. We have been waiting in front of you, our native country, since August 1958. We are not discouraged, because wars have been fought for freedom. Yet today, freedom is still in its embryonic stage. A mere idea. Someway and somehow, this idea must become a reality. How? How?

Look at the children who are waiting here today. They are carrying small American flags, and everybody is dressed in your colors—red, white, and blue.

I have just been asked, "Why did you come back here today?" We know that they don't want us here. We came today for the same reason that we came yesterday. We have a responsibility to ourselves and our posterity to make freedom work. What else can we do? Our fathers and forefathers tried. Roscoe Dunjee tried. Reverend E. W. Perry Sr. tried.

A group came to me last night to tell me how silly we look sitting in places where we are not wanted. They said we look just like a bunch of Black fools.

Some of the children are getting tired of nonviolence. They want us to try just a little violence: "Couldn't we just kill one whitey or stab one?"

"No," I told them. "No, we cannot do that. Violent resistance has only created mistrust and deep-seated hatred, and Jesus told

Peter that he who fights with the sword shall die by the sword. Sometimes I have violent thoughts. I have thoughts just like you. I have evil thoughts, but history speaks to me and says, 'Nonviolence is the way.'"

Your citizen,

Clara Luper

June 1961

Dear America,

I know that you have a conscience, and as I see it, Blacks must become the active conscience of America. But conscience is a drowsy thing. It stirs, turns over, takes another nap, and falls into a deep, dead sleep. "Leave me alone," conscience cries. "Let me sleep, let me sleep," conscience cries. "Let time take care of it—time, time is the answer. Maybe ten years or maybe another hundred years." Oh, no, America, your conscience, like old Pharaoh's of old, will not rest or sleep until we can eat here at John A. Brown's. We will arouse your conscience, and we will not let you rest until we can eat.

Your citizen,

Clara Luper

Dear America,

You must understand that we are yours and "you are ours." We love you. The eyes of the world are on you. Democracy's future is in your hands. We can no longer pretend. You must practice what you preach. We aren't your enemies. We have never betrayed our country. We have not produced any Benedict Arnolds. Even the enemies that you have fed and given aid to talk about your practices, but they never criticize your ideas. Listen, America! Listen!

Your citizen,

Clara Luper

June 1961

Dear America,

Today we're in the Huckins Hotel. We brought a copy of the United States Constitution with us. We have read and reread it. Now, you show us within the golden pages of this Constitution that this nation "was built for whites only." Show us! I dare you to reread the Constitution.

Your citizen,

Clara Luper

Dear America,

Reverend Willie B. Parker, the pastor of St. James Baptist Church, is marching with us today. He has been here for weeks in spite of his knee that has been giving him trouble. Look at him. He has stood there all day with his sore knee. He can hardly walk, but he has his Holy Bible in his hand. He has been reading through its Holy pages. Send someone down here to show us where the Bible justifies and condones discrimination. Tell us that God is not our father and Man is not our brother. We are in the Bible Belt of America. You have commanded us to love one another. The group is now singing "Onward Christian Soldiers," marching as to war.

The children are now repeating Thomas Jefferson's immortal words "We hold these truths to be self-evident, that all men are created equal." That means us.

Did not Abraham Lincoln say "This nation, under God, shall have a new birth of freedom"?

We must have this freedom; we have paid for it in blood, sweat, and tears.

We are here waiting, waiting, waiting. The day has ended, and it has been another sin-filled day.

Your citizen,

Clara Luper

June 1961

Dear America,

I was selected to lead the sit-ins with the assurance of cooperation and full backing of the NAACP and the Blacks in this city. But today, Sallye Harris, Calvin Luper, Marilyn Luper, Areda Tolliver, Betty Germany, Richard Brown, and I are here at Brown's alone. We must take advantage of this day. They all have books. We will read, because "we cannot escape history." Knowledge is power. Frank Wade and his waitresses are really angry. They are pouring coffee on us. We have to sit quietly now. If anyone is to be hurt, let it be me, not my children or my white brother. If any blood is to be shed, let it be mine, not my children's.

Why are the policemen angry with us? We aren't afraid. We're here facing the walls. If we were scared, we would be at home, like "the rest of the niggers," waiting to see what's going to happen. We're going to make something happen.

Blow the trumpet,
Ring the freedom bell.
For all is not well,
Sitting here is hell!
Your citizen,

Clara Luper

August 1961

Dear America,

This morning, James Arthur Edwards started singing "From the Shores of Tripoli." Listen, we are waiting. Waiting for a hamburger, and in that hamburger the whole essence of democracy lies.
Your citizen,

Clara Luper

Dear America,

Today we went to Val Gene's at Shepherd Mall, and the manager told us that someday we could eat. When is someday? He said, "It will not be long." How long is long? Be patient. We made patience. We took patience and made a new word out of it.

P-Promises
A-Ain'ts
T-Talk
I-Ignorance
E-Emptied
N-Nothing
C-Can't
E-Endless

Put it together, it means forever and a hundred more years.
Your citizen,

Clara Luper

Dear America,

I'm back in jail. The police came just like the Hitlers of bygone years and arrested me at Anna Maude's Cafeteria. They called it trespassing or something. I can hear old Judge Sanford's squeaking voice as he says, "You are guilty, Clara Luper." I don't ever want to see him again.

This white community is afraid of us. They were talking about me, and a baldheaded man looked up and saw me and ran.

Sit down, chillun, sit down, sit down.
Old Jim Crow at John A. Brown's got to go.
So sit down, chillun, sit down,
Don't be ashamed,
Because they should be ashamed,
But they have no shame,
And we are not to blame.

Your citizen,

Clara Luper

Dear America,

We upset your false teachings, your old customs and old traditions. Now after what happened yesterday, when you put us all in jail again, you know we will no longer accept segregation as a practice or a philosophy. We have had enough, and "enough is enough."

Your citizen,

Clara Luper

Dear America,

We believe unswervingly in the constitutionality of our case. The sit-ins are self-inflicted wounds that you have placed on your own backs, and now they are upsetting your very butts. I hope you vomit. Vomit up your sour, stinking hatred of people because of their color. Frank Wade, R. D. Cravens, Bishop's, John A. Brown's, and all of the other segregationists in our country are desperately in need of a laxative. Their segregated bowels are constipated. Ex-Lax, Black Draught, castor oil, and Feen-a-Mint cannot move them. Their bowels are locked, traditionally locked, with hatred, fear, frustration, discrimination, segregation, second-class citizenship, and the sit-ins are going to make them move! For years, they have been shooting off hot air—call it a belch or a "poot." They are going to move! Those bowels are going to move because we are children of the Universe and we belong.

This city cannot become a convention city, a tourist city, or one that has a heart until this has happened. So we are going to add pressure.

Your citizen,

Clara Luper

Dear America,

I have just been told that some of the restaurant owners aren't sleeping too well. They are nervous. When they close their eyes at night, they can see us "as black as midnight." Some of them haven't slept for months. We're getting on Mayor Norick's nerves. He looks so tired. The maids said that they are using more sleeping pills than ever. Great! We will continue to use the power that we have. The power to love! We love these white people so much that we are going to make them do right. When we left John A. Brown's, one of the hostesses looked at Lana Pogue for a few minutes and went over to the Skirvin Hotel and started crying. Lana is eight years old now and was repeating this poem that we composed.

> One day I went downtown for a drink,
> Just a little drink of soda water.
> The waitress took a walk and Dan James blew his top
> Just because I wanted a drink,
> Just a little drink of soda water.
> Lord, please fix it. Fix it so a little girl like me
> Can drink a little drink of soda water.

Your citizen,

Clara Luper

Dear America,

The Black people here are acting funny now. I used to be invited to Black churches to speak, but things have changed. I guess they are afraid. Maybe I should be afraid, but fear is not part of my inner structure. They are with me in spirit. They are contributing money to the struggle. But money isn't everything.
Your citizen,

Clara Luper

Dear America,

Your conscience, like old Pharaoh's of old and Abraham Lincoln's before he signed the Emancipation Proclamation, will not rest until you fulfill your promise of liberty, justice, and equality for all.
Your citizen,

Clara Luper

7

GOVERNOR. J. HOWARD EDMONDSON'S COMMITTEE

In March 1960, Governor J. Howard Edmondson announced the formation of a statewide citizens' committee for the purpose of finding a solution to the remaining problems of racial discrimination in Oklahoma. "While Oklahoma has made good progress toward ending racial segregation, I am convinced that more can and should be done to achieve further progress in this direction," he said. He issued the following statement:

I envision the purpose of such a group to function as an advisory committee to me in matters relating to intergroup tensions and situations which threaten harmonious relationships among the various ethnic groups in our state. In this regard, the objectives would be twofold: (1) the prevention of intergroup tensions from arising; and (2) the dissolution of such tensions should they arise.

The committee would further promote unity and understanding among and between all the people of our state: by examining the causes of racial prejudices where they occur; by attempting to eliminate discrimination arising from such prejudices; by promoting educational programs and other activities to aid in the accomplishment of these ends; and by providing an overall statewide vehicle to help solve the basic problems in all fields of human relations in the State of Oklahoma.

I think the actions of other cities, most recently Kansas City, have painted a clear pattern that the removal of this racial barrier is inevitable and everyone is a lot better off if they do it agreeably rather than having to go through this pattern of demonstrations and boycotts.

The pattern on removal of barriers is being followed not only in Kansas City, which is a border situation like Oklahoma, but also some states much more southern than Oklahoma.

His statement, followed by his action, came at a time when we had announced plans for a mammoth mass demonstration, which we felt would bring the long nightmare of the sit-ins in Oklahoma City to an end. Governor Edmondson insisted that the mass demonstration be postponed so that he could have a chance to put the power and prestige of his office behind the efforts to eliminate segregation in public places. I talked to Cecil Williams and Melvin Porter at length about it and warned them not to put off the demonstration unless all the public accommodations were opened.

When I returned from Washington, D.C., where I had mobilized help from a large number of outsiders, I found that the demonstration had been called off. I was so angry that I walked out. I didn't have any faith in the governor's ability to remove the walls of segregation through the committee that had been appointed in spite of the fact that its members represented men and women who were dedicated to the cause of freedom.

The committee went to work and quickly agreed that, in view of the then-current situation in Oklahoma City, the first goal should be to seek a solution to the problem of discrimination against Negroes in public eating places. The question of gaining equal treatment for Negroes in other public accommodations, such as hotels and motels, also was raised. Other areas in which discrimination was felt to be a continuing problem were employment; access to and services in governmental institutions

· ·

The committee consisted of the Honorable J. Howard Edmondson, Dr. Charles Atkins, Mr. Charles Bennett, Dr. Jesse Chandler, attorney Sam Crossland, Mr. Jack Dalton, Mr. Harvey Everest, Mr. Cecil Garlin, Mr. J. R. Gordon, Mr. Ben T. Head, Reverend John Heidbrink, Mr. John Held, Reverend Ben Hill, Mrs. Cecil M. Houck, Reverend W. K. Jackson, Mrs. E. P. Ledbetter, Rabbi Joseph Levenson, Mrs. Clara Luper, Mrs. Augusta Mann, Mr. O. M. McDaniels, Mr. F. D. Moon, Mr. Beverly Osborne, Bishop Chilton Powell, Mr. Cecil E. Robertson, Mr. John Rogers, Mr. Andrew Russworm, Mr. Wayne B. Snow, Reverend C. K. Stalnaker, Mr. James E. Stewart, Dr. W. McFerrin Stowe, Miss Willa Strong, and Dr. R. B. Taylor.

and in such facilities as public parks; and schools, with respect to "real" rather than "token" integration and the loss of jobs by qualified Negro teachers when steps were taken to end school segregation.

With these goals in mind, the committee cited four needs that it felt would have to be met in order to carry on its work:

1. A professional executive
2. Funds to pay salaries for the executive and a secretary and other expenses that might be incurred
3. The need, through various means of publicity, to inform the public of problems and possible solutions
4. Studies of Oklahoma laws and work in the human relations field in other states

Two special problems in carrying on the committee's work also were pointed out. One was the need to extend the work over a broad front, dealing with the existing problems in all parts of the state rather than just in Oklahoma City. The other was the fact that, unlike similar committees in other states, the Oklahoma committee would have no inherent authority, such as the right to summon witnesses and hold official public hearings, nor have any power—other than the power of persuasion and public opinion—to encourage acceptance of any steps it might advocate.

After reaching agreement on its general objectives and immediate goals, the committee proceeded to organize itself. Governor Edmondson named a temporary steering committee to recommend an overall plan of action and to propose a committee structure, and a nominating committee to present a slate of officers. At the second general committee meeting, on April 27, 1960, these officers were elected:

Chairman: Harvey P. Everest, Oklahoma City
Vice-Chairman: Dr. R. B. Taylor, Okmulgee
Secretary: Bishop Chilton Powell, Oklahoma City

Recommendations of the temporary steering committee and subsequent actions of the general committee members resulted in the formation of a number of standing committees and project committees.

The standing committees were as follows:

Steering Committee: Wayne B. Snow, chairman; elected general committee officers: Mr. Everest, Dr. Taylor, and Bishop Powell; Dr. Charles Atkins, John Held, Charles L. Bennett, Rev. W. K. Jackson, and Governor Edmondson, ex-officio

Legal Committee: John Rogers, chairman; Cecil Robertson,
   Dr. R. B. Taylor, Ben T. Head, and James E. Stewart
Research and Education Committee: Dr. F. D. Moon, chairman; Reverend W. McFerrin Stowe, Mrs. E. P. Ledbetter, O. M. McDaniels,
   and Charles L. Bennett

The project committees were as follows:

Food Service, Hotel and Motel Accommodations Committee:
   J. R. Gordon, chairman; Beverly Osborne, Clara Luper, Rev. John
   Heidbrink, Wayne B. Snow, James E. Stewart, and Rev. Ben Hill
State Institution and Facilities Committee: Jack Dalton, chairman;
   Dr. Jesse Chandler, Rabbi Joseph Levenson, Dr. Willa Strong, and
   Andrew Russworm. (Mr. Dalton died in June, and Rabbi Leven-
   son succeeded him as committee chairman.)
Equality in Employment Committee: Rev. C. K. Stalnaker, chairman;
   John Held, J. R. Gordon, Mrs. Augusta Mann, F. D. Moon, John
   Rogers, and Rev. John Heidbrink.

The recommendation that $10,000 be made available from the Gov-
ernor's Contingency Fund for necessary committee expenses also was
accepted. This funding actually became available in July.

The Steering Committee was authorized to hire an executive and a
secretary for him. This was accomplished in July, when Olen Nalley was
hired as executive secretary and Mrs. Jewel Porter as office secretary.
Quarters were obtained for them in Room 305 of the YWCA Building,
320 Park Avenue, Oklahoma City.

As agreed by the general committee, first-priority efforts were concentrated on trying to find a solution to the problem of discrimination
against Negroes in public eating places in downtown Oklahoma City.
While other project committees continued their work, this central problem first occupied the attention of the Food Service project committee,
and soon became the major work of the Steering Committee members
as well. By mid-July, the situation had become so critical that it was the
preoccupying concern of practically all active members of the committee, most of the leaders of the Negro community, many downtown
businessmen, representatives of other organizations, and several civic
leaders who were active solely as interested individuals.

This period of peak activity continued throughout August, when
Black leaders put into effect a campaign of attempts at sit-ins, picketing,

Richard Lebenthal, associate director of the Southwest Regional Office of the Anti-Defamation League of B'nai B'rith in Houston, Texas, told the Governor's Committee that the speedy desegregation of eating establishments would be one of the best ways to ease, if not end, racial problems in the South. He praised Governor Edmondson for appointing a committee to work on the nation's number one problem. "Restaurant owners in other areas who have opened their doors to all people now say that they wish they had opened their doors earlier. Delays and misunderstandings increase tension," he said.

and boycotting of downtown business places. This extended into the month of September.

By mid-September, despite continued efforts among the leaders of the various groups, the situation had reached a practical stalemate. The principal objectives of the Negro demonstrations still had not been achieved; the firms at which these demonstrations had been aimed apparently felt that the "crisis" had passed, and they were less interested in further negotiations; widespread public interest had faded; and the demonstrations had tapered off sharply. While in earlier phases some progress had been made in opening to Negroes several eating places that were of secondary concern, the targets of principal concern remained in status quo.

Hundreds of man-hours were spent in talking with restaurant owners and managers, singly and in groups; in discussions with leaders of the Negro community; in negotiation sessions between downtown leaders and Negro group leaders; in researching similar problems—and their solutions—in other cities; and in spreading the word about how similar situations had been successfully resolved elsewhere. Aid was solicited and obtained from many interested citizens outside the Governor's Committee.

While we cannot report all of these meetings and other work in detail, some highlights stand out and should be listed, at least as examples of the kind of work that was done.

1. In early May, before the second meeting of the general committee, the Food Service Committee devised a plan of action, gained the approval of the Steering Committee, and started to put the plan into action. This plan included conducting

a survey to learn what they had done and what the results were. It also included a series of informal talks with restaurant owners and managers to discuss the pros and cons of their taking similar action. Many—perhaps most—of these restaurant people said they would be willing to serve Negroes provided that a large number of restaurants would take this step at the same time. Many of the restaurant people also said their only fear was that they would suffer economic losses because white customers would stay away if this step were taken.

2. In June, planning was started for one or a possible series of discussion group meetings with restaurant owners and managers. The first such meeting, involving a small group of "key" restaurant people, was held July 6. The purpose of this session, as directed by the general committee, was to convince the restaurant people that there was a need for action and to assure them that the committee was anxious to help find a solution that would entail no economic harm to the restaurants. This session was for discussion only, with no commitments asked. Written material and slides were prepared by the Research and Education Committee, and the presentation was made, at the request of the committee, by Dr. Jack Wilkes, the president of Oklahoma City University, who was interested in the problem as an individual.

About sixteen restaurant owners or managers attended. Two appeared to be antagonistic to the whole idea. The others seemed to feel that something should be done. Several pressed for a decision at this meeting. However, it was felt that this would be moving too quickly, with no guarantee of compliance. It was recommended that a small committee of restaurant owners be named by the governor to work toward a broad, lasting solution to the problem. Several restaurant owners were asked to serve on such a committee, but it proved to be impossible to form such a group; none of the restaurant people wanted to be associated with such a committee for fear of economic repercussions.

Throughout the negotiations with restaurant officials, the prevailing feeling, even among those generally sympathetic to the idea of equal service for all, seemed to be that the restaurants should do the same thing at the same time; if

not, they would be bound to suffer the loss of some of their
white customers who resented the change.

3. In early June, at the request of the committee, a consultant
   team from the Southern Regional Council came to Oklahoma
   City to confer with the Governor's Committee. These men,
   experienced in dealing with situations similar to Oklahoma
   City's, were Dr. John Hope II of Fisk University; Dr. Kenneth
   Moreland of Randolph-Macon College for Women in Lynch-
   burg, Virginia; and Dr. A. Lee Coleman from the University
   of Kentucky. They explained the spontaneous nature of the
   movement and described the current situation as one of negotiation. The committee felt their counsel was extremely useful.

4. A general meeting of restaurant owners and managers
   with Governor Edmondson and several members of the
   committee was held August 2 at the YMCA. Mr. Everest
   introduced Mr. Rogers, who pointed out that the meeting
   had been called in the hope of reaching some agreement to
   open restaurant and lunch counter service to Negroes. He
   presented Governor Edmondson, who asked the press representatives to leave so that everyone might express themselves
   freely. (They did so.)

   The governor appealed for a solution on the grounds of
   justice. He pointed out that the present publicity about Oklahoma City was detrimental to the progress of the city and the
   state, and to the position of our country in world relations.
   He made the suggestion that if the restaurant owners were
   not ready to open to all permanently, they might have a trial
   period of a month or so. If it proved unsatisfactory, they
   could return to their original status. Spokesmen among the
   restaurant representatives said that this would not be acceptable because they would be in danger of losing customers
   who might never return.

   Statements were made by representatives of the Catholic
   Interracial Council and the Christian Family Movement,
   appealing for faithfulness to Christian conscience. They said
   their organizations and others represented included many
   people who were restaurant customers and would prefer to
   eat where all people were served without discrimination.
   Responses from restaurant owners were to the effect that
   regardless of what Christianity or other religion might teach,

· ·

The Governor's Committee received letters from the Oklahoma Christian Missionary Society, the Oklahoma Synod of the United Presbyterian Church in the USA, the Oklahoma Spiritual Assembly of the Bahais, and the following Oklahoma City Christian Church members: Henry Tyler, Northwest Christian Church; Scott Baird, Village Christian Church; Roy Oliver, First Christian Church of Edmond; Jerry Thomson and Ted McElroy, Crown Heights Christian Church; George Bell, Capitol Hill Christian Church; Bill Reece, Britton Christian Church; Marvin Layman, Del City Christian Church; Lloyd Mardes, Highland Hills Christian Church; Charles Lindberg, Hillcrest Christian Church; Howard Chilton, Lincoln Terrace Christian Church; Harold Van Cleave, Midwest Boulevard Christian Church; John Downs, First Christian Church of Midwest City; Curt Tull, Pennsylvania Avenue Christian Church; Loren Swanson, Nicoma Park Christian Church; Garrell Dunn, Putnam City Christian Church; James O. Pearce, University Place Christian Church; and Clarence Pruitt, Southwest Christian Church.

· ·

this was a question of business, and that individuals in the restaurant business—not people in other organizations— would be held responsible for keeping their businesses solvent.

5. In late July, it became apparent that a number of leaders in the Black community were determined that "stronger measures" should be taken to achieve their objective. In conferences and private conversations between various members of the Governor's Committee and other interested white citizens and leaders of the Negro community, three principal points were stressed by the white leaders:

A. While picketing and other demonstrations might serve to focus further attention on the demand for equal treatment, a proposed "general boycott" of downtown stores by the Negro community probably would hamper, rather than help, efforts to resolve the problem.

B. The Negro community could not muster a general boycott severe enough and sustained enough to exert any significant economic pressure upon most of the downtown merchants.

C. Many white people, previously neutral or sympathetic to the Negro cause, might well resent the "unfairness" of a boycott aimed at all merchants rather than at only those who had eating facilities in their establishments and barred Negroes.*

Some Negro leaders agreed that the general boycott would be an error. Their expressions of this view were scorned by other leaders of the movement. The division of opinion brought discord into what previously had been a fairly united front in the Negro community. There was considerable doubt among Negroes as to just what their action plan was to be.

Regardless of some protests and doubts, the apparent trend in the Negro community at that stage was in favor of more militant action, mainly with the hope of exerting enough pressure upon the entire downtown group to cause leaders there to in turn bring enough pressure upon the eating place owners involved to cause them to change their stand.

6. Beginning in the last week of July, and almost daily (and sometimes almost continuously) thereafter for eight weeks, various members of the Governor's Committee conferred steadily with the downtown merchants, other interested white citizens, and various leaders of the Negro community in intense efforts to avert or end the Negro demonstrations. The primary aim was to reach a solution to the basic problem. The secondary aim was to persuade the Negro community that its current course of action was more likely to harm than to aid.

Beginning August 6, mass picketing started, and attempts at sit-ins were made at some restaurants and lunch counters. There were a fairly large number of pickets on the main streets downtown. Rallies in the Negro community stirred support—in both participation and money—to bolster the campaign. Twice postponed to allow time for further negotiations, the boycott went into effect August 20.

---

*When the boycott subsequently went into effect, Negro leaders specifically exempted those downtown establishments whose eating places already were open to Negroes. Later, the demonstrations were focused on only the key objectives of the campaign, particularly the two general merchandise stores that had lunch counters and which had been long-time symbols of the drive for racial equality.

. . . .

Barbara Posey was invited to appear before the Governor's Committee on July 29 to explain why the NAACP youth would be renew-
ing the sit-ins that had been discontinued. Samuel J. Cornelius,
who had been an ardent leader and youth advisor, said: "It's our
understanding that the committee has gone as far as it can, but the
restaurant owners are adamant. We think that we don't have any
alternative but to renew the sit-ins. It has been four months since
they were called off."

. . . .

During this whole period, the efforts to reach a solution
brought into the discussions many civic leaders who had not
previously been active in this matter. Despite the efforts of all
these people and open communications between all groups
concerned being maintained at all times, largely through
the efforts of the Governor's Committee and other human
relations agencies, no solution was reached.

7. At a meeting on August 17, the Governor's Committee authorized the writing of two statements, which were released
on August 18. One reiterated the committee's strong stand
in urging an end to racial discrimination in public eating
places. It also urged white citizens who agreed with this
stand to make their views known publicly, in order to reassure restaurant owners that they would be supported if they
opened their establishments to all.

In the course of the next several weeks, many groups and
individuals did publicly express support for the statement.

. . . .

The Governor's Committee met on August 19 in an effort to avoid
the boycott. Dean Cutchall, president of the Board of Directors
of the Oklahoma City Retailers Association, presented a statement
at the meeting, which restaurant owners were expected to attend.
The meeting was a complete failure as far as opening the restaurants was concerned, because most of the restaurant owners did not
have a central organization. Oklahoma had a restaurant association;
however, most restaurant owners were not members of the Retailers.
The association did not have a policy commitment to anything, and
if they had had one, there would have been no enforcement policy.

. . . .

Officials of Protestant, Roman Catholic, and Jewish congregations, many of whom had publicly expressed their
support before this, were among those who joined in this
new expression. A group of private citizens, responding to
the committee's appeal, obtained signatures and monetary
donations from 826 individuals to finance the publication
of two newspaper advertisements, carrying the names of all
subscribers, in support of the declaration.

The second statement released by the Governor's Committee on August 18 was a copy of an open letter to restaurant owners and managers. It pointed out that their lack of
any central organization that could negotiate and speak for
them collectively was hindering efforts to resolve the problems, and it urged them to form such a group. Copies of this
letter were mailed directly to restaurant owners and managers. No answer ever was received.

8. Sporadic efforts were made after October 1 to find some
course that might lead to a solution. No such course was
found. In late October, members of the committee and other
interested citizens working with leaders of the Negro community and of the downtown merchants reached a tentative
agreement. It would have called for the merchants to:

A. Publish an advertisement supporting the stand of the
Governor's Committee
B. Work with the Governor's Committee in negotiating with
restaurant owners in an attempt to reach a solution to the
basic problem

Officials of the NAACP, who were acting as spokesmen for
the Negro community at this time, would agree, in turn, to call
off the general boycott as of the day the agreement was signed.

Execution of this agreement ultimately failed when the
merchants' leaders asked that a further condition—immediate cessation of picketing—be included. The NAACP would
not agree to this added condition, and negotiations broke
down. Meanwhile, the Negro demonstrations and boycott
continued. Negro leaders insisted that the boycott was having
some economic effect on downtown stores. Some merchants,
at first, indicated that this was true. Later, as the Negro picketing diminished and the boycott lessened in intensity, nearly

all downtown merchants said the boycott had had little effect, and what effect there had been was disappearing. There was no apparent effect upon the primary objectives.

9. In November, members of the Steering Committee of the Governor's Committee began a series of meetings to evaluate what had happened so far and to chart a course for the future.

Because of the crisis nature of the Oklahoma City eating place situation, the major efforts of the committee were devoted to this area alone. However, some other work was undertaken. These activities can be listed, briefly, as follows:

1. A modest survey by the Committee on State Institutions and Facilities aimed at assessing discrimination problems, if any, in those areas
2. The collection of a fairly comprehensive group of pamphlets, clippings, and other publications and treatises dealing with problems of discrimination and their solutions
3. A limited number of talks by committee members to other community groups on human relations problems

The Governor's Committee was organized with the stated purposes of serving as an advisory group to the governor on statewide human relations problems and of working directly on studies and projects designed to help end racial discrimination in the state. However, because Oklahoma City faced a crucial situation in the area of racial discrimination in public eating places and there appeared to be no other organization in the city that was dealing with this problem, the committee was immediately forced to attempt to deal with it. From the beginning, this specific problem absorbed practically all of the committee's effort, consideration, and time. Because of this preoccupying involvement in the Oklahoma City problem, the Governor's Committee had made no substantial progress toward fulfilling the purposes for which it was formed.

In its work with the Oklahoma City problem, the committee may be credited with some rather intangible contributions, both by its very existence and through its negotiation efforts and its public statements. Overall, however, because the key goals of the Oklahoma City effort had not been reached, it must be said that the committee essentially made no substantial achievement in its first nine months of existence.

8

THE OKLAHOMA CITY BOYCOTT

On Saturday night, August 13, 1960, J. J. Boxberger, secretary-manager of the Oklahoma City Retailers Association, met with Dr. E. C. Moon Jr., E. Melvin Porter, Cecil L. Williams, Dr. Charles Atkins, and Dean B. Cutchall, president of the Retailers, to discuss our planned general boycott of all downtown businesses. A mass boycott decision meeting was to be held at Avery Methodist Church on Sunday, August 14. Dr. Moon, a local dentist, read a signed letter from Cutchall, in which he stated: "We are very optimistic about the settlement of our race problem before the Governor's Committee on Human Relations next Wednesday. We have several plans to submit and feel confident one of them will be acceptable to all concerned."

The debate started. Melvin Porter, Cecil Williams, Dr. Moon, Samuel Cornelius, and I fought for the boycott to go on as scheduled, while Jimmie Stewart, Dr. Dowell, Dr. Atkins, and Leslie Brown argued that the downtown merchants should have more warning and we should have more time to organize a boycott. In the name of "common sense," we should give the Governor's Committee and the Retailers Association a chance.

The votes were counted. We lost by forty-four votes, and the boycott was postponed for the second time.

The adults had killed the boycott, but tomorrow, the sit-ins would continue!

Internal strife developed between the members of the Citizens Human Relations Council under the leadership of Dr. Atkins, who had fought for a selective boycott. On August 13, Dr. Atkins resigned as chairman, in the best interest of the total community. He explained that he was a member of the Governor's Committee on Human Relations and the Urban League of Oklahoma City, and both were mediating organizations.

After the Governor's Committee failed to open public accommodations, boycott talk and plans began to come alive again.

Dr. Martin Luther King had stated that we must refuse to cooperate with segregation. We should not pay to be insulted. Segregation is an evil. It is contrary to the will of God, and when we support or submit to segregation, we are condoning an evil. To accept passively an injustice is to cooperate with it.

Therefore, we began to talk about an economic boycott in Oklahoma City. This was a hot issue. The Black community leaders were split down the center as to the kind of boycott, if there was to be a boycott at all. One segment wanted to boycott John A. Brown's only. They held that only Brown's was responsible for the condition, and that other merchants should not be punished because of Brown's. This thought was led by Jimmie Stewart, a member of the NAACP's National Board of Directors; the other group, led by Melvin Porter, Cecil Williams, and me, fought for an all-out boycott.

I told them, "If the business community, led by the lily-white Chamber of Commerce, that group of powerful men that forms the power base of any city, if that group would speak, justice would flow with the speed of an Oklahoma tornado. But their tongues have been glued to the tops of their mouths, and their feet have walked on the other side, while their eyes have only been concerned with segregation facilities and integrated dollars. I mean Black hands putting green dollars in white hands. The Chamber of Commerce's only commitment, as I have seen it, is to the perpetuation of the system. They have been here since 1889 and haven't done anything in civil rights. Boycott the whole area."

Melvin Porter took the floor. He ran his right hand through his curly hair, and a frown covered his face. He pointed his right finger in the air, and the group waited for him to speak. Then, in a thunderous, steady voice, his words began to fall like Oklahoma's April thunderstorms. He called those who were against the boycott Uncle Toms and Aunt Jemimas. He described the things that he had seen, the suffering of the children, and the absence of adult participation. He jumped on the backs of the ministers, and with three exceptions used words to make pictures out of them.

Then Cecil Williams spoke. He went into detail about Tatums, Oklahoma, the all-Black town where he grew up. He told how his family had moved to Oklahoma City, where they lived in a poor, rat-infested neighborhood with a path to the outhouse. He said coming from a background like that, he felt that we had no other choice. "We must boycott everything and everybody."

Wild applause went into the air. A motion was quickly made and seconded that the decision to boycott be made at a public meeting, which was to be held at St. John Baptist Church, at 801 Northeast Second Street.

A committee was appointed, in which Dr. Atkins was to prepare the reasons for the boycott. The downtown eating places were given an ultimatum on August 10, 1960, two years after the first sit-ins, that if the public accommodations were not opened by August 15, an all-out boycott would go into effect. In the meantime, I announced that the NAACP Youth Council would continue the sit-ins, in which we would constantly say "Behold the walls," and if the walls of segregation could not be removed by August 15, the youth would join the adults in an all-out boycott. So we picked Brown's, the Skirvin Hotel, Bishop's Restaurant, the Huckins Hotel, and Anna Maude's Cafeteria. The guards at each door stood with their ropes in their hands and with backup help, ready to use the strong arm of the Oklahoma City Police Department to perpetuate segregation.

As I stood with Father Robert McDole, Theodosia Crawford, A. Willie James, Cecil Williams, and a small number of children and youth from six to twenty-one years old, I wondered how long we would have to stand before the walls would vanish.

In the meantime, I could hardly wait until August 15. This was going to be the "battle of battles." As we entered St. John Baptist Church, I wondered how many people would really show up and how strong the opposition was. The crowd poured in. I kept wondering what Reverend W. K. Jackson would say and do. Reverend Jackson, a soft-speaking, calm minister, knew power and understood how to use it. Would he speak? I knew that Reverend J. S. Sykes, the proud, popular NAACP Youth Council advisor, would vote with us. I was proud to see Eddie Stamps, the well-dressed car salesman. I was hoping that Leslie Brown, the hard, detailed, questioning-answering prediction advisor, would keep his mouth shut. My thoughts were lost in the music that was now filling the air as we sang:

We shall not, we shall not be moved.
Just like a tree planted by the river
We shall not be moved.

Willie Johnson stood and said, "Come on, you all, let's sing."

It looked as if everybody was singing. I saw Mr. Wisener, the owner of Wisener Business School, clapping his hands. I kept watching the opposition camp. There were some disturbances over the presence of certain representatives from the city and the police department. I watched the crowd as people continued to join in. To my surprise, the Blacks who were totally against the sit-ins were arriving in large numbers. I heard whispers: "Those hotheads are going to get us in trouble." "I work downtown, and I'm not going to lose my job." "We'll see."

I was hoping that the singing would continue. Harold Woodson, Edmund Atkins, Calvin Luper, Zella Hull, Areda Tolliver, Carolyn House, Alma Faye Posey, Richard Brown, Doris Powell, Samuel Craig, and Brenda Crawford were in the front of the church leading the singing.

I ain't going to let nobody turn me around.
I ain't going to let no white man turn me around.
I ain't going to let no Black man turn me around.

Dr. E. C. Moon Jr., who was president of the Oklahoma City chapter of the NAACP, was there. I looked at him and tried to read his stand. What would he do? Suppose it was a tie. How would he vote?

Samuel Cornelius, the YMCA's physical education director, had arrived. There was nothing he enjoyed more than a good debate. He said, "I'm not going to speak. I'll just watch you all. I hope that the best side wins."

Dr. Moon presided. He went over the problems that we had encountered and thanked everyone for coming. He called for a discussion of the proposed boycott.

Dr. Atkins was the first to speak: "We have gathered here tonight to make a decision that will ultimately affect the history of our people and our city. At the very outset, I must admit that two wrongs do not make a right. I don't believe a genuine boycott will benefit this city; therefore, I do not think that all of the downtown merchants should be boycotted.

"The downtown merchants have, through the years, extended credit to our people and have given them employment. These are two facts that cannot be overlooked. This boycott could backfire in our faces! If we boycott all of the downtown places, we will lose support, and this action will cut off the areas of communication between the races. These avenues must be kept open.

"We should be realistic. These downtown merchants don't own the restaurants in question. I believe in boycotting, but in boycotting the people who are responsible for the evil that exists. In other words, boycott the people who are responsible for the discrimination. We all have to live here after this thing is won. We've got to win other battles after this battle is won."

I wrote in my daily diary, "A man has a right to change his mind, doesn't he?"

Dr. Moon called me as the next speaker. The crowd responded with a loud roar and cheers. "I have listened with a great deal of interest to everyone that has spoken," I said, "and especially to Dr. Charles Atkins. I share Dr. Atkins's concern in keeping the avenues of communications open. Yet I feel that he deliberately refused to tell you how long the so-called avenues have been open. In fair play, then, I must tell you. They have been open for eighty-one long years, and for eighty-one years Black people have taken their money downtown, contributing to the growth and development of downtown. So the age-old question appears before us. For what? What have we gotten? The right to eat in the back of restaurants or in the streets. We are all educated, or uneducated, paper-sackologists. Now the whites are sitting and eating, and we are out in the streets eating out of paper sacks. What kind of avenues of communication would you call that? The downtown merchants openly admitted that this is not their problem and they have no interest other than spiritual or moral interest in this struggle. We have to take their word for it. Now I'm asking you to give the merchants a chance to change their 'economic interests to spiritual interests.' We won't boycott them in spirit! Just in finance. Then we will be speaking a language that the downtown merchants will understand. Freedom is everybody's business. And if it takes a general boycott to help, I am willing to go all the way. Now, I know that we don't have the buying power of the Blacks in Montgomery, Alabama, or in Memphis, Tennessee, but we do have a little buying power, and Aunt Hattie told me that every little bit helps. The people at John A. Brown's, Anna Maude's, the Skirvin, Bishop's, and Huckins, according to the restaurant owners, do not want to eat with Blacks. They haven't disputed the restaurant owners, and therefore it must be true. So we have no other choice but to vote tonight for a general boycott, which is another step in our desperate struggle to be free. Some Blacks would say 'Give them more time.' Time for what? The clock on the wall says the time is *now*! We will wear old clothes and walk with new dignity."

Melvin Porter, Archibald Hill, and Cecil Williams spoke in favor of the boycott. Dr. A. L. Dowell and Jimmie Stewart spoke against it. Mrs. Ira D. Hall pleaded for Black unity.

The crowd voted for a general boycott. Hundreds of adults, led by Dr. Moon, volunteered to carry picket signs. Thousands of Blacks and a large number of whites agreed to discontinue using their charge accounts or to cancel their charge accounts. Others agreed to furnish transportation; others to write letters and make telephone calls. Everybody had agreed to carry their part of the load.

TOMORROW IS ANOTHER DAY, AND WE'RE READY
TO BOYCOTT THE WHOLE TOWN.

On the way home, a carload of whites threatened Barbara Posey, Alma Faye Posey, Mrs. Alma Posey, Calvin Luper, Marilyn Luper, and me. They ran us down Eastern Avenue and on to the Posey home, where we ran inside the house as they made it to the porch. We knew now that things were really getting worse instead of better.

On October 4, 1960, Dr. Moon spoke at a "Mothers in Support of Nonviolent Protest" rally at the Greater Cleaves CME Church. He told the group that the NAACP was preparing for a long boycott, maybe a year or a year and a half. We were now planning especially for Thanksgiving and Christmas, because those are the heaviest shopping seasons, and we intended to keep Black people away from downtown until every eating place in Oklahoma City opened its door to Blacks. There was profound gasping among the audience. Dr. Moon spoke in deep tones. "We shall not stop until segregation in public places becomes a memory," he said. We were proud of Dr. Moon that day, and our hearts were beating with gratitude.

• •

Dr. E. C. Moon Jr. was a sensitive man of rare qualities. The youth loved him. He personified the idea of a freedom-loving dentist in the fullest sense of the word. He was a leader, a man of conviction and compassion. To him, justice was more than a word: it was a responsibility. His was a continuation, not a spasmodic operation. He maintained a constant interest, and added a new dimension to the movement with the participation of his beautiful wife, Bobbie, and his daughter, Carletta. He sacrificed his practice for the cause of freedom.

• •

The group met at Calvary Baptist Church at 201 Northeast Second Street to start the boycott. The crowd who had voted to have the boycott were conspicuous by their absence. There were only thirty Blacks there. A few of us had stayed up until 3:00 a.m. making signs. Isaac Hargrove, a commercial artist, had volunteered to make a large number of signs and had delivered them to Calvary.

Cecil Williams had been appointed as chairman of the boycott committee and had the names of a large number of adults. Cecil had said that he didn't want any youth on his committee or any picketing. The youth would continue their sit-ins, he said. It was 8:45 a.m., and we were scheduled to leave Calvary Baptist Church at 9:00 a.m. I kept watching Cecil as he walked in and out of the church, nervously waiting for the adults.

Dr. Moon led the group in singing "America." Reverend W. K. Jackson, the minister of St. John Baptist Church, led the prayer, saying, "Oh God, we invite Thy guidance, Thy direction, and Thy leadership." Dr. Moon explained that the slogan of the boycott was "Don't spend first-class dollars for second-class citizenship." He explained the purpose of the boycott.

Dr. Dowell offered encouraging words to the thirty-five people who had arrived. "In the time of Jesus, he didn't have a big crowd of followers, but his messages were no less important because of that," he said. It was obvious that although Dr. Dowell had voted against the general boycott, he was there doing his part, while those who had voted for the boycott were absent.

Dr. Moon and Cecil Williams gave the final instructions. The group was divided into pairs. There were to be two on each side of Main Street. They were to remain on the sidewalks. The group was not to block the doorways and would not talk to anyone while carrying a sign.

Dr. James Cox, the Black psychiatrist, was chairman of the printing committee and was in charge of the signs. Their originality and appeal stood out:

PRENTICE GAUTT CAN'T EAT HERE

LET EVERYBODY EAT

KHRUSHCHEV CAN EAT HERE, AND WE, THE CITIZENS AND
     TAXPAYERS, CAN'T

WHAT'S WRONG WITH BEING BLACK?

IF DEMOCRACY IS TO LIVE, SEGREGATION MUST DIE.

Not only was Dr. Cox proud of his signs, but he had distributed leaflets to Black churches and organizations, urging Blacks and their white friends not to shop downtown, and explaining to them the purposes of the boycott.

The exceptions to the boycott were the Katz and Veazey drug stores, the YWCA, the House of Chan, the Roberts Hotel Coffee Shop, the Downy Flake Donut Shop, the Oklahoma City Steak House, the S. H. Kress Co., and the Biltmore Hotel.

It was now time to leave. I walked downtown with Dr. Cox, who insisted on carrying two signs and walked as if he were in a race. Because of the lack of adult participation, I thought about the implications of what had happened at St. John Baptist Church. None of the most powerful citizens in Oklahoma City had voted against the boycott, and I didn't believe that they would use their influence in supporting it. However, time would prove that I was wrong. Our problems were to come from an entirely different direction, and we were going to fight anyone who stood in our way, be he Black, white, or polka-dot.

The boycott was on, and a large number of Blacks continued to shop downtown. They would walk by us and sometimes stop. One lady had purchased some school clothes for her children. She stopped and said, "Clara, I'm praying for you all."

I said, "I'm glad that you are praying for us, because you surely aren't helping us."

She held her head down and walked away.

One fat Black woman rushed into John A. Brown's, crossing the picket line. Two youths and I followed her inside. She bought some big old white panties. We were so angry with her. If she was not going to cooperate, she at least could have bought some black panties.

A white clerk at Brown's asked a Black schoolteacher if she knew that the Blacks were boycotting. She said, "No, I didn't."

The clerk said, "You know it now."

We purchased school bells, and every time we saw some Blacks shopping in a store, we would walk up behind them and ring our bells and keep walking.

We purchased ten cameras and started taking pictures of Blacks who were shopping downtown. We put the pictures on display in strategic locations.

The boycott continued until July 1961, and was an effective weapon in bringing Oklahoma City into a full awareness of how important all her citizens were.

· ·

The Purpose of the Oklahoma City Boycott

By Dr. E. C. Moon Jr.

Dr. Martin Luther King has awakened the people of America to the fact that when you cooperate with evil, you become a partner with those who would practice evil. The boycott here in Oklahoma City represents an awakening ON the part of the Negro citizens of this community that they are supporting their own humiliation and embarrassment when they shop in areas that deny them service in public accommodations. That a community should arbitrarily, without provocation, deny a whole race of people the convenience and dignity of service in a public place of accommodation is an outrageous and immoral practice on its face, but for Negroes themselves to cooperate and support this injustice is the very height of stupidity.

The purpose of our local boycott then becomes clear. We are attempting to offer an effective program for Negroes who value and demand their rights as first-class citizens and for all citizens who value and are concerned about this experiment we call "democracy."

To some extent, but not yet enough, this purpose is being accomplished in the Oklahoma City community.

· ·

9

PERSPECTIVES ON THE OKLAHOMA CITY SIT-INS

Let's Step Forward

By John C. Heidbrink

In 1958, most of us were traditional ministers from the demonstrations which dotted the American religious landscape. Churches, both Black and white, are a harmless part of the American cultural scene: someplace to go for forgiveness, a baptism, marriage, and death. The government even allows special tax incentives for "giving to the church." This indicates how harmless the church has been in American political life.

To go a step further, we can even say that good citizenship is equated with responsible discipleship. None of us had suffered one moment's inconvenience because of our religious convictions. Even our teachers and pastors (and lots of priests and rabbis, too) trained us to equate our religious attachments with loyalty to the nation. Such distortions have paralyzed the church for generations, and in all nations and states. The historical alignment between Lutheranism in Europe, more especially Germany, and the nation-state eventuated in the emasculation of the church in the face of Hitler's rise and momentary success. Thus, we are prepared by reading even a few pages of modern history to expose the churches in their loss of the salt which, at least in the early centuries, traded the revolution of liberation for protection and tax incentives by the secular state.

This is where we found ourselves in 1958 as Roman Catholics, Protestants, and Jews. We were the polite people protected by our Anglo-Saxon privileges and hereditary correctness. We were, by and large, whores in Babylon and the church, while the fatest of all the whores mothered us comfortably. Even our racism and color superiorities received nothing but increase in the church we called Jesus today.

But something was blowing in the late 1950s. What was it? In a small effort to describe it, one must say that "the old order was changing," and no one realized it except maybe the Black folks, and they were unprepared to live further ahead than one day at a time. There we were, all of us, Black and white preachers, the comfortable Black and white middle class, and a revolution of sorts was tugging at our preaching robes.

The Black folks in some quarters, not all quarters, were weary of the work they had been doing, sick of the pay they were receiving, revolted by the second-rate educations they were receiving, insulted by the eating and sleeping areas assigned them by the ruling class. Of course, many Blacks had reacted to these conditions for ages, and a few came through bearing the watchfires and the leader's torch. But few were ready to move. Fear had molded generations of timid and obedient servants who, though free in the abstract, hardly lived or breathed the freedoms enjoyed by the majority of the republic. Some of them were wondering why.

The group nearest me in 1958 who were wondering the loudest was the Youth Division of the NAACP coordinated by Mrs. Clara Luper, a teacher at Dunjee High School way out in the red dirt country of eastern Oklahoma City. Mrs. Luper was saying some things the newspapers were picking up, the *Daily Oklahoman* in particular. I was the chaplain of Presbyterian students at the University of Oklahoma in Norman. Soon the newspaper carried the shocked byline that the Youth Division had been contacting restaurants, motels, hotels, and small cafés in the interest of integrating the facilities, which were public and could not legally be segregated. Laws were consulted and traditions examined, and nothing could be marshaled to delay any longer. Private clubs, yes, could be restricted because of a different tax structure, but places like John A. Brown's and its lunch counter and other places I did not believe could legally be segregated. To do so would be against the law. And the Youth Division of the NAACP was out to test the law. But, like in state after state, traditions had been permitted priority growth and, like jungle vines, were choking the Constitution and its foundations of society.

All of this amounted to scandal and sacrilege. The churches had not once opened an eye or raised a voice. But it took a small band of Black kids and a Black teacher with vision, poetry, love, and caring to open up the sick body. And open it they did, and in the process called some of us off our carved pulpits and out into the street.

The call came after some of us were attending, in good white liberal fashion, the NAACP youth meetings in Oklahoma City, because, after all, "the colored people deserve one hour of our time a month; they're such good people."

In our innocent condescending fashion, which bloomed because we felt we were the good white enlightenment who needed to show off our liberal minds, we suddenly had to put our mouths where our feet were; no more waiting and sending the NAACP dues each year and attending the Urban League banquets, where we heard how much the whites had done to sustain "separate but equal" advantages for Blacks, and where a few whites were honored each year for stepping out briefly but harmlessly from the safe herd. Suddenly, we were asked to help a small band of nonviolent kids and their courageous leader. And we were asked to help by standing and walking with them with signs and attitudes which suddenly planted the great Indian movement of Mohandas Gandhi in Oklahoma.

We were asked to loan our bodies and carry signs but examine our hearts for anything which might queer the purposes we sought by invoking a violent response or an ugly sneer. We were taught by Mrs. Luper to turn our cheeks if insulted and smile when we wanted to spit and swear. We were led into workshops where nonviolence as a technique was taught us that the power of love could overcome the bitterest actions. This went on for weeks and months. John A. Brown's lunchroom resisted and became for the entire state a symbol of white exclusiveness fringed by an elitist desire to live only with "my own kind." And this kind was denoted by something as revoltingly superficial as skin color.

Preachers, priests, and rabbis joined hands and worked together in a way no one had a notion they could. A movement of unity between religious groups was forged. Black pastors, always the last to come forward because of their years of depending financially on white churches, began to throw survival to the winds. There we were, and no one knew what would happen from day to day. Nuns soon came to join in. The governor, J. Howard Edmondson, appointed a biracial Commission on Race and Equal Opportunity, and some of us served on it. But we soon learned that the American Indian, insofar as Oklahoma was concerned, was also segregated.

Where had all of these whites come from, and for what reason? Was the land theirs because they had numbers and know-how? Soon we began to find out why the resistance. The City Council began to meet.

The mayor was appointing this one and that to begin liaison with Mrs. Luper and the Youth Division. But by this time the Youth Division had enlisted great numbers from the Black community of Oklahoma City who were ready for the push. The adult NAACP group began to organize for action, too.

How it all ended belongs to others to tell. Some of us moved away and became active and strong civil rights people in our own denominations. We would like to think that the eventual March on Washington and its ensuing influence on the civil rights legislation of the 1960s began, for many of us, in towns like Oklahoma City back in the '50s. This was our schoolroom; this was our laboratory of human growth as we learned how others were treated and how they resisted with a great spiritual power found only in the soul of people. These years in Oklahoma and the situation there which nourished us, the people like Mrs. Luper and the Youth Division of the NAACP who were our teachers, became for some of us "our growing up in the human family." And it will always remain for us an initiation into peoplehood, our family of mankind.

The Oklahoma City Sit-Ins, 1961: Why I Got Involved and Stayed Involved

By James C. Shields

My first knowledge of "victory" came at the end of several significant events one morning, and it was unexpected. I stumbled into it after some duties were done.

The night before, the phone call came late. I was already mostly asleep.

"Would you make a call on bereaved parents?" the friend asked. "They're here from the coast for their son's funeral in the morning, and they feel left out with the service the wife has arranged. There's tension between them. They want a minister of their own denomination."

"Yes, I'll go by to see them," I replied. "Give me the details."

I had planned to drive from Norman to Oklahoma City the next morning anyway, to see a student friend from the University of Oklahoma who was recovering from surgery. The man's funeral was at 9:00 a.m. Arriving early, I asked to see the parents before the service began. We visited rather tensely. I stayed for the funeral and offered a bit of consolation and solace afterwards before they left for the burial.

I went next to the hospital, to see the OU friend. Her operation was comparatively minor—though very important to her and her feelings about herself. Her recovery was quite fast, and she was restless and bored with staying in the hospital. She wanted to go back to school, to see her friends. She wanted to talk, and the visit was relaxed and fun.

It was close to 10:30 a.m. as I drove away from the hospital to head back to Norman. The car needed gas, and so as I came down Broadway to Third Street, I decided to turn left and go over to a station that I'd recently seen in the northeast section of town. Only in the last few months had I gotten acquainted with the northeast part of Oklahoma City, even though I'd gone to high school in Oklahoma City. My first parish after seminary was in Oklahoma City. Northeast Oklahoma City was Black; I was white.

Standing on the corner as I turned the car onto Third Street was Clara Luper. She obviously was looking for a ride, so I stopped and asked if there was someplace special she wanted to go. She needed to meet some people at the Eastside "Y" rather quickly.

Clara, more than anyone else, had introduced me to northeast Oklahoma City's Black people and the Sit-In Movement.

She was excited as we drove to the "Y," for she'd just come from a visit with Mrs. John A. Brown, whose cafeteria in Brown's Department Store had been closed to Black people and to Blacks and whites coming together asking to be served. Mrs. Brown had just said she'd work out something and open her cafeteria to everyone, no matter what other cafés and cafeterias might do.

At the "Y," Clara and other Black leaders of this freedom movement conferred quickly, and Clara made phone calls to other owners and managers of eating places.

By lunchtime the Sit-In Movement had its victory. Oklahoma City eating places would begin to integrate.

It was a morning that's still vivid in my memory after fourteen years. It began with a death visit. The hospital visit was joyous, as an individual was thrilled with a personal victory and accomplishment. And then happening by the right corner at a significant human rights victory celebration! How did I happen to be at that corner? How did I happen to know Clara? How did I happen to get involved in the Sit-In Movement?

John and LuAnn made it happen—at least that I got involved at all in sit-ins, and that I met Clara. John Heidbrink was director of the Westminster Foundation for Presbyterian students at OU while I was director of the Wesley Foundation there for Methodist students. LuAnn Massengale Atkins was assistant chaplain for Methodist students at Oklahoma City University. Out of talks with them, I got involved.

The first visits to the Calvary Baptist Church building at Northeast Third and Walnut in Oklahoma City were uneasy ones for me. I don't enjoy socially tense situations—and obviously the scene into which we would go following these briefing meetings was both tense and hostile. The sit-in briefings each Saturday morning talked about courtesy to people in asking to be served, responding with kindly persistence to rebuffs or insults or even hostile actions, being a disciplined group, and moving in ways as directed by either the group's leaders or police. While these sessions relieved some anxieties and convinced me of the religious motivations of the group and their training, discipline, and peaceful resistance in the face of angry reactions, still there was some tenseness in going into oppressive social structures and confronting people there who were strongly committed to defending them.

But we went. Also we persisted. It wasn't easy.

It wasn't easy to face restaurant managers who stood silently and stared blankly through the Black and white pairs who came to the entrances asking to be served.

It wasn't easy to be challenged by a local counselor in a Norman coffee shop who attributed sit-in motivations only to "jealousy of the rich." Eating and freedom were the issues, not "jealousy" or poor vs. rich.

It wasn't easy to be challenged by a local businessman in the congregation where I worshipped who accused us of trying to destroy Oklahoma City businesses. More business was offered to public restaurants, not the closing down of white businesses.

It wasn't easy being accused by a minister friend of simply being "angry." There were times of anger at seeing persons ignored and maltreated simply because they were Black, but simple "anger" says nothing about the Fatherhood of God and the common humanity of all persons of all races.

But there were compensations besides these difficulties. Support and defense came from relatives, several colleagues, church officials, and local laypeople. The support and defenses helped, but there wasn't much encouragement, for most of them felt tensions about whether the "church" or "clergymen" ought to get involved in controversy.

Still, I couldn't help but wonder how so many people could participate in worship—stressing love of God and neighbor as self—but never walk for justice for neighbors, Black and white. Actually, the most encouragement came from seeing Black young people willing to ask for their rights with resolution and courtesy, and from several key conversations and experiences with Black leaders, especially Clara Luper.

The NAACP Youth Council people were marvelous. They were committed. They sang joyfully as they walked for freedom. They were polite, disciplined, and self-controlled, even when abused and provoked. Only once or twice in those long weeks did I ever see a young person cry from the stress of the hostility they met or return a harsh word when abused. They were pushed and cursed by hate-filled whites, arrested by police, and generally condemned by the prevailing white society, but they continued with courtesy and courage.

The courage was contagious. Their courage helped me. It also helped my friends Milton Propp, the Oklahoma City University chaplain, and LuAnn Atkins, the OCU assistant chaplain, as well as Father Robert McDole, a Roman Catholic priest in Oklahoma City, and the few white students from OU and OCU who joined us.

The NAACP Youth Council members I remember best were Barbara Posey and Calvin and Marilyn Luper. There were many other young people from the Black community coming to the sit-ins. While I've forgotten the names of many of them, I recall a number of faces vividly, and most of all the courage they embodied.

The most memorable conversation for me was with Clara Luper one Saturday afternoon when we were locked in at a downtown Oklahoma City hotel coffee shop. We entered the coffee shop a while before noon. Rather than serve us the coffee and cold drinks we requested, the hotel people locked us in and departed. There were six or eight of us, Black and white, youth and adults.

We hadn't much to do, and so we talked about the meanings of what we were involved in. There was not a doubt in Clara's mind about the rightness of what she was doing, nor about the peaceful but persistent tactics. There was no doubt in my mind either about the rightness of what we aimed for. I'd been taught by parents, churches, schools, and the American Constitution about "liberty and justice for all." What anxieties I first had about the methods of seeking justice quickly went away with the setting in the church building, the prayers, directions, and songs that preceded each Saturday's march and sit-in.

Clara made notes in her journal as we talked and speculated about why so few white people were coming into this movement, so obviously based upon the Judeo-Christian tradition and American ideals. It troubled us both—and disappointed us, too. Both of us believed that an easy majority of white Americans were fair and non-bigoted, but they were silent. The conversation lasted a fairly long while. About midafternoon, hotel officials and Oklahoma City police arrived at the locked door, opened it, and asked us to leave their unusual confinement cell. That was the only time I've ever come out of a coffee shop more hungry than when I entered.

I concluded some years later that the reason so few whites got involved in freedom movements at the beginning was that they were trained by both religion and culture to be uninvolved Americans rather than Good Samaritans. Being "good" in both religious and civic terms meant being uninvolved in trouble, even to help socially wounded people. Whites had been taught to be "good"; they had not been taught how to be "effectively good" to other people in tense circumstances.

Another helpful "conversation" in continuing to participate in sit-ins was seeing Dr. L. J. West Jr., a white psychiatrist in the OU Medical School, and Dr. Chester Pierce, a Black psychiatrist in the OU Medical School, with the actor Charlton Heston—three physically very large men, walking Oklahoma City Main Street sidewalks, wearing placards about freedom and justice. They talked with other marchers and made conversation as they walked with interlocked arms among the watching crowd and passersby. Seeing and hearing them helped reassure some of my fearful relatives.

As I reflect back on the Oklahoma City sit-ins from the perspective of the events of almost fifteen years, they really seem quite tame and mild now. Oklahoma City was confronted by a number of Black adults, a substantial group of mostly junior high youth, and a few white adults, including some white college students. Oklahoma City was lucky. Freedom to eat in public restaurants came without the bombs of Birmingham, the dogs of Selma, the bullets in the night of many other towns, or the martyrs like Medgar Evers and Martin Luther King.

Oklahoma City was lucky that freedom for oppressed and oppressors came so easily and peacefully—but Oklahoma City wasn't very smart. Oklahoma City learned about "open eating places" but not about "open housing," and so Oklahoma City has school and "busing for balance" problems. It's doubtful if sit-ins or picketing can solve the housing problems. We do not seem to know the answer, or tactics, for that yet. What we do know—however dimly perceived—is that until all of a city's people live freely and well, few of a city's people live freely and well.

The victories for Blacks and whites in Oklahoma city in 1961 are gladly remembered as much as the plights of Blacks and whites in Oklahoma City in 1975 are sadly viewed. Thanks, Clara and friends, for a good past; I wish we knew where to go now.

Meet Father McDole

The Rev. Robert G. McDole is a native Oklahoman who lived at Stillwater until he was twenty-one.

He studied at Oklahoma State University, a Roman Catholic seminary at Bethany, and a seminary in San Antonio before coming to Sacred Heart Parish in July 1958.

He attended the University of Oklahoma for one year beginning in September 1950, and received a music degree.

The redheaded priest has been at Corpus Christi Parish, 1005 Northeast Fifteenth Street, since July. He is assistant pastor at that church now.

Catholic Priest Tells "Why I Joined Sit-Ins"

By Reverend Robert G. McDole

Last July, soon after I came to Corpus Christi Parish in the northeast part of Oklahoma City, my awareness of the evils of racial segregation and discrimination began to change through personal experience to a strong personal response of deep indignation.

I have realized better day by day ... that injustice is assured only when those who are not injured feel as indignant as those who are.

... The northeast section of our community has been undergoing radical and profound change for some time.

What this means in terms of social relations would fill many tomes. But what it means to a parish priest who sees his fellow citizens and his brothers in Christ humiliated, persecuted, and even hated is very simple.

A call to leadership, self-giving, and action according to the advice of St. Paul, "Be not overcome with evil, but overcome evil with good."

Late last summer, the Young Christian Workers section, of which I am chaplain (it includes both Caucasian and Negro young people), held an inquiry into the problems of integration.

The action which resulted was assisting those in the sit-in effort taking place on Saturdays in downtown Oklahoma City.

When the first Saturday for carrying out the action arrived, there were, as I recall, four YCW members assembled to go to Calvary Baptist Church for the pre-sit-in rally, and I went with them.

Except when prevented by other parochial duties, I have been going every Saturday since.

It has been a source of great joy to me to be associated with fellow citizens and fellow Christians—although of different faiths—in this effort to secure justice for all citizens of our community.

The dedication and generosity of Mrs. Clara Luper, Willie James, the Reverend John Heidbrink, Mrs. LuAnn Atkins, and others has been instructive and inspiring.

I feel a great deal has already been accomplished by the fact that although we cannot worship together, we can join our efforts to make this community a better reflection of God's will and a better expression of the purpose and prescriptions of the American Constitution.

A counsel of Our Lord Jesus Christ was "Work, for the night is coming when no man can work."

In our world community of today, the leadership of our Western and Christian cultural tradition has fallen to the United States. We are on trial before the large part of the world that is non-Western, non-Christian, and, I might add, non-white.

The ideas we profess in our Constitution and express in our patriotic songs, and even more so in our religious songs, are very real to us who take part in the Sit-In Movement.

They are so real and meaningful that we recognize the great need of proving them to the world by our witness to the fact that they are sometimes outraged and that we protest the fact.

My Bishop has stated that we do not have much time to grant that full equality to all citizens which justice commands and right conscience demands.

We who sit in, or more accurately look into, the restaurants and other eating places we are not allowed to enter are trying to make the best possible use of the little time we have to serve our Western civilization.

"Why Did You Do It?"

Dr. Louis J. West

Last Saturday afternoon I went downtown with a small group of distinguished Negro colleagues. Later, as I sat on the cold, muddy marble outside a "service-to-whites-only" cafeteria, I couldn't help thinking of a line from Ibsen: "You should never wear your best trousers when you go out to fight for freedom and truth." Having committed this sartorial error, I am now called upon to state whether my becoming a white participant in a Negro "sit-in" demonstration was not also an error. Hostile anonymous telephonists and anxious personal friends ask the same question: "Why did you do it?"

That such a question should be put to a physician in this country nearly a century after Lincoln described us as a nation "conceived in liberty, and dedicated to the proposition that all men are created equal" is not so much astonishing as anachronistic. That it should happen to Oklahoma City, one of the most progressive and forward-looking communities in the United States, is of only passing significance. In a few short years, such incidents may be regarded as historical curiosities, and participants in these demonstrations will perhaps be considered as having been moved by the spirit of their time, rather than having themselves contributed significantly to progress. If this be the case, why bother to demonstrate? There are three major reasons for my doing so; three principles involved.

ETHICAL REASONS: the Christian Principle. As a product of twentieth-century American culture, with its great debt to the Old and New Testaments, I sometimes call myself a Christian. To me this means a moral commitment to the ideal of the brotherhood of man. Am I my brother's keeper? I must try to be. However, like Voltaire, I am very fond of truth, but not at all of martyrdom. Well, so I love my neighbor enough to risk helping him when he is reviled, persecuted, demeaned, or humiliated because of the color of his skin? If not, I fail to be true to myself; I violate the Christian Principle as I understand it, and my conscience bothers me. If another man's understanding of Christianity differs from mine, I cannot help it. Byron said man's conscience is the oracle of God. Mine may be neither prophetic nor divine, but it tells me to speak out in public against racial discrimination. To this voice I must respond; it speaks louder than all other voices because it is closest to my ear.

POLITICAL REASONS: the Democratic Principle. In the dawn of the Republic, our first president prayed that all Americans would "entertain a brotherly affection and love for one another." Today a few individuals, by their persistent refusal to treat citizens of all races as brothers, impugn Washington's wisdom. My call openly to oppose their discriminatory practices, even when they are seemingly condoned by law, is as old as the call to democracy on this continent.

An encroachment upon the dignity of any man debases mankind. Nobody is entitled to "reserve the right" to violate the principles on which our democracy is based, and from which all our freedoms derive. Any such violation threatens to alienate those rights, including equality, declared inalienable by the founders of our political system. Therefore, by defending the rights of any citizen, one defends the rights of all. Can the responsibility for this be delegated by me to a Negro organization? No, because it is not only a struggle for the dignity and equality of the Negro in which I am engaged; it is for my own and every man's. If freedom is deserved only by those who are willing to fight for it, then I must take a personal part.

NATIONAL REASONS: the Patriotic Principle. Our country leads the free world in the most terrible struggle in the history of mankind, against a monstrous tyranny that would bury liberty forever. The battle is global; it is joined; men and women and children are suffering and dying in it in Europe, Asia, and Africa. We are numerically inferior to our opponents, and we are losing ground steadily. Today our best hope for preserving religious freedom, free elections, free speech, free press, free assembly, private property, private profit, and private cafeterias is to persuade the uncommitted peoples of the world to join us in our fight for a free way of life. These peoples are of all races; whites are a small minority.

Already Western civilization has reaped whirlwind after whirlwind of hatred from the seeds of racism it has sown. Now, tales of racial discrimination in the United States are being used against us by the communists with vicious effectiveness far and wide. These propaganda weapons, employed in the battle for the minds of men, can destroy us more surely than atomic weapons. Can freedom as a way of life survive, and with it our nation? If so, colored people in every land must come to know that democracy offers them something precious, worth winning and preserving. But we must exemplify democracy, proving its value by truly living it. Viewed in this light, any insistence upon prolonging racial discriminatory practices in the United States can be seen as giving aid and comfort to the enemy.

Whether it be treason or merely stupidity, cynically profitable or indignantly righteous, emotionally prejudiced or blandly traditional, northern or southern, public or private, racial discrimination in America serves the cause of communism everywhere. As patriotic citizens, and in the national interest, we must all work quickly to end racial discrimination in this country forever, and pray that it is not already too late.

Segregationist vs. Integrationist

1. It takes time to work out these things.
2. It will cause trouble.

3. I will lose my white customers.
4. You aren't going after it the right way.
5. I have no recommendation.

6. I heard that you all were satisfied.
7. Why don't you build a restaurant?

8. This is my private business.

9. You should be tired, you have been trying for a long time.

10. You are going to start something.

---

1. You have had 342 years.
2. Theaters, schools, parks, buses, trains, the City Auditorium, the zoo, and 116 other places have opened, and there has been no trouble.
3. The places that have opened have not lost any business.
4. What would you recommend?
5. Then we will do what we know to do—openly protest.
6. Sorry, you have been terribly misinformed.
7. We will when the Germans build one for the German-born Americans, the Irish for the Irish, and the Mexicans for the Mexicans.
8. Yes, but you have a public license, and your business is advertised over my radio, in my newspaper, in my telephone directory, and I can read your signs.
9. We have just begun. We are training our members as soon as they are able to talk to say "freedom," and to work for freedom.
10. No, we use nonviolence.

A Call to Action

By Clara Luper

While the restaurant owners sleep, let the city fathers remain silent, and whites shift their responsibilities; let the Negroes pretend that things will work themselves out, and see what will happen to our city.

Oklahoma City has embedded the ideals of freedom, justice, and equality into all of her citizens; therefore, every citizen has a responsibility to help in this struggle.

We are brothers. I don't think that the Oklahoma City restaurants are bigger and more influential than the freedom-loving, God-fearing people of Oklahoma City.

As you answer this call, remember that the great cause of human liberty is in the hands of God, and it's God's will that men should live together as brothers.

10

TULSA, OKLAHOMA

To receive a call from Shirley Williams was not a surprise. I had always called her my "little girl." She always affectionately called me "Mother dear." She was quite a star and could shine in any area, from orations to music, from organizing to implementing. She was the daughter of Mr. and Mrs. Portwood Williams and the granddaughter of Mrs. Acorns, a citizen of the community who always helped us.

Shirley Williams had married and moved to Tulsa, where she had become involved with an activist group that wanted to break down segregation in public accommodations. She called me and asked if I'd talk to the group that was meeting over at her house. The group had expected active participation from Tulsa's Black community and was disgusted and discouraged.

"What do you do when the people don't cooperate with you?" she asked in a high-pitched voice.

"I just use what I have. So if we have one minister, whether he is Black or white, I thank God for him. I don't spend a lot of time worrying about the people who aren't participating. I just spend my time in trying to determine what to do with the people who are participating."

Shirley said, "Mother dear, will you come over and lead a demonstration for us? I don't know what will happen. The only thing I do know is that these people are crazy. Stone crazy. They might do anything to you. They are living back in the seventeenth century. Will you come? Then we can tell everybody that you are coming, and that will increase our crowd. You can tell us—I mean show us—how you are doing in Oklahoma City."

"If you think that I can be of some service, I shall be honored to come. I appreciate the opportunity to come to Tulsa. I'll probably get to see my cousins Sarah, Dorothy, and Brother," I replied.

"You come on. I wouldn't promise you that you will get to see your cousins where we are going."

We completed the minor details as to the time with an "I'll see you real soon."

The NAACP Youth Council chartered a Greyhound bus, left our segregated places in Oklahoma City, and headed for Tulsa. On the way, we talked about the Tulsa race riot, which took place in June 1921. We discussed how over thirty blocks in the Black part of town were completely destroyed. We argued over whether 85 or 175 Blacks were killed. The "hearsay" doctrine was vividly used with a direct confrontation. We were joined in freedom songs, spirituals, and our state song.

Arriving in Tulsa, we joined about four hundred in a freedom march through downtown. Whites and Blacks were shocked at this march, and a few jeers were heard from the crowd. The parade was climaxed by a rally in Boulder Park. The thirty members of the NAACP Youth Council from Oklahoma City joined in leading freedom songs. I was featured as the guest speaker. My speech was concerned with voter registration. I continued to quote from Frederick Douglass, "The quickest way to freedom is by way of the ballot box." The message was, "We are not afraid. We have marched in Oklahoma City for years, and we have marched in Tulsa today, and we are now ready to go and eat. Where are we going to eat?" The crowd went wild with applause, and we had a quick caucus and decided to go to Borden's Restaurant in North Tulsa.

We arrived at Borden's and went straight to the front door. The door was slammed in our faces, and we were told that we could not eat there. It was at that time that we decided to go to the back door. "Since we have been used to going to back doors, I'm sure we can get in the back door," I told the group. And to the surprise of the manager, we walked through the back door, through the kitchen, and into the serving line. Immediately all the doors were locked.

I got in a heated argument with the manager over a tomato. As he was telling me all the things that Black people couldn't do since they were so inherently inferior, I told him that he had no creative intelligence. "For example, that tomato tells me in simple language that you can't make a tomato."

He said, "Why, that's silly, Clara Luper, you can't either."

"Now, if I can't make a tomato and you can't make one, evidently we are in the same category, and I have as much right to eat tomatoes in this restaurant as you."

One of the waitresses said, "She's too damned smart."

We started singing and waving our beautiful American flags. Then we recited the Twenty-Third Psalm over and over. In the meantime, a large group had gathered outside, and they were pledging their allegiance to the American flag and singing "America."

It was interesting to watch some of the customers who were in the cafeteria when we arrived as the employees tried to let them out and the Blacks tried to squeeze through the door. Newsmen were slapped and pushed. One employee grabbed a television reporter's camera, and there was quite a scuffle.

The crowd outside consisted of a large number of White Citizens' Council members who had been denied a parade permit by the city. They were very angry because the Blacks had been permitted to stage a march. I looked out the window and counted sixteen motorcycle officers. Policemen were equipped with teargas along the side street.

Mr. Leroy Borden, the owner of Borden's Restaurant, signed a complaint for our arrest. I looked around, and a detective took me by the arm and led me out of the cafeteria. The boos and slurs from the White Citizens' Council sounded loudly in the subfreezing weather, which was turning into sleet. The chairman of the Student Committee on Human Rights at the University of Tulsa was dragged out of the restaurant. He was kicking and screaming. I saw four officers throw him into the paddy wagon. Assistant Chief Don Phillips and twenty-four other officers took thirty-two to jail very peacefully.

The ride to the police station was quite enjoyable, as we all talked about the weather and some of the problems that this country was facing.

When we arrived at the police station, I explained to the two white officers that I could not get out of the car because I had just been to Nilar Jewel's Beauty Salon, where I had paid her to dress my hair. If I got out, my hair would go round and round and squat as firmly to my scalp as the '89ers squatted for land. To my surprise, the officer said, "I'll go and tell Police Chief Jack Purdie, because if we drag you out, it will only add to the tension that is already mounting here."

The officers left, and in a few minutes Chief Purdie came out with an open black umbrella and escorted me into the jail. I liked Chief Purdie from the very outset—if for no other reason than that he was kind to me that day. Before I was locked up, I met Police Commissioner Bennie Garren and City Attorney Charley Norman.

The Tulsa women's cells were unusually clean, and I was put into a cell with two white women, later joined by Shirley Williams Scoggins. I found out from Shirley that thirty-three had been arrested. Shirley talked about a committee that the mayor had working on human relations, which she called a "tea-sipping," do-nothing committee. The committee had been set up in November 1961, and it had handled integration problems by mediating disputes. It had passed a public accommodations resolution in December, which made it clear that it was a policy of the city of Tulsa that all public places should be opened to all races. There was no penalty for ignoring or disobeying the policy. The city had turned down a strict public accommodations ordinance that included a penalty clause dictating a $100 fine or revoking of city licenses for those businesses that did not want to comply.

We spent over an hour in jail and were charged with trespassing. We were released to the custody of Mr. Ed Goodwin, an attorney and the publisher of the *Oklahoma Eagle,* a weekly Black newspaper in Tulsa.

After our release, we found that we had really upset the Tulsa community. Vincent Dunn, the president of the Tulsa NAACP Youth Council, denounced the demonstration and stated that it was inspired by CORE and by those of us who had come from Oklahoma City. Other Black leaders in Tulsa felt that additional time was needed to prepare for the demonstration. White leaders argued that integration in Tulsa had suffered a temporary setback because of the sit-in and that further demonstrations would lead to trouble. Commissioner Garren said, "Ultimate integration has come to be accepted by most Tulsans who have chosen to look the other way."

Shirley Scoggins stated, "We don't understand what ultimate means, but we know that direct action is now our policy. There is only one way that demonstrations can be stopped, and that is by the immediate opening of all—*all*—public accommodations in Tulsa."

Members of the Vernon AME Church, Reverend B. S. Roberts, Reverend Ben Hill, and attorney Amos T. Hall congratulated us and vowed to support us.

The picketing continued as the small groups bumped up against all odds until the walls of segregation fell in Tulsa!

Speaking to the Association of Women's Studies on February 22, 1961, Dr. John Paul Duncan, a University of Oklahoma professor, compared the Sit-In Movement to a nagging wife:

> Where nagging has worked in the family, this sort of demonstration can work for integration.
>
> People do not like to live in families or societies where they feel that there is a moral wrong. If there is something more than a sheer wall of physical violence in a community against this action, there should be some results from sit-ins and picketing.
>
> Picketing points out that segregation is a serious moral evil. To others, it is like walking around with a "rock in your side." But just because a great number of people don't participate in these things doesn't mean that they aren't any good.
>
> Causes have to be fought by people who can devote all their energies to this activity. Everyone has his own ax to grind.
>
> If you want to change a condition such as segregation, quiet negotiations, writing, talking, and taking action to draw attention to the condition will put a little social pressure on it.
>
> I'm tired of hearing "wait until people's hearts change and let it work out gradually." After all, how long is gradually?

11

DOE DOE AMUSEMENT PARK AND THE MARCH TO LAWTON

The mingling of races at Fort Sill was a small part of a greater movement toward understanding what would happen in a military-oriented town. It seemed inconsistent with democracy that Fort Sill's soldiers had a long history of defending democracy all over the world and yet could not defend democracy beyond Fort Sill's gates in Lawton, Oklahoma. Black and white soldiers who had fought together could not swim together at Doe Doe Amusement Park in Lawton. This condition in 1966 was not a newly discovered truth but a hard, cold reality. The United States Army, through its leaders and officers, was silent on the discriminatory policies that Black soldiers faced in Lawton.

Discrimination in Lawton had been expressed in various ways by different people again and again. Essentially, it could be reduced to a theory that goes like this: The whites in Lawton were prepared to perpetuate segregation at all costs. They knew that Blacks were victims of apathy and were afraid to stand up and be counted. They also knew that it was difficult to awaken the large number of Blacks from the long sleepy nights of segregation. And so the city of Lawton had resorted to a systematic method of building walls, visible and invisible, that had kept the Blacks out. After the walls were built, they would spoon-feed one or two Blacks, and this was what they called good race relations in Lawton, Oklahoma.

State Representative Archibald Hill Jr. had talked about Lawton. He referred to it as a twentieth-century town with seventeenth-century ideas and leaders. Upon his arrival, he found that Blacks in Lawton were completely segregated in spite of the fact that Fort Sill was there. Men from Fort Sill were going off to fight for democracy all over the world, and yet Blacks in Lawton couldn't enjoy first-class citizenship. He said, "Man, Lawton, Oklahoma, is Jim Crow's headquarters, and we've got to do something." He immediately checked the voter registration list of Blacks in Lawton and found that there were only 603 registered voters and not even a Black postman. He reorganized the NAACP, which had 16 inactive members, and increased the membership to 125. He called this "a shot in the arm." Spurred on by Dr. C. Owens, Reverend Jones, and others, three thousand new voters were added to the rolls within a few weeks. Archibald Hill had upset freedom's waters. The waves of oppression started flowing toward him until finally he accepted the challenge of moving to Oklahoma City, where he established a lucrative law practice and continued his civil rights work. He organized a local chapter of CORE and became involved in everything that meant progress for poor people in Oklahoma City.

Twenty-five marchers met at New Zion Baptist Church in Lawton and marched with U.S. flags and placards to Doe Doe Amusement Park. Ben Hutchins Sr., the owner of the park, met the group at the gate and said, "Get off my property. I don't want you on my property! Officer, arrest these people for trespassing!" Sharp words and fistfights followed. No one was seriously injured, but tensions were high.

"That was an angry, mean-looking man," Hill stated.

Some Blacks jumped over the rope to the beat of "Hey, Hey, Freedom."

Over a hundred Blacks formed a circle in the street in front of Doe Doe Amusement Park and sang:

He's got the whole world in his hands,
He's got the whole wide world in his hands,
He's got old Ben Hutchins in his hands,
He's got the whole wide world in his hands.
He's got Mayor Gilley in his hands,
He's got the white City Council in his hands,
He's got Old Man Hutchins in his hands,
He's got the whole world in his hands.

A week later, we went back to Lawton. When we arrived there, we went on to Sheridan Road and marched seven blocks to Doe Doe Amusement Park. We marched to an army cadence count and sang

Oh freedom, oh freedom,
Oh freedom over me,
Before I'd be a slave, I'd be buried in my grave,
And go home to my God and be saved.

We chanted "We want to swim in Doe Doe Pool." Some of the smaller children were chanting "We are on our way to Doe Doe Park; we are going to swim in Doe Doe Pool."

As we entered the park, I continued to ask, "What kind of man is Ben Hutchins?" I had heard that he was a tough man and loved Negroes in their subservient roles. I had heard that he had vendors and other investments in the Black community. He was the one that a large number of Blacks and whites were afraid to cross.

As we entered the park, I looked up to see two men standing there, looking straight as us. Dr. Owens told me that the two were Ben Hutchins and his attorney, Lawton Burton. They both looked as if they were mad at the whole world. I told Senator E. Melvin Porter, "If Ben Hutchins is as mean as he looks, he will say 'Welcome!'"

"Are you a fool, Clara? He's going to act like a peckerwood and say 'Go home!'" Porter said.

"He would be a handsome man if he would remove some of those frown lines from his face," I said.

Silence fell over the crowd as Dr. Owens spoke, saying politely and softly, "We want to swim in the pool. May we swim today?"

Ben Hutchins looked at me. His face looked as if he had not smiled in fifty years. Continuing to stare into his eyes, I said, "We want to swim and we have paid our dues. Every time a Black brother died on a battlefield, that was a down payment, and we have a right to swim."

Hutchins was now looking over the large number of Blacks who were standing in front of him. He spoke loudly and sharply. "This is a privately owned park, and I have the right to enforce a segregation policy." His lawyer nodded his approval, and Dr. Owens repeated the request to swim in the pool.

I looked back to see a whole army of police coming toward us. One of the officers displayed copies of a city ordinance pertaining to obstruction of sidewalks.

"This is my dream," Hutchins said, "and I worked day and night to make my dream come true. I built this park, my park, my park, with my own hard-earned money. Money that I worked hard for. This was my dream. A dream to have a beautiful place for white people and for white church groups and white schoolchildren, and you all are trying to ruin my dreams."

I replied, "We have dreams, too. I dream of putting my big black feet into that blue water. And my dream is quilted into every piece of the Great American Dream of freedom, justice, and equality."

Police Chief Hennessee interrupted by asking us to leave. He repeated, "This is your last chance. If you don't leave, we'll have to take you to jail."

We did not leave, and we were placed under arrest.

"Yes, Porter, we are riding in style in a good old paddy wagon."

E. Melvin Porter (Oklahoma's only Black state senator), Reverend William G. Hayden (a white Catholic priest from Lawton), seven youth from Oklahoma City (Barbara A. Hill, Marilyn Luper, June Roy Spivey, Carolyn J. House, Royce Frazier, Sylvester Smith, and Freddie L. Edwards), and I were charged with violating the city ordinance prohibiting obstruction of streets or sidewalks by a crowd. Some children from Lawton were also included.

Ten of our children between the ages of five and thirteen were taken into custody and placed in the juvenile ward. To my surprise, the jailer came up and said, "Mrs. Luper, the chief wants to see you." He unlocked the door, and I was taken into the chief's office. As I walked in, I realized that the chief had a very serious problem. He tried to explain to me how the ten small children from Oklahoma City had to use the bathroom frequently and that they wanted water and food.

I said, "You're the chief, and I know that you know how to handle that, so if you'll be kind enough to take me back up to my cell, I shall be very appreciative."

He said, "Oh, no, you understand children, you're a schoolteacher."

I said, "I don't teach elementary students; my training has been confined to secondary education."

He said, "Well, I don't care about that. I'm letting you out of jail, and you take those little children and get back to Oklahoma City!"

I started laughing as I said, "Chief, may I have a conference with one of my lawyers?"

The chief said, "Yes, you can call him."

I said, "No, he's in jail. E. Melvin Porter is my lawyer."

The chief immediately took me upstairs, where Senator Porter was jumping up and down. When he saw me walking around, he started fussing and blaming me for getting him locked up. He said, "I'm sick. I'm suffering from claustrophobia. I've got to get out of here!"

Freddie Edwards said very slowly, "Senator Porter, this is fun."

Porter said, "It may be fun for you, Freddie, but it's hell to me!" He continued to put on a show as he jumped up and down, yelling, "Let me out, let me out!!"

I said, "Porter, I just came to tell you all goodbye; the children and I are on our way back to Oklahoma City."

Porter said, "No, you won't leave me down here! I've got to get back to my office. I've got to get back to District 48. I cannot serve my people down here. I represent the people in my senatorial district. I've got to get back home. I have some meetings."

I said, "Goodbye, Senator. The legislature will not open until January." I left him screaming and went back where Dr. Owens was paying all of our twenty-dollar fines.

We left Lawton and went to the NAACP's National Convention in Los Angeles, California, where we won the Isabel Strickland Memorial Award and received commitments from various NAACP youth groups to assist us in a mammoth march to Lawton.

In the meantime, Major William Rose, director of the state's Human Rights Commission, spoke out against segregation at Doe Doe Amusement Park, saying, "As long as the citizens are exercising their constitutional right to protest and are doing it in a peaceful manner, then we can't object to it. Segregation is morally indefensible."

The freedom-loving people of Lawton responded with letters. Mrs. Margaret Gover wrote an open letter to the citizens:

12 June 1966

Dear Fellow Citizen:

I am Margaret Gover, an interested citizen of Lawton, spokesman for nobody, in charge of nothing for the group who demonstrated at Doe Doe Park Saturday.

I am a wife, a mother, a church member, a taxpayer, a voter, a consumer, and a civic-minded individual. I have a good job. I live in a comfortable house in a nice neighborhood. It would be very easy for me to withdraw myself into my little nest and fluff my feathers and say "This situation at Doe Doe Park does not concern me."

Why does it concern me? *Because* I am a wife, a mother, a church member, a taxpayer, a voter, a consumer, a civic-minded individual. I have a good job. I live in a comfortable house in a nice neighborhood. I am a partaker of the good things our democratic society has to offer, therefore I must accept the responsibilities that go with the joys. When my babies were born, they were beautiful—a gift of God. In order to experience the joys of motherhood, I had to accept the responsibilities that went with it. For every baby kiss, there was a bottle to fix, a diaper to change, clothes to wash, hurts to mend. It was also a beautiful gift of God that I was born into a free society. For the joys incumbent to this happenstance, I must also accept the responsibilities. I am a part of "We, the people" spoken of in the Constitution. I am a part of the "whosoever" that Christ gave his life for. I am a pretty important person—and so are you. There are really only two of us in this whole big world, and we are responsible for it all. Those two are me—and you.

I am not going into the opinions rendered by the Justice Department and the attorney general in regard to the operation of Doe Doe Park. They are opinions only, one favoring Mr. Hutchins's contention, the other favoring an unsegregated operation.

The morality of his position is a question that we must concern ourselves with. It is inconceivable that a business dependent upon the public for its existence could be considered as private as your own house. When I spoke with news reporters yesterday at Doe Doe Park, they asked me if I felt that I was trespassing. I asked them if they felt that they were trespassing. We were standing very close to each other. They asked me how I would feel having people barge into my living room or my backyard uninvited, and they told me that Mr. Hutchins's pool was as private as his backyard or his living room. I informed the reporters that I had been swimming in Mr. Hutchins's pool, that I had skated in his skating rink, that I had picnicked in his picnic area, and that I have never received a phone call or a letter from Mr. Hutchins inviting me over to swim or skate or picnic. I have always been required to pay the entrance fee. I don't charge admission to my house, do you? I also find Doe Doe Park listed in the yellow pages of our telephone directory under "Swimming Pools—Public."

Mr. Hutchins is not solely responsible for his actions. The two of us, you and I, are responsible. We have sat back and done nothing about passing a public accommodations ordinance in our city. We have allowed our elected servants, the City Council and Mayor Gilley, to drag their feet—our feet—on this important legislation. We have sat back and said "Gee, we should build some municipal pools," but we haven't built any. Our public servants thought about it—they even have a committee. But it isn't all *their* fault. It comes right back to two people who have failed our duties—me and you.

In order for our government officials to fulfill the duties of their offices, we must let them know what we expect. In order to know what the issues are and how we stand on them, we must know about them. Our news media have a particular responsibility in this area. Their responsibility is to inform the public completely about the issues. This is news. They certainly have the right to editorialize their convictions on any given subject, but this is editorializing, not reporting the news, and should be so marked.

I believe that the local news media thought they were serving the public interest by simply ignoring the Doe Doe Park issue, and finally they were misinformed in regard to opinions about the operation of Doe Doe Park. They failed to get the complete story. I believe that this was a sincere effort on their part to prevent public demonstrations and bad publicity for our city.

To the people of Lawton, I would like to express my thanks and appreciation for the kindness, sincerity, and dignity you accorded us as we made our pilgrimage. The police were extremely courteous and efficient as they carried out their instructions. It was obvious that they did not relish their task of arresting and incarcerating little children, ministers, and other people sincerely dedicated to the cause of "liberty and justice for all."

Yesterday, when I spoke to reporters, I did not represent myself as spokesman for the group, as being in change of publicity, or as anything other than an interested citizen. I did not say that the group was willing to be arrested for publicity. What I did say was that nobody wanted to demonstrate, that every conceivable effort had been made to inform the people—that's you and me—of the segregated conditions at Doe Doe Park without avail, and that there had been no other way than by demonstration to bring it to the attention of the public.

I believe that we, the people of the United States of America, of Lawton, Oklahoma, must take a common stand against the policy of segregation at Doe Doe Park or anywhere else. How can we ask the soldiers, red and yellow, Black and white, we are training at Fort Sill to defend our freedom when some of them are not free to choose whether or not to swim at Doe Doe Park? How can we uphold the ideals of democracy in another country when we deny equality to ten percent or more of our own people?

Last week, I wrote letters, I called people on the telephone, I talked to people. Nothing was accomplished. Other people wrote letters, called people on the telephone, talked to people—nothing was accomplished. Yesterday, I walked. Other people walked— some went to jail. Today I am writing letters, calling people on the phone, talking to people. I hope others will do the same. I hope something will be accomplished soon. Pray God I don't have to walk again.

Sincerely,

Margaret L. Gover

At a demonstration at Doe Doe Amusement Park on June 18, 1966, a proposed city ordinance requiring integration of privately owned facilities was handed to the mayor and the City Council. The council was silent on the subject as large numbers of Blacks attended council meetings to speak on behalf of the ordinance.

We were invited by Dr. Owens to join in the picketing of City Hall. A demonstration was staged. They borrowed a speaker from Levi Pressley, and a freedom rally was held at City Hall.

Dr. Owens, Reverend N. H. Jones, Reverend Al Kelly, Reverend Egan Miller, and Reverend James Miller spoke before the City Council. Reverend Miller's dramatic plea closed with a beautiful prayer.

The council finally passed a public accommodations ordinance that excluded privately owned and operated swimming pools and amusement parks.

One hundred and ninety years ago, Thomas Jefferson wrote the immortal words "We hold these truths to be self-evident, that all men are created equal, and that they are endowed by their Creator with certain unalienable rights, that among these are life, liberty, and the pursuit of happiness." Happiness to the Blacks in Lawton, Oklahoma, meant the right to swim at Doe Doe Amusement Park. So on July 4, 1966, a mammoth Fourth of July march was staged in Lawton.

Since the highway patrol had the overall responsibility for providing safety to the marchers, I felt that we were on the wrong issue. We had to find out what highway patrol chief Lyle Baker was going to do. Senator Porter and I went out to see him. He finally got around to his plan. Chief

Baker was going to assign a limited number of patrol cars to the march. One would precede the march and one would follow the marchers. A plea to all motorists to drive with extra caution would be made. He stated that a member of the highway patrol would address the marchers at 5:30 p.m. on the south steps of the Capitol.

As we left the commissioner's office, I asked Porter, "How in the world did you come up with the technique, and how did you get all of us to follow you?" He went into detail and explained that Doe Doe Amusement Park was a national crisis and should receive national attention in order that the walls would fall.

"Here is the permit that will allow you and your army to march through Oklahoma City," I said. "I went to the city traffic control office, and Martha Moore gave me the parade permit."

"At least your 'ride-in' didn't work out," Porter said. "Remember you had made arrangements to set up tents at 'Doo Doo' Park." He smiled then and said, "I mean Doe Doe Park."

We talked about how Dr. Guy Bellamy (the chairman of the Human Rights Commission), Dr. Frank Belvin, Monsignor A. A. Isenbart, and William Rose (executive director of the Human Rights Commission) had gone to Lawton to try to get Mr. Hutchins to open the park to all. Bellamy had sounded discouraged because the commission did not have the support of the legislature or of the people of Oklahoma.

Porter said, "We had better stop talking about the commission and get everything ready for the march." We rushed out to GEX, and he bought a pair of striped coveralls with pockets where he could rest his hands. I bought some blue denim coveralls.

Porter went to Chickasha on Tuesday and made preparations for a food, medicine, checkup, and rest shelter to be set up at the halfway point. At one time, he had suggested that one group of marchers would walk to Chickasha and another group would march from Chickasha to Lawton. But because of the compassion that the NAACP Youth Council felt for the Black soldiers who were training at Fort Sill for duty in Vietnam and being denied the right to swim at Doe Doe Park, we all agreed to march until we couldn't march anymore.

Willie J. Cole, one of the NAACP Youth Council workers, had been killed in Vietnam the first week of June 1966. He was twenty-three years old, an Oklahoma Citian by birth, and had graduated from Douglass High School. His death struck the Youth Council members like a clap of thunder. It was only fitting that the one-hundred-mile march to Lawton from Oklahoma City would be in his memory.

Vera Pigee had called from Clarksdale, Mississippi, and had organized a prayer group, which consisted of Reverend Rayford of Clarksdale, Mrs. Mary Lee, and others. I said, "We really need it, Vera." She
offered to come if I thought it would help. I said, "No, you keep fighting
in Mississippi, and every lick you hit in Mississippi will help us here."

"Will Trudy participate in the march?" she asked.

"Vera, we couldn't march without Trudy, our freedom-fighting dog.
Trudy has not missed a single march. You know she is black, and a
black dog understands Black people's problems. In fact, she will lead the
march," I said.

Vera talked briefly about James Meredith and his lone march through
Mississippi.

I looked at the clock, and it was 5:30 p.m. "I'm sorry, Vera, I've got
to be out at the State Capitol at six. Bye-bye, Vera, I'm on my way to
Lawton."

Oklahoma's State Capitol grounds were covered with friends, news
reporters, and one hundred marchers who had pledged to walk to Lawton. Mark Roseman, the national youth director of the NAACP, had
flown to Oklahoma City from New York City to participate. Roseman,
Melvin Porter, Cecil Williams, and I spoke briefly.

Geneva Smith, the versatile schoolteacher, sang "From Clouds to
Rainbows," and we started marching. Senator Porter, Mark Roseman,
Nancy Davis, Trudy, and I were in front. Porter was all smiles. "Isn't this
a beautiful sight? Oh, thank God for this day. We are together!"

Morgan Mallard, a high school football player, stepped in front of
Senator Porter. Porter told him to stay behind because he was going to
lead this march right into Lawton and would arrive there on Saturday.
Morgan smiled and said, "Senator, I'll be right in your footsteps."

We were now marching west down Twenty-Third Street. Freedom
songs were being sung in different areas. There were a large number
of hecklers following us. Their obscene and profane language could not
dim the sincerity of this march.

Silence fell over the crowd. Now only footsteps could be heard marching on the streets of Oklahoma City.

I missed Senator Porter from the front of the line and heard on the
radio that the leader of the march was no longer leading the marchers.
He was about one-fourth of the way back. As we approached Southwest
Twenty-Ninth Street, according to a radio commentator, Porter was near
the end of the line. The commentator stated that the senator was now
leading the march from the end of the line. I sent Porter a note that

read "General E. Melvin Porter, if you continue to slow down, you'll be 'burned in effigy' by the group that you organized and motivated."

Morgan Mallard said that Porter read the note and stuffed it in his pocket, and his steps were extremely short. "Mrs. Luper," Morgan said, "I don't think the senator will make it to Lawton." The marchers started laughing and beckoning for him to come on. Porter started skipping.

At Reno and South May, three young whites carried signs that read:

ROSES ARE RED, VIOLETS ARE SWEET.
USE YOUR HEAD, NOT YOUR FEET.
CLARA LUPER, WHEN YOU GET TO LAWTON—STAY.

From Southwest Twenty-Ninth Street, we marched west to Depot Boulevard and south toward Tuttle. Mr. Fred Davis followed us in an old '50 model Chevrolet truck. The truck was loaded with food, fruit, pop, and water that he and a group had donated and solicited. His seven-year-old son, Calvin, was the youngest marcher in the group, and Nancy Lynn, his daughter, was one of the song leaders. Nine-year-old Jawanna Johnson, their cousin, had come from Cushing to join them on the march.

Night had finally fallen over the state. Ruth Tolliver, Lillian Oliver, Mary Pogue, Dorothy Stewart, Ophelia Cooper, and Jewel Porter had prepared a special supper for all of us. We talked, sang, and prayed. The weather changed almost instantly. It began to rain lightly.

Senator Porter came over and told me that we needed to have a caucus. I said, "Okay." He told me that because of the weather, we should go back to Oklahoma City for the rest of the night. Then we could start the next morning. I said, "Senator, you are the general of this march, and if you have any messages for your troops, you had better tell them yourself."

He said, "Okay, I will."

He hastily called the group together and spoke very slowly. "It's beginning to rain now, and I didn't know it was going to rain when we started this march." The youth looked at him as he began to repeat himself. He said, "Clara, you ought to teach these kids to respect their elders" as the children began to laugh. I laughed, too. He got mad and said, "I expect the adults to cooperate, and Mrs. Luper, when you laugh, you contribute to the rudeness of these kids."

I did not answer as the kids yelled, "Come on, Senator, speak to us, we're listening."

Porter continued, "As I was saying before I was so rudely interrupted by the supposedly intelligent youth advisor, Clara Luper, it is raining and I didn't count on it raining, so I feel since you all might take a cold or the flu or pneumonia, I'm recommending that we all go back home and get out of the rain so none of us will get sick." He stopped abruptly and coughed continuously. He continued, "Well, what do you all think?"

They said, "Senator, you believe in democracy, don't you?"

"Why, sure, I believe in democracy. If not, I would not be here," he said in a sharp, cold voice.

"Then let us vote on whether we shall stay here or go back," John Jordan said.

After a lengthy discussion, Porter agreed to let the marchers vote. The vote was ninety-nine to continue to march in the rain, with Senator Porter casting the lone vote against continuing. "Let's go," he said. "It's beginning to rain, and if we're to make it to Lawton Saturday, we had better get started."

The rain continued to fall. There were only two raincoats and no umbrellas. We were completely soaked, but the children started singing.

> I'm not going to let nothing turn me around,
> Turn me around, turn me around,
> I'm not going to let no rain turn me around,
> I'm headed for the Promised Land!

Porter limped toward the children and said, "Oh, yes, you are going to let something over which you have no control turn you around. Now every one of you is soaking wet, w-e-t!"

The children stood like soldiers and listened to their leader. There were some girls who had covered their heads with sheets and blankets. They pulled the sheets and blankets away from their heads and listened carefully.

Porter continued cautiously with concentrated energy, "Now, kids, it's really going to rain today, and I'm afraid we are all going to catch a cold. I mean bad colds." He coughed. "The cold could lead to pneumonia. This is D-Day. Decision Day. We have a decision to make—to stop or to go ahead with the march."

He continued to talk as if he were suffering from intense pain. "I'll feel terribly responsible if some of you should catch pneumonia. You could die from an acute case of pneumonia. Mrs. Luper is over there grinning, and she doesn't have one dime to buy an aspirin, let alone pay a hospital bill. You're out here as wet as a bunch of rats singing about freedom. You'll be free in Rolfe's, Temple's, or Mrs. McKay's funeral home. As I was saying, it's Decision Day, and I've made a decision. Since I conceived this march and organized it, my decision is to stop the march until the rain stops."

"You're just looking for an excuse," Larry Farmer said.

"Young man! The excuse is the rain, and it's visible. This isn't an average rain. This is a rainstorm. It might turn into a hurricane, I mean a tornado."

The children stood aghast in silence for several minutes. Senator Porter looked toward the ground. Everything was quiet. Only the sounds of the raindrops could be heard. Only the sounds of the raindrops until he continued, "If you all don't stop the march, we could call for some raincoats."

"How long will that take, Senator Porter?" Rebecca Mallard asked.

"I don't know. It's seven now. Maybe ten or eleven p.m."

The group stared at him.

"All right, let's vote."

The vote was ninety-nine to one again. Porter looked dejected, disturbed, and embarrassed. He turned, hopped over to his jacket, put it on, flopped a white Panama hat on his head, and yelled, "OK, we might as well get on with this march!"

So the march continued. We marched until we came to a Mobil service station, where we stopped to make use of the restrooms, which had miraculously been left open that night. We decided to spend the night on the ground near the service station. It was a tough night. We turned in our sleep and waited. We were cautious of the travelers who were passing by, along with stray dogs that came by in large numbers. There were makeshift pillows, which rustled and creaked as the children moved about. We collapsed on the ground without undressing. The ground felt as voluptuous as it looked.

I awoke early, in spite of the fact that it was pitch dark outside. I watched the sun as it rose in the East; its face was soon covered by the clouds. The children began to wake up, and one by one we plunged our hands into the cool water trying to rub up a lather from the soap that was on Mr. Davis's truck.

"C'mon, c'mon, we have gotta eat breakfast," Marilyn Luper said.

Bouncing back and forth from the restroom, some children walked cautiously on their swollen bare feet, avoiding the rows of children who were still sleeping.

Nancy Davis, Mary Pogue, Ruth Tolliver, Esther Watson, and Dorothy Stewart arrived from Oklahoma City with toast, bacon, eggs, cereal, fruits, orange juice, and milk. All heads were bowed reverently in prayer.

Nancy Davis prayed softly at first, then she lifted her voice as if she were in True Vine Baptist Church and prayed that God would take care of us on "this long, tedious, and dangerous march." When she finished, the children sat on the grass and enjoyed their morning meal. This was followed by a singing period where the songs provided a feast for the intellect and stirred the emotions of our souls.

It was time to leave. Senator Porter had slept through breakfast, and the children were now moving to the sounds and rhythm of the music that originated from his snoring. "Shall we leave him here or wake him up?" asked LeRoy Jackson, a fourteen-year-old Black Spencer youth.

Someone said, "Let's wake him up."

Waking up Senator Porter was a very difficult, almost impossible, task. Calvin Davis, the seven-year-old lad, jumped up and down on his back. Porter finally attempted to get up, but fell back to the ground. The children roared with laughter.

"How old are you, Senator?" Linda Pogue asked.

"It's none of your business," Porter answered incoherently.

"Well, you look and move around as if you're eighty-nine this morning," Larry Farmer said. Porter then got into a verbal argument with Larry. Harry Farmer and the rest of the youth gathered around, and some attempted to lift Senator Porter and help him stand up, but he would not cooperate.

The march continued. We marched down U.S. Highway 62 and turned west on State Highway 37, stopping only for a drink of water. Senator Porter fell flat on his face and was thrown in the back of a pickup truck, where he was panting in pain.

Just before we crossed the South Canadian River in Canadian County, there was a freshly painted sign that read "The Ku Klux Klan wants you!"

Marilyn Luper looked down and said, "I'm glad someone wants me."

Sylvester Smith looked at his American flag and started singing "America."

Mr. Victor Porter from Okmulgee, the father of Melvin Porter, joined the march near Tuttle. "I don't know if I can make it. I'm aching all over," Senator Porter said. Laughter filled the air as he lay flat on his back in the pickup truck.

I went in and made arrangements for the group to eat at Chaney's Café on Main Street.

Mark Roseman spoke in Tuttle, saying, "We are marching to arouse the conscience of America and to bring Lawton into the Union of

Brotherhood. We are marching because we are thoroughly opposed to segregation in any form. We are marching because we want America to remove the hampering walls of prejudice and discrimination."

I remember the huge open highway with the horizon shimmering with warm raindrops and rows of cars with people staring at us, but always overhead there were the vaults and domes of the sky where rain-filled clouds continued to float by like fish, and in another view one could see the endless open, beautiful sky.

Tuttle was a town of about one thousand white people. Some of us had walked there, and a few had ridden in cars or trucks. We had received a cold reception, and a number of white teenagers heckled us as we entered Chaney's Café. As we left, a group of white boys shouted, "Hey, niggers, what are you doing in my town? This is my town and I don't need any niggers in my town."

The marchers began to separate into various groups as we left Tuttle. Several white groups stood on the sidelines in complete silence.

Four Grady County deputy sheriffs, four highway patrolmen, and the Tuttle policemen watched for possible trouble. They carried riot helmets in the back seats of their cars. Tuttle city marshal Wes Welchel talked to us. He said that he had noticed that there was more tension in Tuttle than he had ever seen, and the police were there to soothe the exacerbated tempers.

LeRoy Jackson had walked every step of the way into Tuttle. He was talking to two white youth, John Governale of Guthrie and Dan J. Davis of Oklahoma City.

We continued to march on that long, sultry, cloudy day. My feet began to swell, and I started counting the blisters. There were twenty blisters on my feet. The Davis truck arrived with medical supplies, so I went over, received foot medication, and continued to walk. An airplane flew by overhead, and rows of curious travelers with car tags from California, Michigan, and Texas passed us.

LeRoy caught my hand and said, "Come on, Mrs. Luper."

The meaning of the march became clearer with each step. Only God could support and sustain us. We continued to call on God. We walked and pondered over the cost of challenging the might of segregation. Travelers stopped and brought candy, cookies, and cold drinks. We were now headed to Chickasha and were scheduled to stop at the city park. When we arrived at the park, we had never seen anything like it. The Blacks had turned out en masse, and we entered the park singing

Freedom, freedom,
Everybody wants freedom.
Chickasha wants freedom.
Lawton wants freedom.
Everybody wants freedom.

I was so overcome with emotion that I went behind Fred Davis's truck and cried. The crowd came around us, and we were all treated as if we were celebrities. The tables were filled with fried chicken, barbecue of all kinds, beef roast, baked ham, a multitude of cakes and cookies, hot rolls, potato salad, fruit salad, and all kinds of drinks. Chickasha, Lawton, Oklahoma City, Norman, and other towns had contributed the food, and it continued to come in. There were handwritten notes wishing us luck. A white friend had sent me a green swimming suit in order that I could swim at Doe Doe Amusement Park in a brand-new swimming suit. An old-fashioned freedom rally was held at the park. Speeches of welcome were delivered to us by various Black leaders in Chickasha. I thanked the people for what they had done. Senator Porter spoke briefly and said that every bone in his body was tired, swollen, and sore. The crowd roared with laughter. Mrs. Fletcher, Mrs. Stevenson, and my sisters from the Zeta Phi Beta Sorority were in the crowd that said goodbye to us.

As we left Chickasha, I wrote, "I've never seen such a crowd as this one. There was a special feeling of closeness. I have never felt so small and yet a part of something so big, so different, so wonderful, and so good." I had a feeling of pride for the people, the young and the old, the Blacks and the whites. There was a sense of satisfaction and triumph in the audience that could be felt.

In the faces of these people, there was a new sense of hope for the future. They actually believed that the march to Lawton would bring a new day for Blacks, and it could be seen in their faces and in the tenderness of their conversations. Their love poured out into smiles and emerged into our hearts.

Along the highway, people stood in amazement as we passed. We walked and we rode. Each step we took demonstrated the American dilemma, which was the contradiction of racial bondage, inequality, and injustice as practiced by Doe Doe Amusement Park. Our swollen, bloody feet were insignificant as compared to the real acts of heroism and sacrifice by hundreds of Americans from the very beginning of American history. We were just passing through another "Red Sea" looking for the Promised Land. So we traveled on.

Daylight faded into darkness as the silent stars reminded us that it was night. The men, led by Fred Davis, Cecil Williams, and Victor Porter, went up into the Wichita Mountains Wildlife Refuge to find a place where we could camp for the night. They enumerated the perils and problems that we would encounter. To make things easier, they had placed wood, rocks, and guards around the camp, which was divided into two sections, one for females and one for males.

After the usual freedom rally, we went to bed a little after 1:00 a.m. Mother Earth became our bed, and our pillows were rocks covered with blankets. We had been told to beware of the snakes in the Wichita Mountains. We saw only one snake and a couple of lizards. The croaking of the frogs reminded us that we were sleeping out in God's great garden.

Oh, I shall never forget the joy of that glorious night. We all were part of a divine miracle, because eighty-eight of us slept on the ground in the mountains, and not a one was bitten by mosquitoes, ants, or any insects. We were guarded by the men who stood all night while we slept, and we were protected by the God of the Universe. The next morning, we got up and fell down on our knees and thanked God.

After breakfast, the transportation committee had fifty cars lined up, and we left the mountaintop inspired and rededicated to the completion of our task. We rode into the suburbs of Lawton and headed to Elmer's Park, where a large number of Lawtonians had prepared food, drinks, and other refreshments. Our feet and bodies were tired and dirty, but our souls were happy and refreshed. We had walked for freedom and had given it all that we had.

We joined Dr. and Mrs. Owens, Reverend N. L. Jones, John Henry Nelson, Herbert King, Elmer Stewart, Mr. and Mrs. R. L. Dewberry, Rita, Levi Pressley, and Mr. Mackey and marched to Doe Doe Amusement Park. When we arrived, we were greeted by a large number of policemen. The crowd increased with every passing minute. Freedom songs, flag salutes, patriotic songs, and spirituals were the order of the day.

We waited, and the crowd continued to increase. Well-wishers and friends arrived from different cities, especially from Lawton, Chickasha, and Oklahoma City. Georgia Moore, Ophelia Cooper, Dorothy Stewart, Ruth Tolliver, Oneita Brown, and hundreds of others arrived from Oklahoma City. I talked to Blacks from Holdenville, Tatums, Ardmore, Boley, and Okmulgee, and they continued to come.

Ben Hutchins and Dr. Owens moved toward me. Hutchins was now ready to negotiate. They wanted to talk to our lawyer. We started looking for Senator Porter. The crowd was so large that it took a great deal of time. We all became frightened that Oklahoma's lone Black senator might have been kidnapped.

Negotiations with Ben Hutchins went on without Senator Porter. In the meantime, John Jordan had fallen into the muddy pond at the side of the park.

Mayor Wayne Gilley came to the park and pledged immediate action. He stated that a recently created human relations commission would take up a proposed ordinance to eliminate discrimination in all public places on Tuesday.

Our goal had been achieved.

As we were preparing to leave, Morgan Mallard and LeRoy Jackson found Senator Porter on the other side of the park in his automobile fast asleep. I wrote:

Sleep on, Senator Porter,
Sleep on.
The work has been accomplished
And the day is done.

The citizens in Lawton gathered around us, and with tears in our eyes, we left Lawton, knowing that history would record that we had struck a blow in the ultimate struggle for freedom.

12

THE SANITATION STRIKE

After the Sit-In Movement ended in 1964, Cecil Williams and I were appointed by the city manager to a new Minority Employment Committee. This committee was to study and recommend to the city manager methods of increasing minorities in the employment forces.

We met monthly and went round and round and always landed in the same spot, with Blacks excluded by carefully calculated patterns of segregation. We succeeded in getting the assistant city manager to prepare a detailed monthly progress report, which would statistically show the number of Blacks and other minorities. Frank Cowan, Reverend Ora Compton, Marion Craig, Cecil, and I continued to pound on "Let's start at the top." The committee's meetings were finally postponed and died a slow death two years later.

In July of 1969, City Manager Robert Oldland decided to resurrect the Minority Employment Committee and put some real productive teeth in its functions. Cecil and I were reappointed to the committee. Mr. Oldland in his memorandum stated that if any city department or firm had an inequitable balance of minority group employees, the committee was to pinpoint it and then assist in correcting the situation.

I missed the first meeting and was told that Wesley Kirk, director of the Opportunities Industrialization Center, had questioned the committee's objectives. "If we're not going to deal directly with the problem, we're wasting time, and I don't have time to be playing with issues," he said. Kirk was assured by Assistant City Manager Joe Whorton, the committee chairman, that the committee would carry on a simultaneous investigation of private firms and city departments.

At the next meeting, I opened a "can of internal worms" by insisting that the city should clean up its own house first, before requesting or demanding that private firms do the same. For example, the city manager's office and the municipal counselor's office were still lily-white. The Sanitation Department had 324 employees, over 80 percent of whom were Black, and there were no Black supervisors. Excuses began to come in. The municipal counselor, Roy Semtner, stated that he couldn't find any Blacks who wanted to work in his office and that he had been out looking for them. The meeting ended in complete confusion.

During the next week, I was in constant contact with the sanitation workers, who had brought some complaints of discrimination to the NAACP Youth Council's office at Freedom Center. I asked the workers why they didn't go the city manager. "Who, Robert Oldland? That man has no concern for the poor. His head is in the air!" one sanitation worker said, and the others agreed.

"He couldn't be that way; he is our city manager. He is our highest-paid official, and you should go to him," I told the group.

The conversation continued. I listened as the men talked about their obscure conditions. The majority of the group felt that violence or burning the whole damn garage down would be the only way that they could get any attention. "We're the *nobodys* in this city," they said.

"Oh, no, you're the most important workers in this city. Your job is a profession, just like the city manager. You exhibit skill, physical strength, and patience with the citizens. You are somebody. You're the backbone of the city," I told the group.

"Will you go and tell Robert Oldland what we want?" they asked.

"I'll be happy to do it, but I wonder if you can't find someone else to be your spokesman," I stated.

"No, we want *you*," they said.

"I'll tell you what to do. Go back and meet with all the sanitation workers, Black and white, and you all get together on what you actually want. I want the whole group to decide on the person who they want to speak for them."

They thanked me and left. George Kerford, the executive director of Freedom Center, and I discussed the pros and cons of the sanitation workers' complaints. "George, I'm sure the men will find someone else," I said.

Kerford threw his long yellow arms up in the air and started laughing. He said, "We'll see tomorrow."

Tomorrow came and brought over two hundred sanitation workers to my office. They said they wanted me as their leader. They were shy, with the exception of about four. I told them that if they really wanted me, I'd go and speak for them, but they would have to do something for me.

"What?" they asked.

"First, develop a positive self-image and show some love and appreciation for yourselves."

Before I knew it, the office became a classroom, and I started teaching the men a lesson in self-image. We began to repeat:

> I might carry garbage,
> But, I am, I am,
> I am somebody.
> I might be underpaid,
> But I am, I am,
> I am somebody.
> Hold up your heads,
> There is as much dignity in carrying garbage
> As in being a city manager.

A steering committee was appointed, consisting of a group including Mr. Radford and Mr. Boone. We started working and going through all the complaints that had been given to us. George and I contacted Cecil Williams, Senator E. Melvin Porter, Councilman A. L. Dowell, and Reverend W. K. Jackson, among others.

I could hardly wait for the next meeting of the Minority Employment Committee. I had in my purse an itemized list of complaints and the signatures of 276 sanitation workers who had asked me to represent them at City Hall.

The meeting was called to order by Joe Whorton. When the regular agenda had been completed, I called the committee's attention to an emergency that had developed within our Sanitation Department, stating that I would like the committee to request that the city manager meet with the sanitation workers to solve the following problems.

Whorton interrupted, asking, "What do the sanitation workers want?"

"Joe, I just happen to have a list of grievances. The group is seeking a five-day work week instead of the present six-day work week. They would like to spend Saturdays with their families or working to supplement their low salaries. They would like an immediate end to the practice of making workers help out on other collection routes when they have completed their own assigned routes. They want specific job assignments. They want the trash collection separated from the garbage collection. They want a salary increase. They want an enforcement of the city ordinance regulating customers' placement of garbage cans. They want the doors fixed on the toilets at Westwood, and they want to be respected as *men*. If Blacks represent nearly eighty-five percent of the workforce, they should be represented equally in administrative positions."

The committee refused to act and asked for additional time to review the complaints before any kind of action could be taken. Joe Whorton promised that he'd take it to the city manager.

Three days later, we received an answer from the city manager's office, which stated that the city would consider a trial five-day work week, a three-man collection crew, and a special curb crew to pick up grass, and would consider a plan to compensate those who volunteered to work extra time to help out on a route other than their own. They assured us that the sanitation workers were paid in proportion to other workers. The committee meeting sounded like an early-day town meeting, with Wesley Kirk, Cecil Williams, Frank Cowan, and me fighting for the committee to take action now. "This information is as cold as ice," Kirk stated, "and I know that the sanitation workers will not be pleased with the report."

I apologized because I had stated that the sanitation workers were receiving $290 per month instead of the new pay minimum of $360. The report further stated that I was uninformed or misinformed. I reacted by saying that it was the person who had prepared the report, namely Robert Oldland, who was misinformed or uninformed.

Wesley Kirk objected to the report and stated that it was primarily aimed at me and seemed to indicate a personality conflict.

Joe Whorton attempted to make me give him specific examples of grievances, with names, times, and places, which he would then be happy to investigate. I said, "Joe, do you think I'm crazy? I'm not going to expose the men. I'm not going to have those men crucified. I move that we vote to reject the report from the city manager's office."

Cecil Williams immediately seconded the motion. When it came time to vote, the committee voted 4–4. The Blacks voted to reject the report, and the whites voted to accept it. The committee was split, and the members left the meeting. The lines were clearly drawn. An assistant city manager had just been hired, and Joe Whorton stated that out of the eighty who had applied (Black and white), none were qualified, and the job had gone to Mrs. Dorotha Babb, a twenty-year city employee. One thing was for sure: according to the criteria, no Black would qualify, because since 1889, no Blacks had been hired.

I said, "I wish the city would be honest and say, 'We just aren't going to hire any Blacks or other minorities.'"

We left the meeting and went to Freedom Center and started to work. We called the regional and national offices of the NAACP, and they pledged their support. Ken Brown, a member of the National Board of Directors, flew down the next day. He had been instrumental in setting up strikes by garbage collectors in Baltimore, Maryland, and Memphis, Tennessee. Meetings were set up at Freedom Center, and Ken went over the complaints that had been filed in the NAACP office. As a consultant, he gave us the expertise that we needed, telling us that Oklahoma City's garbage department sounded like the same old song-and-dance routine that the NAACP had heard all over the country.

On August 2, 1969, I called a public meeting and invited Robert Oldland to come to the NAACP Youth Council's headquarters at 1910 Northeast Twenty-Third Street. He said I was uninformed, and I said he was uninformed: "Robert Oldland is a coward, and I don't believe he has the courage to face me. This is the time for direct action. The City Council is being asked by the city manager to raise the salaries of some bigshot city workers, and I think it's time for the city to give that same long-overdue raise to all city workers."

In the meantime, A. D. Taylor, a Black man, had been appointed to the position of field supervisor over forty crews and four foremen. Now he was placed under Clarence Taylor, the new white director of the department.

Tensions continued to build, and the fight between Robert Oldland and me continued. "She cannot speak for the sanitation strikers," Oldland continued to emphasize, and every time he mentioned my name, he threw gasoline on the burning fire of unrest.

Reverend W. K. Jackson, president of the Coalition for Civil Rights, had given me a go-ahead signal at the beginning. Now he called and told me that we must meet with the city manager, and there were times when I was just too radical. He called Frank Cowan, the Urban League executive director, and a meeting was arranged. Along with me, it was attended by Reverend Jackson, Frank Cowan, Cecil Williams, and Leonard Benton, executive director of the Oklahoma City Urban League and a member of the Black Panthers.

Reverend Jackson was the spokesman, and his presentation was clear, informative, and direct. He related how Black people had supported bond issues through the years and how the bond promises of yesterday had become today's nightmares. "We are tired of promises," he said.

Robert Oldland and I had been frowning at each other, and I continued to stare him in the eyes. He told me that he didn't recognize me as a spokesman for anybody. I told him that through the years, we had worked with city managers and had prevented some serious problems. I related the Otis Abner case and cases of other men in the Street Department. If he and the sanitation workers had such a good relationship, I asked him, then why had they come to me? "Your grievance committee is not worth the paper that it is written on," I told him.

He was turning red and got so angry that he called me a liar. I said, "Robert, don't you do that. Let me tell you something. Those men told me to tell you they aren't going to carry any more Pampers, Kotex, maggots, dirty rags, and, and . . ."

Cecil Williams cut in and said, "They told us that they aren't going to carry any more *shit*."

I yelled, "After August 19 . . ."

Oldland yelled back, "Any worker who walks off the job is dismissed automatically, and I will replace those who refuse to work. There will be no strike!"

"It depends upon you. We are prepared to stand or lie down in front of the garbage trucks. If you drive over us, we'll gladly give our lives for the cause of justice, democracy, and fair play," I told the group.

Cecil said, "You know I'm an old paratrooper and I don't mind dying for the cause."

Reverend Jackson said, "Let's go!"

I said, "Yes, it's unfortunate that we have a closed-minded uninformed or misinformed bigot for a city manager."

We walked outside and were greeted by ten Black Panthers wearing dark-colored berets. Everybody was curious to know what role they would play. They said that I would serve as their spokesman. They said that they had been working underground, but were ready to come out into the open.

Committee meetings and conferences were going on all over town. On August 12, we submitted the following demands to Robert Oldland and gave him one week to take some action.

> A minimum starting salary of $460 monthly will be sought. Presently, sanitation workers start at $360 per month.
> A "cost of living" clause also will be requested so that salaries will increase automatically as the cost of living increases.
> A five-day, forty-hour work week. Presently, there are three-man crews.
> Enforcement of ordinances relating to dogs and the accessibility of garbage cans.

> Employment of Blacks in administrative positions in the department and regular promotions for all employees. About 80 percent of the department's employees are Black.
>
> Men with early routes should be allowed to go home after completing their routes. If they work on a route other than their own after having completed their own route, they should be paid for it.
>
> Reinstatement of the policy under which a man is paid for the job he does if that work is above his own job classification. For example, a refuse collector who drives a truck during the regular driver's absence should be paid what the driver earns.
>
> A "new look" at the sick leave rules.

Finally, we asked for an end to "snooperism," the practice of supervisors secretly checking up on employees.

I assured the group that the NAACP would support the sanitation workers at its national, regional, and local levels. "Oklahoma City has a heart," I told the workers. "When the people find out the things you are suffering, they will do something." (Oldland did not attend the meeting.)

While we were fighting on one front, Dr. A. L. Dowell, the councilman from Ward 7, was fighting on the other. He was raising questions about a complete revision of the pay range for lower-echelon employees in a discussion of proposed pay rate changes for higher-paid employees. He urged the city administration to look into promotional procedures in such divisions as sewer, street maintenance, and sanitation. He said, "This needs to be done because I believe that we need to see that long-time employees aren't being passed over for promotion."

Vice Mayor Rowe Cook defended the city manager and asked for specific examples where this had taken place.

Ward 2 councilwoman Patience Latting wanted to know the reason behind the pay raises just for certain employees.

The city manager sent Jeff Ray, assistant director of public works, out into the field to discuss problems that the workers had.

Gail Parker, president of the NAACP Youth Council, appointed a special committee called Children and Friends of Sanitation Workers. The purpose of this committee was to march, demonstrate, and work on behalf of the sanitation workers.

Robert Oldland continued to talk about the role that I was playing. "Unfortunately, she has assumed a role that cannot be; she is not a spokesman or representative of any portion of the city's workforce," he said.

"I'm speaking as the advisor of the NAACP Youth Council, and I'm just telling the fool what is going to happen," I told the group.

I was informed later that day that the city personnel director, Harold Stephens, was working on a trial program. I had told Stephens that I had no confidence in his ability to integrate anything in Oklahoma City. His tenure as personnel director only and publicly revealed those ironclad facts.

On Tuesday morning at the City Council meeting, the sanitation problem was placed in the hands of Nelson Keller, George Sturm, Patience Latting, Rowe Cook, Ben Franklin, Bill Bishop, and John Smith. The council tossed it back to Robert Oldland.

Nonactivity led to the sanitation strike on August 19, 1969. We worked until 3:30 a.m. in order that it would start on schedule.

Reverend Oree Broomfield, the energetic pastor of the Greater Cleaves Memorial CME Church, was the first minister to become personally involved in the sanitation strike. The first sanitation rally was held at his church, where a vivid account of the first day of the strike was given. The church was packed, with people standing around the room. I explained to the crowd that when we went to Westwood, where the garbage trucks were kept, we were standing on the sidewalk and something happened. I couldn't begin to describe what happened there. I was standing near the gate, and a young Black man was standing in front of me. He looked up to see a big blue truck driven by a white man. He yelled, "That's my truck!"

By some magnetic force, we stepped right in front of that truck, while people yelled "Move out of the way! You'll be crushed!" "Move, Clara, move! Move out of the way!"

For some reason, I didn't want to move. The sanitation workers needed help, and I was a part of them, so I stood in front of the truck. It rolled right up to us, until our bodies rested against the front of the truck. Then we were all arrested.

Senator Porter spoke: "We've got to stick together. White people are smiling in our faces and stabbing us in the back. It's time that we tell these white folks like it is. Our garbagemen are the backbone of this city. They have been carrying our garbage, and I mean garbage, for nothing. We can't do it. Most of our backs are too weak, and we wouldn't carry it for the money that they have been getting. These men shouldn't go to jail. We should do it ourselves!"

He walked across the stage, raised his arms, and said, "Let's not let these men go to jail tomorrow. Let's do it ourselves." He pointed out toward the audience and waved his hands, saying, "Let's do it ourselves. I'm willing. Are you?"

Attorney Archibald Hill stood, and the crowd cheered. He related and identified the kind of segregation that we were fighting. He turned his head from side to side and looked to the ceiling of the church and yelled, "I'm going to participate in the demonstration tomorrow."

James Brown Jr., the national director of the Youth and College Division of the NAACP, described to the crowd how the police department had overreacted, then later said, "They supported it. Those policemen should realize that if the sanitation workers get a raise, they will, too. At least, I talked to one policeman who realized it. The policemen should realize that the sanitation workers and the police department are in the same boat!"

We were at Westwood Yard every morning at 5:30 a.m. I had the opportunity to walk in the shoes of the sanitation workers, and I didn't like it.

We threw up a human barricade in front of the sanitation trucks. We were backed by busloads and carloads of people. James Brown had come down from New York. He and Richard Dockery, the NAACP regional director from Dallas, were arrested.

I had not eaten in two days and was physically exhausted. I went to the jail, and a series of meetings were arranged with the mayor and the chief of police. I went from office to office. Afterwards, the chief of police, Wayne Lawson, was very kind and recognized how tired I was. That day, I was the only woman arrested. Everyone was real kind to me once I had gotten off the elevator. The hospitality that I had received in the past had changed. The jailers knew that we were fighting a fight that would result in a raise for them. Although my bond had been paid, I refused to leave my cell. I needed to think and to meditate and to thank God for everything that He had done for me. He had been so good to me! I had never known physical pain, and I hadn't had a headache in over twenty years. I had worked three jobs in order to provide things for my family. Circumstances beyond my control had wrecked my marriage and sent me to the divorce court. A few years earlier, I had prayed to live. I had wanted to see my children, Calvin, Marilyn, and Harold Green, finish school. But my prayers had changed. I just said, "Thank you, God." During the sanitation strike, I had seen men consume beer, wine, and whiskey like camels drinking water. I had heard more unorganized and misfitted curse words than I had ever heard in my life. I had seen and talked to more hypocrites than one could imagine.

One day, we were at City Hall, and a well-known Black leader told me that he was going to talk to the mayor on our behalf. A news reporter followed him into the mayor's office and came back with a tape on which he said that he was in full support of the city manager and not of Clara Luper and the sanitation workers.

I had seen Reverend Jackson and the people of St. John use their church as a headquarters for the sanitation workers. I had seen hundreds of dollars raised by Ira Hall, F. D. Moon, Reverend Joe Edwards, and other members of the financial committee for the workers. And I had heard Reverend Jackson and other ministers being cursed out by some of the sanitation workers. I saw people and worked with people who were more interested in rumors than facts. I saw Uncle Toms and Aunt Jemimas by the dozens.

Yes, I was tired and I needed the rest, and I needed to say thanks to God.

Senator Porter rushed down to the jail. His eyes were popping, and he came down in an aristocratic role to order me to leave the jail at once. He was so excited. He told me that he had just left the NAACP Youth Council office, and the sanitation workers were angry because they believed that I was being mistreated in jail. "I have assured them and reassured them that you are all right," he said.

I said, "Porter, now that you have seen me, you know that I'm not being mistreated. So go back and tell them that I'm all right."

He said, "Are you crazy, Clara? Do you think that I'm going back over on the east side without you? Those men asked me, 'Where is she? Why isn't she out of jail?' Clara Luper, this town is going down in ashes! One sanitation worker looked at me and said, 'If you don't bring Clara Luper, you'll be going to Rolfe's Funeral Home or Temple's or McKay's. We'll blow your head off if you don't bring Clara Luper back.'"

"Oh, Lord," I replied. "This is the biggest mess I've ever seen. So you decide. If this sanitation strike doesn't end, do you realize where I'm going to be? Well, I'll tell you. I'll be in Coyne Campbell's Mental Hospital. I'll be stone crazy."

Porter said, "Oh, no! I can't afford it. I'll be in Central State Hospital. Come on Clara, you are going to leave this jail now!"

"Senator Porter, why don't you stop playing your court role and tell me, what do we do now? How much longer?" I asked.

"I know what we're going to do. We're going to get out of this jail, and I've got to go face the sanitation workers and prove to them beyond a shadow of a doubt that you have not been beaten up or hurt in any way. That's my assignment, and it comes from the King of the Sanitation Workers. You are the advocate of nonviolence, and by staying down here, you are creating violence."

"I'm ready!" I said.

As we left the elevator, I had no idea about the kind of ovation and reception that the sanitation workers and their wives would give me. I had an experience that day of being wanted, loved, and respected. You'd have thought that I had been gone for a year. Once worker took a puff off of his cigarette and yelled, "Everything is going to be all right because *Clara Luper is back!*"

Reverend Ralph Abernathy, president of the Southern Christian Leadership Conference, arrived in Oklahoma City on August 24, 1969, under strict police protection. He led a march through downtown, from Northeast Second and Stiles, in memory of Martin Luther King, directly to City Hall. He had met with leaders of the strike and was determining in what area SCLC could best help the sanitation workers.

He spoke to a crowd at St. John Baptist Church. "I've been to jail twenty-eight times fighting for the rights of my people, and I'm ready to make it twenty-nine right here in the capital city of Oklahoma. I've come here to tell City Manager Pharaoh to let the sanitation workers go free, to tell Mayor Pharaoh to let my people go!" he said as the crowd stood with raised salutes and wild "Amens." He complimented the middle class, the whites, and the ministers and told the crowd that he would send Reverend T. Y. Rogers, director of the SCLC Department of Affiliates, into Oklahoma City on Tuesday.

Reverend Abernathy, Reverend Jackson, Cecil Williams, Frank Cowan, and I went to the municipal building and straight up to Robert Oldland's private office. The door was locked, and he refused to meet with us. Reverend Abernathy said, "Things are not well here in Oklahoma City, and Robert Oldland does not have sense enough to run this city."

I said, "No other city, either. I think he is a self-conceited, low-thinking, immature person, and from the gossip that is spreading, he is really having some personal problems."

Reverend Abernathy was warmly greeted in Oklahoma City. He stood on the steps at City Hall and said, "I'm willing to fight and die here in Oklahoma City to settle the sanitation strike."

We left City Hall and attended three other strategy meetings.

During the strike, we marched to Robert Oldland's home out on Ski Island Lake. I rang the doorbell. Reverend Jackson left one of his cards. Reverend Rogers, the SCLC official from Atlanta, left a note saying "We will be back." Harold Woodson left a note saying "You'll never sleep until the sanitation strike is over." Cecil Williams promised to return with some roaches and maybe some rats to feast on the green grass. We sang "We Shall Overcome" as the neighbors watched from their boats, windows, front yards, and the tops of their houses.

Frank Cowan, the Urban League director in Oklahoma City, spoke to over five hundred people at St. John and urged everyone to get involved. "Call City Hall," he said. "We have the determination, and we're willing to go through anything to win this battle."

On August 30, 1966, over five hundred Douglass High School students marched to City Hall during the noon hour. Henry Floyd, president of the Senior Branch of the NAACP, followed and snapped pictures, admiring the students' courage and nonviolent approach.

State Representative Hannah Atkins stood proudly in front of the garbage truck and was arrested. She and city councilman Dr. A. L. Dowell were both arrested on complaints of obstructing a street and failure to disperse, along with Lee Etta Hawkins, Eddie Stamps, Pauline Edwards, and Janice L. Hall. Charles Lewis was arrested on a complaint of failure to yield to a motor vehicle. Their bonds were set at forty dollars each. Representative Atkins remained in jail after her arrest, where she prayed and meditated.

Chief Lawson asked me to let him see my press card after I tried to interview a sanitation worker, and he then refused to give it back to me. I wanted to knock his head off. I was so angry that I started crying. Archibald Hill came over and put his arms around me. Chief Lawson told him that I had used the press card when I went out of the U.S. and I didn't need it anymore. "She's not a reporter," he said.

I said, "One thing's for sure, you are the police chief, and it would be inappropriate for me to tell you what I think of you!"

Representative Hill said, "Chief, you know you're violating the law. The issue is not whether she needs it or not."

"This is such a trivial thing," Lawson said.

"It might be trivial to you, but it is very important to me," I said.

The chief walked off with my press card and my picture that I had purchased for my card and never returned it.

That same day, I was given two traffic tickets, one for violating a city anti-noise ordinance by blowing my car horn, and one for impeding the normal flow of traffic by driving too slow and too close to the Westwood Yard.

The two hundred sanitation workers demanded a meeting with Forrest Keene, the public works director. After two hours, they asked him to find a remedy for their demands within twenty-four hours or face the consequences. The City Council instructed Robert Oldland to draw up specifications for contracting with a private company to provide city garbage service.

Phil Savage, a tri-state NAACP director from Philadelphia and a cofounder of the Student Non-Violent Coordinating Committee, arrived in Oklahoma City on Thursday. We all attended a meeting at the Skirvin Hotel, where Savage said, "Sometimes we arrive at a very strategic point where walking is stupid, and it is at that very time that we have to hit the streets. And I want you to know that the NAACP is ready to go all the way. This city can't imagine what it's like having garbage on the sidewalks, roaches, ants, and stink."

Henry Floyd announced that NAACP units in eighteen other Oklahoma towns had promised to join the Oklahoma City demonstrations for as long as it took to get the job done. NAACP chapters in Louisiana, Texas, and Arkansas were all on "standby," ready to come to Oklahoma City whenever they were needed. Richard Dockery, the regional director from Dallas, said, "If sanitation workers feel that they need some refined articulation, we're going to furnish it to them. We've threatened no one. We act as good Christians should. We warn our adversaries, and we aren't afraid of nobody and nothing!"

Reverend N. E. Kabelitz, pastor of the Redeemer Lutheran Church, asked Oklahoma City to invest its money in people and not in a convention center. He said, "There is something desperately wrong here when a city can vote a $119 million bond issue and urge all citizens to get out and work for its passage and can't take care of its own people." The sanitation workers, dressed in dingy blue city-issued coveralls or similar work clothes, commented on how sturdy and warm the room was and what a cool reception King Oldland had gotten. As they left for their various meetings, they walked by the toilet and found that a new door had been installed.

The men immediately called me and related that at 5:45 a.m., a police canine unit had been stationed outside the gate at the Westwood sanitation station, and that Mr. Oldland had told them that their demand for a

$100 raise was not justified at this time, but the city was now reviewing its salary scales.

Clarence Taylor, the superintendent, tried to talk to the men about the main problems, and they said, "Man, it's money. Money is the problem. I make $360 a month, and every two weeks I take home about $107. Do you understand?"

On Wednesday, the Coalition for Civic Leadership heard from five city councilmen and the city manager, who met at St. John Baptist Church for a roll call vote. They voted to support the NAACP Youth Council, which had pledged to stand or lie down in front of garbage trucks. The CLC was composed of representatives of all the major civil rights, social, civic, and religious organizations on the east side of Oklahoma City. Jimmie Stewart, a member of the NAACP's National Board, made the motion, and the crowd went wild.

Robert Oldland announced that Oklahoma City was ready and could substitute trash crews if necessary. James Blassengill, a sanitation worker, said, "Who is he trying to fool? He can't find three hundred people to carry trash for the price that this city is paying."

Oldland submitted a progress report to the City Council, and the members urged him to make the same report to the workers. On Wednesday morning, Oldland stood in front of two hundred workers at the Westwood sanitation barn in his gold-colored slacks and white-skinned shoes and outlined the new job conditions, which included a five-day, forty-hour week, starting September 2, and a few other insignificant changes. When he had finished, he gave each employee a copy of the report. He then asked for questions. The room was so quiet that you could have heard a pin drop. One tall Black worker stood up and said, "We certainly appreciate your interest, but we have chosen a representative to speak for us, Mrs. Clara Luper."

The whole group applauded.

Oldland said, "I've told you, there is no representative outside this division."

They said, "Then we don't have any comments."

On August 16, the city set up a special committee to study ways in which Oklahoma City could obtain more money to raise employees' salaries. The City Hall committee consisted of five representatives from each of the city's five area Chambers of Commerce plus two representatives from the NAACP. The NAACP committee members were Reverend Oree Broomfield and Lawrence Green. The Chambers of Commerce members were as follows:

Oklahoma City Chamber: Patrick P. Lyons, Paul Strasbaugh, Lowe
Runkle, F. M. Petree
Northeast Chamber: Curtis E. Moutrey, Aster R. Barber, James E.
Hope, Miss Lucyl Shirk, Mrs. Hannah D. Atkins
Capitol Hill Chamber: Carlton V. Myhro, Al O'Connor, C. I. Knight,
Guillen W. Nourse, W. L. Weldon
Citizens' Chamber: Fred W. Spencer, Leroy W. Kirk, Mrs. Nilar Jewel
Phillips, Willie Dunn, Melvin F. Luster
Northwest Chamber: Robert L. Medley, Don Wages, John H. Hum-
phrey, J. H. White, Bill Cornell

Although the committee would be studying ways of getting money
to benefit all city departments, not just the Sanitation Department, the
primary concern of the members was the salary demands of the garbage
collectors.

Reverend J. C. West, chairman of the Ministers' Alliance, requested a
meeting with Robert Oldland and was turned down. Reverend West told
the ministers, "It's no use, he won't see us." Oldland announced that he
would replace the three hundred strikers if they were not back on their
jobs by the next Monday. James Blassengill, a very outspoken sanitation
worker, said, "Who does he think he is? We are somebody, and we're not
going to turn around. We want to take care of our families. Our families
need some vitamins, too, and some meat sometimes."

Ralph Jefferson, the lead negotiator for the group, said, "Sanitation
workers are just as important as other city officials. To make it plain, we
are just as important as the city manager, and we deserve a raise and a
five-day work week. I'd like to go to the zoo on Saturdays. But once you
make those hours on Saturdays, your whole day is ruined."

Kirby Radford not only spoke for the sanitation workers but appealed
to the city to put Blacks in policy-making positions. "We're tired of being
snooped on and treated like children," he said.

Dr. W. K. Jackson told the members of the coalition, "I'm praying over
it, and if it is the Lord's will, I'll go to jail tomorrow."

When he said that, I jumped up and started clapping. "That I want to
see. I sure hope the Lord will grant you permission. I have been waiting
a long time for this moment." Reverend Jackson tactfully told me to
shut up and that nobody had pressured him into anything. He would
enter into secret prayer and then have a conference with his attorney,
Senator Porter.

I could hardly wait until the next morning.

It was 5:00 a.m. A large number of policemen were at the Westwood garage. We started singing "We Shall Overcome." Reverend Jackson, Reverend Edwards, and Reverend Kabelitz arrived. Reverend Jackson had on a long black robe with a matching cape and a black turban. In his right hand, he carried a large black Bible. I marched with the ministers for a few minutes and then walked over to the sidelines for a conference.

I saw Reverend Jackson open his Bible and fall down on his knees with the other ministers. A big garbage truck was headed toward him at a slow but steady speed. "Oh, no, you had better not run over them!" Profanity came from two sanitation workers who had never shown any kind of emotion. One said, "I'll kill the —— if he runs over those preachers."

A group of policemen rushed over to Reverend Jackson and commanded him to move so the trucks could pass. Reverend Jackson continued to read from the Bible. I heard him say, "Thus sayeth the Lord." The policeman grabbed him and dragged him to the car, tearing his black robe.

I couldn't take it. I started crying and couldn't stop. I had to get myself together. Why was I crying? I had seen hundreds of arrests. But I couldn't stop crying. Just yesterday I was talking about the preachers; now I was crying. I was not alone. The sanitation workers, the children, and some of the police were crying also. I said, "Something has happened here that we'll never forget."

We rushed down to the city jail. Reverend Jackson and Reverend Edwards said they were going to stay in jail. Reverend Jackson told us to go back and continue to picket. We obeyed him. In the meantime, people who had never prayed started praying. When we finished picketing, we went back to the city jail and serenaded Reverend Jackson and Reverend Edwards. They stood in the window and waved a prayer sign.

Senator Porter and I went up to the cell, and Reverend Jackson told us that he was not ready to get out. He had some spiritual work to do in the jail. We found out that he had put up bond for everybody in his cell after he had prayed and counseled with them. He said that he was doing "God's work," and that we couldn't understand because God had not revealed it to us.

We took his message back to the people outside, and we prayed outside the jail under the ever-watchful eye of the police until after midnight. Reverend Jackson and Reverend Edwards remained in jail, where they fasted and prayed. It was two days later when they were released. They both stated that "new dimensions had been added to their lives."

On August 20, the following state charges were filed:

Inciting to riot:	Howard Ray Leake
Disorderly conduct:	Elbert Earl Leake, Lafayette Washington, Leroy Lynn Malone, Cleve Lewis, Herman Lee Moore, Eddie Eugene Myres, Shirley Gaines, Haywood Boone
Obstructing the street:	Clara Luper, Conway Liddell Jr., Arthur Bee Daniels, Arthur Lee Cato, John Ira Mitchell, Richard Lee Dockery, Leo Dean Reynolds, Robert Wilkins, James O'Neal Northerton, Marion Alton Williams, Morris Harold Leake, Leonard Wayne Smith, Worthy John Farris, James Robert Simmons, Mort Glassner, James Brown Jr., Cornell King, Charles Barnett Guylon, Frank Stiggers, William Fletcher Stewart, Maurice Cudjoe, Louis Samuel Johnson, Windell Lottie, Jimmie Ray Atkinson, Cassandra [?], Gail Parker, and fifteen youth who were taken to the Berry House*

Police protection was given to all garbage trucks. What a sight—a police car driving behind a garbage truck!

Strikers demonstrated in the rain on August 29. I led the freedom fighters in an old-fashioned snail dance, which was a slow, sophisticated march that we used to do in what we called our West Africa—Hoffman, Oklahoma.

Mrs. Clara Robertson was pushed or bumped by a garbage truck. She grabbed a windshield wiper and was carried about fifty feet before she was thrown off. She was arrested, fingerprinted, and photographed by officers. She was hurting all over and could hardly move. They dragged her to the paddy wagon and threw her into it.

William Woodward held a small plastic American flag to his chest as he lay on the ground. He was sixty-seven years old. Police wrestled with him and took his flag and dragged him to the paddy wagon.

Fifteen demonstrators were jailed that day: Haywood Hill, Barney Gerald, Lloyd Cale Beatty, Wesley Wayne Gresham, Mrs. Bobby Belts from Atlanta, Opal Alundelta Cooper, Oberia D. Dempsey, William C.

---

*Editors' note: Berry House is a local juvenile detention facility.

Woodward, Inola Carter, Clara Mae Robertson, Debra Vennetta Heath, Estelle P. Berry, Jann C. Nickerson, James Blassengill, and Erick Delbert James.

On Thursday night, Mayor Norick called an emergency meeting of the City Council and issued an emergency proclamation prohibiting the congregation of three or more persons in certain areas of the city, especially City Hall, sanitation truck garages, the emergency operations center in Lincoln Park, fire stations, the fairgrounds, and the water and sewage departments.

After discussing Norick's proclamation, I had the crowd recite the freedoms guaranteed by the U.S. Constitution. Freedom of speech, press, religion, and assembly—this is the heart and the meat of this country. This is what democracy is all about. For these freedoms, Black men and white men bled and died on yonder's bloodstained battlefields, and no short bow-tie-wearing mayor was going to destroy the U.S. Constitution by taking those freedoms away from us. So we concluded that Mayor Norick's proclamation was not worth the paper it was written on.

Mrs. W. K. Jackson had hung up the black robe that Dr. Jackson was to wear. His cap, which resembled a rabbi's, was on the table. Reverend Jackson had answered the telephone so much that he sounded like a tape recorder. "Yep, Sister Clara?" he answered in a voice that sounded frostbitten.

"What do you think will happen tomorrow?" I asked.

"Sis Clara, I don't know," he answered.

"Why, if you don't know, I don't know who to call," I said.

"Well, Sis Clara, I'm just going to let the Lord take care of it, because I'm going to sleep!" he said. "But you just do what you are supposed to do, and I'll do what I'm supposed to do. You hear me, don't you?" he said.

As I hung up the telephone, I was so angry with him. Why did he have to be so blunt? He was always like that. Always looking through you to your most hidden motive. I know what I'll do, I told myself. I'll just call Senator Porter and we'll talk about Reverend Jackson. The nerve of him telling me to just do what I'm "supposed to."

At that moment, the telephone rang. It was Senator Porter. "Clara, is everything ready for tomorrow? I'm just calling to let you know that the police force, the state troopers, the FBI, and all are ready for you tomorrow. Strange armed people are checking in at motels all over this town," he said.

"Oh, that's great. Then in case you and the prophet Dr. Jackson are killed tomorrow, we'll have a march in both of your memories. We'll start downtown, and when we get to St. John Baptist Church on Northeast Second, you and Reverend Jackson will have parted. The prophet will have gone to heaven and you'll be burning in hell!" I said.

Porter started laughing and couldn't stop. He said, "I can see my pastor waving his little cap on his way to heaven. Clara, I wish you could have heard the pastor on Sunday. He really preached. You know, I get a kick out of watching him since he has been in jail. While he was in there, he bailed out all the men who were in his cell. I hope that he'll bail you all out tomorrow, because I have no plans to go to jail."

"If you don't make it through Black Friday, Clyde Madden will run for your seat if Cecil Williams doesn't decide to run. Goodnight, Senator."

Hanging up the telephone, I looked at the clock and realized that I had to go to sleep. It was past midnight, and in reality it was August 19, 1969—Black Friday. I picked up my pen and wrote:

Black Friday, Black Friday,
Tell the Blacks to stand up today,
This is not just another day,
This is Black Friday,
And when this day is done,
Downtown, Capitol Hill, and Nichols Hills, too,
Will know that this is
Black Friday.

I opened the door, and it was black dark outside. I had seen Black Friday, and it was black dark.

By 5:00 a.m. I was down at St. John Baptist Church. There were only a few of us. We began to sing freedom songs. I started counting the youth. Gail Parker, Reginald Irons, and I were assigned various areas and schools. My assignment was the young people.

It was nearing 5:45 a.m. The crowd was picking up. St. John was humming with activity. We left the church and went down to the Westwood garage. We stationed ourselves in front of the trucks. The crowd was tense. Representative Archibald Hill had recommended a change of plans. He had suffered bomb threats, the bombing of his car, his house had been broken into, and his life was constantly being threatened. He was now carrying protection bombs that would scare off the offenders with a peculiar smell. In spite of all his precautions, the night before he had accidentally dropped a protection bomb in the basement of St. John Baptist Church, which had led to a rapid evacuation of the building. Representative Hill had hired a guard, and now he was standing in front of a huge garbage truck.

Dr. Dowell had used every ounce of power that he had as Ward 7 councilman to legally settle the strike. He had held conferences with Robert Oldland and other councilmen. After he had tried everything, only to run into dead ends, he was now standing in front of the garbage truck with Roland Betts, a Southern Christian Leadership Conference field organizer who had been in Oklahoma for several weeks working with the sanitation workers, and William Woodward of Oklahoma City. They were standing in front of us talking. We were singing "We Shall Overcome." Dr. Dowell was extremely tired. This was all part of his long, hard struggle. All hell had broken loose for him when he attempted to enroll his son Robert in Northeast High School in 1961 and went to court. The Dowell case had completely legally destroyed all-Black and all-white schools in Oklahoma City. His case had brought about a new kind of busing in which white children were being bused to Black schools and Black children were bused to white schools.

The Dowell case had integrated faculties, janitors, secretaries, cooks, etc., and this had made him a continuous target for the white bigots and the Blacks who were trying to turn the hands of progress back. I can hardly remember what he said that morning because I was just thinking how Oklahoma City should be honoring him. Black teachers and especially Black principals and assistant principals should say thanks to him every day.

I saw Archibald Hill standing there. His freckles seemed to be more visible than usual. He was immaculately dressed, and his high-heeled boots were shined so brightly that one could easily have used them as mirrors. The Westwood barn was a mass of confusion that day. Policemen were stationed in all directions, with a policeman hanging on some kind of mechanical device way up in the air.

I looked up to see the police officer who had arrested me a few days before for blowing my car horn between 1:00 a.m. and 6:00 a.m. I still had the ticket in my pocket. I said to Cecil Williams, "What is going to happen now?"

Looking up, I saw that Dr. Dowell, Archibald Hill, Roland Betts, and William Woodward were under arrest. "That's all right, you can't stop this movement, God is on our side," Dr. Dowell said as the police car took them away.

This was Black Friday, and three of our main leaders had been arrested. We immediately divided up. Senator Porter, A. Visanio Johnson, and a group went down to the city jail, while Cecil and I went back to St. John Baptist Church.

When we arrived at the church, I had a quick conference with Dr. Jackson, who was calm, cool, and collected. Then the telephone rang. "Oh my God!" Reverend Jackson said. "What law?" he continued.

Looking at his face, we knew that something was wrong. He said, "Okay, we'll get them out."

Reverend Jackson told us that Dr. Dowell, Archibald Hill, Roland Betts, and William Woodward had been charged under a 1910 statute for inciting a riot, and the fines were $5,000 each. This meant basically that we would have to come up with $20,000 cash or find someone with some clear property. This created problems that were really mounting up. I was told to get on the telephone. Senator Porter and Visanio Johnson were sweating and working. Reverend Jackson's telephone continued to ring. I called attorney James Barrett, and he told me that he'd get the money. He would have to call.

"Okay, we're on our way," I said.

In the meantime, Porter had gotten Earl Temple, the owner of Temple's Funeral Home, to put up the money and some property. I thanked Barrett and told him to thank all of his friends who had helped him and left him standing in the courthouse with all of the cash money.

We rushed back to St. John Baptist Church, and it was so crowded that we could hardly get in. Reverend Jackson gave us a signal, and we followed him to his office to give him a complete rundown on what had happened. He said, "Take the youth up to Fifth Street Church and go over the details of what we have to do. I don't want any violence! You all hear me, don't you?"

Before we could answer, Eddie Stamps walked in and said, "Pastor, they are sure coming." Cecil and I rushed out and told all of the youth to follow us. We marched directly up to Fifth Street Baptist Church, where the welcome mat was out for us. We went directly into the church and started to sing:

Oh, when the saints
Go marching in,
Oh, when the saints go marching in,
Oh Lord, I want to be in that number
When the saints go marching in.

Cecil was assigned to take care of the marshals. Armbands were given. We had over three hundred marshals. I went over our nonviolence rules and explained that we could not afford any violence. If anyone was going to die, let it be those of us who had organized the march. I said, "We want this march to be nonviolent, because we are marching in order that young people will live in a city where they will be respected and their work will be appreciated. We don't own any oil wells; we don't own any big corporations; we don't have anything but our children, and we can't afford to get them killed or crippled. Violence does not solve problems, it multiplies the problems that we already have and divides our strength. Just remember we are on our way to victory, and we're not afraid because God is on our side."

Different youths spoke. The audience gave Gail Parker, the president of the group, their attention. When Gail had finished, I said, "I'm recommending to the Coalition of Civic Leadership that after Black Friday, we will march in the stillness of the night. The hours from twelve midnight to six a.m. We'll only use two thousand marchers, with five hundred going to Capitol Hill, five hundred to the Village, five hundred to Nichols Hills, and five hundred downtown. We'll make the nights long and black, and when the white brothers look out their windows, they'll see Blacks moving during the black nights, and we'll be singing 'Joshua fought the battle of Jericho, and the walls came tumbling down.' We'll carry one garbage can, and we'll beat on that garbage can. This we'll do only if Black Friday doesn't work!"

The NAACP Youth Council gave me a round of applause as I thanked everybody for "just being here." I knew that we didn't have to worry, because "young people want to be free now."

Gail Parker led the group down to Washington's Park, and I couldn't believe my eyes. The people were of all ages, sizes, and colors. A student from Douglass High School came up and told me how the students had gone to their first- and second-hour classes, and at the end of the second hour, nearly a thousand had walked out. He wanted to know how many came from Northwest Classen. I looked out and saw a whole army of white and Black students. A white student from Northwest Classen walked up to me and said, "I had to come."

Classen, Central, Star Spencer, and all of the high schools knew it was Black Friday because the Black students were not there. An irate white patron immediately filed a lawsuit against Mr. John Sadberry, the principal of Douglass High School, and me for forcing the students out of school and having them participate in a demonstration.

People continued to come. The students, Cecil Williams, Melvin Porter, Gail Parker, and Harold Woodson were calling the Black teachers names like Principal Toms and Teaching Toms. "No!" I said, "They are just 'Scared Toms.'" Scared they would lose their jobs.

"I see you are here. How did you get off?" Nancy Lynn Davis asked.

"I told my principals, Mr. Cheney and Mr. Crain, that I would not be in on Friday. I had to face reality. Since I was Black before I was a teacher, and since this was for the benefit of Black people, my Blackness forced me to be on Black duty today." Both men had looked as if they understood. If they didn't, I didn't have time to worry about them. So what if I had sacrificed one day's pay for the cause of freedom.

Our conversation was lost in the cheers that were going up with the arrival of Dr. Jackson, Reverend Kabelitz, and Reverend W. B. Parker. There was a whole line of ministers. We couldn't believe our eyes. Dr. Jackson gave directions. From the park, we marched west on Northeast Fourth, left on Stiles to Northeast Second, Second to Main, and on to City Hall. I was in the middle of the crowd as Dr. Jackson yelled for me to come up front. So I marched to the front with him, Senator Porter, Reverend Kabelitz, and others.

Cecil brought us the first official count—two thousand. He and his marshals were running back and forth, and by the time we arrived downtown, we had ten thousand people participating in one way or another.

As we marched along Northeast Second Street, people applauded. One drunk staggered into the line and said, "Hell, I don't know where you are going, but I'm sure going!"

Cecil said, "Oh, no you aren't; you're going to stay and wait until we get back."

When we turned on Broadway, we received the message that most of the downtown stores had been closed for the rest of the day. Policemen and onlookers were on top of the buildings. People in automobiles looked as if they were in a state of shock.

Freedom songs removed some of the tension. We had been marching for an hour now. We had just passed John A. Brown's, and standing in the next block and a half were Chief of Police Wayne Lawson, District Attorney Curtis Harris, law enforcement officers, and news people. I looked at Reverend Jackson. Sweat covered his face. I looked at Porter, and he pointed straight ahead toward City Hall. I started laughing and couldn't stop. Reverend Jackson said, "All right, Sis Clara, things have been going too good to mess up. Let's keep on doing what we're doing."

I said, "I'm sorry," and continued to march.

I noticed that Reverend Jackson was chanting a prayer, so I moved over closer to him. Senator Porter was trying to get closer to his pastor, and as we were talking about positions, we found that we had stepped ahead of Dr. Jackson, Ben Tipton, and Reverend Joe Edwards. Now we were face to face with a mob of police officers and news people at Main and Walker, which was the area that was restricted under Mayor Norick's orders.

Chief Lawson looked extremely tired. His skin was a pale red, and he looked as if he had not slept for days. He spoke nervously. "Senator Porter, you are aware of the city ordinance that prohibits demonstrations from crossing this line. I'm asking you to tell your people to turn around and go back."

I waited for Porter to explain why we couldn't turn back. Now the crowd was gathering around us. Porter looked Chief Lawson straight in the eyes and said, "Sir, I'm awfully sorry. I'm not in charge of these people; Mrs. Clara Luper is in charge of this march." He raised his head proudly and looked straight at me.

I started to say, "Senator Porter has just misrepresented the facts in this particular case," but being a seasoned politician, I knew better than to argue with him. Chief Lawson moved over toward me.

An informal command post was established on the steps of City Hall by Chief Lawson, Fire Chief Byron Hollander, Chief of Detectives Major C. C. Miller, and Highway Patrol Chief Bill Mayberry. I was asked to tell the people to turn around and to go back to the east side. I spoke quickly, sincerely, and sharply. I said, "Umbo Umbo umbo umber. Quis umbo umbo umbo umber. Ochee Ocheo Ocku okro okmu. Shoo owon hu chkon chun. Mung ming oh umbo umbo!" and continued to walk.

Chief Lawson backed up and said, "Senator Porter, what is she saying?"

Porter yelled, "She is talking in that Hoffman, Oklahoma, Swihini."

Porter joined me, and tears were rolling down his cheeks. I looked at Reverend Jackson, and I couldn't see anything but teeth. I didn't see anything funny. Reverend Jackson said, "Why, you have just seen a miracle!"

The group was now singing "We Shall Overcome" as we turned and moved toward City Hall. The state troopers were there by the hundreds. We went on to City Hall, where Reverend Jackson and I spoke very briefly, and then we walked back to St. John Baptist Church.

There had been no arrests during the march and no violence. Governor Dewey Bartlett congratulated the coalition leaders, the city, the marchers, the mayor, the law enforcement officers, and the City Council.

Black Friday had ended. It affected the schools, paralyzed the businesses, created employment problems, and moved over four hundred police officers and troopers into the downtown area, where they were armed with riot sticks, teargas, and shotguns. The state and city had demonstrated their power, and Black Friday had made the state troopers and policemen look like strangers to the American way of life, which guarantees to citizens the right to assemble peacefully and to protest.

Yet the arrests of Dr. Dowell, Attorney Hill, and Roland Betts clouded the day.

After Black Friday, the leaders of our city were willing to talk and to yield to the demands of the sanitation workers. Stanton Young, the co-owner of Pepsi-Cola, and Paul Strasbaugh, the executive director of the Oklahoma City Chamber of Commerce, were among those who met with Dr. Jackson and a committee to work out the details of the settlement.

• •

Stanton Young: "Where does true power lie? Can it be found in life's tornadoes, or does it happen in the quietness of one's soul?" Young was quiet, reserved, and powerful. He moved with the skill of an eagle, and like a spider he captured both friend and foe in his web of understanding. He was brave, courageous, and tolerant. He loved and radiated love. This was firmly demonstrated as he pulled every visible and invisible method to end the sanitation strike. From the mayor's office to the governor's mansion, he worked for his dream of freedom, justice, equality, and equal employment for all.

Paul Strasbaugh felt helpless during the sanitation strike. He was a shrewd public-relations man. His greatest asset was his technical ability to talk about Oklahoma City, and with slow, moving words, he described the city's positive points. He readily admitted its negative points, too, but with a quick, sincere smile, he would explain to you how this particular problem would be solved through cooperative action. As an employee of the Chamber of Commerce, he worked unceasingly to end the sanitation strike.

Tim Tolliver was in the power structure and was part of the Black community. What role should he have played? What action could he have taken that would have been accepted by the city manager and the sanitation workers and the leaders of the Black community? Though short in stature, Tolliver stood tall during the sanitation strike. He refused to give up his Blackness and worked to improve the lot of Blacks and other minorities in Oklahoma City.

• •

The sanitation strike was just another wall that we saw and tried to do something about. It took a large amount of work to keep it together. We were not able to get more than three hours of sleep a night during the strike. Now it was over. The sanitation workers had improved the lot of city workers, and another wall had fallen.

13

WALLS IN EDUCATION

The walls of segregation separated Black and white students in education because of laws passed by the first state legislature. Under the law, white teachers were prohibited from teaching Black students, and Black teachers were prohibited from teaching white students.

Ada Lois Sipuel removed the walls of segregation at the University of Oklahoma and other state colleges and universities.

Oklahoma, under the leadership of Governor Johnston Murray and Governor Raymond Gary, furnished straightforward, farsighted leadership that led to acceptance of the 1954 Supreme Court decision that eliminated legal segregation in all public schools.

Leaders like Roscoe Dunjee, Jimmie Stewart, Dr. H. W. Williamston, and the NAACP continued to call for the complete integration of schools.

Local school boards did not back up at compliances, but implemented the decision by releasing Black principals and teachers. These teachers left Oklahoma, and their educational skills enriched other states. Token Black teachers were placed in some schools. It took a life member of the NAACP Youth Council, Robert Dowell, and his father, Dr. A. L. Dowell, to integrate the Oklahoma City schools, and it took Judge Luther L. Bohanon, a strong, strict Constitutionalist, to destroy the all-Black and all-white schools in Oklahoma City.

This was done in spite of the anti-busers, including a white patron, Yvonne York, who defied a federal court order, and John Smith, a city councilman who held a "hammering bus demonstration" in the neighborhood of Capitol Hill, where he led in the hammering of a school bus.

Religious whites sold their churches on the east side, took their Bibles, and moved westward, selling their pulpits and buildings to Black churches.

Neighborhood schools became all-Black schools.

Real estate dealers had a field day. Whites continued to nervously watch for Black home seekers. Neighborhood groups were organized.

A few whites tried to stay. A group was organized to prove that whites and Blacks could live together, which proved to be successful.

Blocks became half Black and half for sale, and finally 99 percent Black in most northeast areas.

Yet the schools were supposed to become integrated.

The Board of Education had the responsibility of integrating the schools, and Foster Estes, the Capitol Hill representative, was the wall that we had to behold.

The Board of Education was a powerful body of white men who demonstrated to Jimmie Stewart, Reverend W. K. Jackson, attorneys Henry Floyd and Archibald Hill, Mr. F. D. Moon, and me what "white power" really meant. They did it with professional charts, reports, maps, and "future plans," as they called it.

I especially observed Foster Estes, the unannounced leader and the most influential board member. His tall, plump figure had not been impaired by the court order that he had been wrestling with and speaking out against. His gray suit with matching shirt and tie announced his taste, activity, strength, and enthusiasm. His face was filled with different expressions, and one could see that he was extremely shrewd, intelligent, and powerful. He was not as handsome as Clark Gable, but his features were attractive, with strong masculine appeal and sensitivity. His eyes were romantic, and his countenance sometimes lightened into a reddish hue. He exemplified dignity and concern. His looks and calm voice did not harmonize with what I had heard or read about him.

He talked to the group about how his whole life had been spent working for quality education. He believed in neighborhood schools. When the issue of busing came up, he was just like a tiger, and his eyes flashed back and forth. His arguments against busing were long, antiquated, cold, and extremely dull.

When he finished, I was tempted to get up and walk over and strike him. I wanted to silence the busing champion forever, because Oklahoma City had never practiced neighborhood schools. Foster Estes knew that Blacks who lived in West Town had been bused to Douglass High School, and that whites who lived on the east side had been bused to school on the west side of town.

I decided not to embarrass the superintendent of schools, and especially F. D. Moon, so I just sat and listened to him. He continued to insist that he was not prejudiced, but he just couldn't go along with busing children across town. He believed in quality education, but not in busing, he continued to repeat.

I just sat and watched him. When my time came, I spoke along with Jimmie Stewart, F. D. Moon, and Henry Floyd. I said, "It's not the bus, it's the Blacks. Forced busing is not an issue. Never has been and never will be. No federal court has ever used the terms or said that any child has to ride a bus. The phrase 'forced busing' is a wall used by racists and bigots like Foster Estes to camouflage the real issue. There is nothing in the court order that would keep a parent from personally transporting his child, to engage in a carpool as most of the students who are going to private and public schools do. If it's the bus, how do you explain the large number of students' automobiles that are parked in our schools' parking lots?

"In the state of Oklahoma, we have had laws since 1920 for busing. Laws that permit a child who lives more than a mile and a half from his school to legally ride a school bus. State aid is specifically provided to take care of busing.

"Where were those proponents of forced busing when little Black children were being bused from within a few feet of white high schools for several miles to Black schools prior to 1954? In some cases, they were bused past the white school, out of their county to some Black schools. In some cases, they were bused past three or four schools.

"Was it wrong then to bus these children? Why didn't we hear anything from those who espoused the great cause of neighborhood schools? If it's wrong now, why didn't they say it was wrong prior to 1954? Is it because prior to 1954, Blacks were bused to Black schools and whites were bused to white schools? If that's the reason, why don't you, the proponents of such attitudes, be honest with yourselves and admit that you are racists? And that you strongly object to busing when it mixes the races on buses and in classrooms?

"Are we sure that busing will not work? We are sure that segregation didn't work during the legal days of the 'separate but equal' doctrine. Because those were the separate and unequal days.

"Black people have always been adjusting. Black people have been adjusting since 1619. Black people had to adjust to legal slavery, which was wrong. Are you going to tell me that the white man can't adjust to legal integration, which is both morally and religiously right? What's wrong with doing right?

"The 1954 Supreme Court decision was handed down not by Blacks, but by nine white men in long black robes—men who had been appointed to their positions by white presidents who were elected mainly by white people. The judges were approved by an all-white Senate that was elected by a majority of white people. Now, are you going to get on my case about busing?

"I'll tell you, as Reverend Lee Massey used to say to an old dog down in Hoffman, Oklahoma, 'You are barking up the wrong tree.' We bused yesterday, we're busing today, and we'll be busing tomorrow. So join us in getting on down to the serious business of education, which is the way to eliminate crime, diseases, and prejudices; because when we get the George Washington Carvers and the Thomas Edisons of this day together in the same classroom, we're going to experience the fruits of a fair, uninhibited society."

After I finished, Foster Estes and I got into a heated argument, which was the beginning of years of arguments and verbal fights between us. Over the years, I gained respect for him, and even learned to love him, but I continued to disagree with him on his busing stand.

Black students, teachers, bus drivers, cooks, and custodians were transferred to previously all-white schools as a result of the Dowell case and the Bohanon decision. I was transferred from Dunjee High School in the extreme eastern part of Oklahoma City, known as Spencer, to Northwest Classen High, the home of the famous Knights, in the northwest part of Oklahoma City.

This made news all over the state. The days that followed were filled with hate calls and threats. I was constantly reminded that no "nigger jailbird" would teach at Northwest Classen High School.

My first day at Northwest Classen was quite memorable. As I walked down the hall to my classroom, a group of white ninth-graders were down at the end of the hallway. They began to chant:

Here comes a nigger
Here comes a nigger

I walked straight down the hallway and said, "Did you young men call me?" I was not smiling. I said, "My name is Mrs. Clara Luper, and remember I'm your teacher."

Those young men held their heads down and apologized to me. I never had any more trouble out of the students at Northwest Classen.

Many of the teachers extended a warm hand of welcome and went out of their way to assist me. One teacher came to my room one morning and very nervously asked me what she should call me. "I don't understand. What do you mean?" I asked.

She said, "I mean, do you want me to refer to you as a colored teacher, a Negro teacher, or a Black teacher?"

I saw that she was sincere and frightened, so I said very calmly, "You'll make that decision, but in making it, consider your own health and future as an educator. Don't be misled by anything you've heard about the nonviolent Clara Luper."

She left my room, and to this day she very distinctly calls me "Mrs. Luper."

Demonstrations against busing were staged outside my classroom, and groups paraded up and down in front of my windows chanting "Nigger, get out of our classroom." Fortunately, my white students put their arms around me and said, "This is our teacher, and if she leaves this classroom, we'll leave, too."

One day during the sanitation strike, Mr. Cheney, the principal, called me to his office. His face was red, and he looked as if he were completely exhausted. He said, "Clara, I don't know how to tell you this, but my office is being flooded with calls. And from what I'm hearing, the parents are going to take their children out of your classroom."

I said, "Good, this will be a great year for me."

He said, "You aren't concerned or worried about it?"

"Of course not. Life is too short for me to worry about people who do not even know me."

"I just thought I'd tell you," he said. I thanked him and went back to my room. I lost only one student out of my regular classes because of parental interference. I overheard one student explaining to his friends why he always got his history lessons. "She loves me," he said.

My two years at Northwest Classen were inspiring and exciting. One day before school closed, Mr. Cheney called me in and congratulated me for a job well done, and we talked over my next year's schedule.

I worked hard during the summer preparing for my next year's work. About three weeks before school started, one of the assistant superintendents, Dr. Lunn, called me and told me that he wanted to see me. A luncheon date was arranged. I had always had a great deal of respect for Dr. Lunn, a very scholarly man. He told me that he had good news for me.

I could hardly wait for the good news. "You've been promoted. I have been sent here to tell you that your teaching assignment has changed. You're now the associate director of the Media Research Program."

"And what is that?" I asked. In a long, roundabout way, he explained it. When he finished, I asked him if he knew my father. He said no.

I told him, "My father was an outstanding man, although he did not have a formal education. He loved his children, and he taught his children to work. He also taught us not to take 'bull corn' from anyone. I've worked hard in the Oklahoma City school system, according to your own evaluations and the North Central Association evaluators, so I'm just not going to take any 'bull corn.' So thank the Board of Education for me and tell them that I'll not take that assignment. First, it will take my heart out of me. You have to understand that my heart is with the children, and in an office without the children, I'd dry up just like a 'raisin in the sun.' That job has no appeal to me. It's a dead-end street."

Dr. Lunn tried to continue the conversation, pointing out all the advantages, like a raise, but it had no value or interest to me, and I decided definitely not to take the job.

When the news broke that I had been transferred against my will, Dr. W. K. Jackson called a meeting of the CLC, and people like Mrs. Jessee Moore, Dr. F. D. Moon, Jimmie Stewart, Reverend J. W. West, and others became involved. All the Black teachers in Oklahoma City, along with a large number of white teachers, supported me and were willing to make personal sacrifices in my behalf.

The teachers offered to contribute part of their salaries to help me. The ministers said, "We are here." Reverend W. B. Parker took the floor and spoke in my behalf.

I really felt happy inside because the teachers were actively involved. What a day! I received telegrams and telephone calls from all over the United States, including calls from the National Education Association and other teachers' associations. I was flooded with job offers.

Dr. Cheney mailed certified letters telling me that I had to accept this new assignment. I answered each letter by reminding him that my contract was a teaching contract.

I received a final ultimatum: I would have to report the following Monday to the Media Center. The following Monday, I was in New York City, attending the Miss Black America beauty pageant. When I returned to Oklahoma City, Dr. W. K. Jackson gave me a good scolding and told me to call Dr. Lindley.

Dr. Lindley invited me in for a conference. He was completely relaxed, and when I left his office I had agreed to work at Northeast High School under the most promising principal in Oklahoma City, Mr. Melvin Todd. I worked there until I transferred to John Marshall High School, where I am now teaching and enjoying every moment of it.

• •

Jewish, Red, Black, White—It's History

By Kay Dyer

Oklahoma City Times, Wednesday, January 8, 1969

Involvement is a word used often by Mrs. Clara Luper. And it is more than just a word to her. She has applied it to her own activities and to the high school students she teaches in American history classes at Northwest Classen. The civil rights leader, who has made some history herself, is teaching at the northwest Oklahoma City high school this year after 17 years at Dunjee, where she taught history, mathematics, geography and government at various times.

Though Mrs. Luper has been criticized at times for her civil rights activities, Northwest Principal Jim Johnson says he has heard no complaints about her as a teacher. "And the kids like her."

Mrs. Luper says she was not apprehensive at the move from Dunjee to Northwest, though she did face some problems in not knowing her pupils. But she says other teachers have been helpful. "The caliber there is so good, they go out of their way to help you. There is no way in the world a teacher can feel unwanted."

The students, she says, are different than those at Dunjee economically. Most of the pupils she taught at Dunjee were from disadvantaged areas, she explains, "but their minds are the same. Kids are honest with you. They want to be heard and they want you to listen to them. They want to be disciplined. They want you to help them. And this isn't just a racial thing. It's all kids. They want to find themselves, and if you listen to them and their problems, it helps them find themselves."

Mrs. Luper says the value of integrated schools—integrated racially as well as economically—is that students can share insight with others who have never had the same experiences. She explains that at Northwest Classen, many of the students have traveled extensively. "When we studied about Mount Vernon, one student brought slides he and his parents took on vacation. "This helps students relate to a situation." At Dunjee, she says, pupils had not had the advantage of travel. "There you had to help create a world—artificial situations which they had never experienced." By the same token, she says, students who have never known what it is like in the poverty areas could benefit from experiences shared by pupils who live in those areas.

Mrs. Luper says she told parents of her Northwest students that she is teaching all kinds of history—Jewish, red, black and white, "because it is the diversity of its people that is the beauty of America."

Northwest students, she says, have been "very curious about my role in civil rights. But they're going to have to understand the whole history of the Negro in America." She says, "Too many people take this (civil rights movement) out of context. You can't take it out of the context of its place in Negro history and the history of America and expect to understand it. I want them to compare what I say with what others have written and said about the movement, not just take my word for it. They should get the facts and then decide what their reaction is going to be. I don't try to make them believe the way I believe. If they want to be bigots, they can be bigots. People in this country have a right to be whatever they want to be."

Mrs. Luper says she does now, and has in the past, tried to keep her students from generalizing about groups of people. If someone refers to "those Jews, those Negroes or those Indians, I need to know what Jews, what Negroes, what Indians." The same generalization, she says, occurs among Negro people. "I'd hear kids at Dunjee saying something about 'those white people' and I'd always ask, 'What white people?' I try to teach them to look at people instead of their race. We can get all the scientific knowledge we can absorb," she says, "but if we don't learn to live together, we've created a monster which will destroy us."

History, she says, is her favorite subject, though it took a back seat to mathematics when she went to Langston University. She holds a graduate degree in history and secondary education from the University of Oklahoma. "I had a decided interest in the social aspects of things," she explains, and "math was too exact. History includes the social aspects."

She has set objectives for her history students: "I try to make them aware of what we have—the type [of] government we have, how we got it, why we got it and the problems we had in establishing it." For students to become aware of this, she feels they must become sensitive to the problems faced by the founding fathers of the country and actually become involved in these problems.

As students proceed through the history course, they take different roles and act out the events they are studying. A visitor to her classroom will see how far this student involvement extends. In a recent ninth grade history session, a youth who had the role of John Quincy Adams apparently wasn't prepared to answer all the probing questions his "constituent" classmates were asking. A friend stepped forward saying: "Speaking for John Quincy Adams, I'd like to answer that question." But the classmates would have none of this and replied: "He's the one running for president. We don't care what you have to say; we want to hear his answers."

Students in Mrs. Luper's classes elect a president who names secretaries of various cabinet posts as well as ambassadors to different countries. Current events are handled by the ambassadors and secretaries who report to the president on the latest developments in Czechoslovakia, France or England, plane hijackings and other events which might affect the United States government. Ambassadors must be versed in history so they can explain operations of the U.S. government to the countries they are sent to.

• •

• •

Mrs. Luper Called "Superior" Teacher

Tulsa Tribune, Thursday, October 9, 1969

The Oklahoma City school teacher who was a leader of the garbagemen's strike, Mrs. Clara Luper, has done nothing to merit being fired, a top school official said Wednesday. "Her political activities do not disqualify her as a teacher," said Dr. Jesse Lindley, director of secondary education.

Mrs. Luper, a longtime leader of the civil rights movement in Oklahoma, teaches social studies at Northwest Classen High School. School officials were criticized from some quarters in the wake of her role in the recent—and still continuing—garbagemen's strike. Mrs. Luper has not been prominent in the strike since school opened.

Lindley noted that not too many years ago a teacher's job depended on her being able to please everyone in the community. "To prevent that sort of pressure on teachers," Lindley said, "we have set up a code which is part of the state law that describes the grounds and methods by which a teacher can be fired." He listed as the grounds immorality, willful neglect of duty, cruelty, incompetency, teaching disloyalty to the American system of government, or any reason of moral turpitude. "Mrs. Luper has not violated any of those requirements," Lindley said. He described Mrs. Luper as "a superior teacher," and the president of the Oklahoma City Teachers Association, Mrs. Eve Williamson, agreed.

Lindley said Mrs. Luper's arrest during the garbage strike was a misdemeanor charge, "the same as a traffic violation. We don't fire people for that."

"I feel strongly that every teacher has a right to be a first-class citizen and to participate in political activities," Mrs. Williamson said. "Until those political activities interfere with her ability as a teacher in the classroom, she is free to advance any cause she desires."

• •

14

SUNDAY, 11:00 A.M. TO 12:00 P.M.

America's Most Segregated Hour

It was a Sunday. I found my way to the First Baptist Church on Robinson Avenue with Glendale Brown, Marilyn Luper, Leslie Brown, Areda Tolliver, Arnetta Carmichael, and Calvin Luper. As we walked in, the people looked at us as if we were Black devils. A coolness spread over the church. Reverend Herschel Hobbs preached, and the big moment came when he "opened the doors of the church." Three whites went up and were welcomed and received. Glendale Brown, a very handsome young Black, walked up, and it was as if all hell had invaded the beautiful church. "Oh, no" could be heard in the crowd. Reverend Hobbs, an internationally known minister, told Glendale that he could not accept him as a member at this time, because his motives would have to be checked out. A committee visited Glendale's home and questioned him and his parents, Mr. and Mrs. Leslie Brown. They asked such questions as "Do you belong to the NAACP?" "Why do you want to join First Baptist Church?" "Wouldn't you be happier with your own people?" After the committee reported back to the church, Glendale Brown's membership application was prayerfully rejected.

Cecil Williams and his pregnant wife had decided to join the Christian Church. Dr. Donald Yates invited them to join his church. They were promptly turned down. This led Dr. Yates to a historical "Picket and Prayer Campaign" against the segregated walls of the church. This action stirred up the ministers, Black and white. I was happy and honored to join Dr. Yates in picketing the churches. This was different. We learned one unexpected lesson: that church people could curse, frown, step over you, and then go inside the church, read the scripture, sing, listen to the preacher, and come outside and curse like people who had never heard the commandment "Thou shalt love thy neighbor as thyself."

The First Unitarian Church of Oklahoma City, in a resolution prepared by minister Frank O. Holmes and members of the Board of Trustees, called for an end to segregation in Oklahoma restaurants. This was progress, because there were white ministers who had told me that they had wanted to come out openly and support the sit-ins, but they were afraid of what their congregations would say. I said to them, "I can understand what you white pastors are saying. Your first priority is to please your lily-white congregations, who own the segregated restaurants and hotels. To you guys, preaching is just another job, just like show business. Put on a good show Sunday. Remember that we will be demonstrating Monday." So I created a wall between the ministers and the sit-inners, and Dr. Yates made it worse by picketing the churches.

15

FREEDOM CENTER

The NAACP Youth Council continued to meet in my home after the sit-ins. We worked hard on voter registration, "get out the vote" campaigns, War on Crime programs, and tutoring programs. We opened up new jobs. The Youth Council members always returned to my home, where they would always leave my refrigerator clean—clean out of food.

Lillian Oliver and I started searching for a permanent home for the Youth Council. We readily accepted rebuffs and insults. We just had to find a building. We couldn't continue to tell Harold Woodson, Gail Parker, and the other youths that we couldn't find a building.

One day, we stood at Northeast Twenty-Fifth Street and Eastern Avenue, and Lillian said, "This is the spot. This is the place that we shall buy." How were we going to do it? We knew that the NAACP Youth Council could not buy property, so standing there we decided to organize Freedom Center. We called a meeting at the home of Mr. and Mrs. Al Kavanaugh in Nichols Hills. Lillian Oliver, Linda Pogue, Harold Woodson, A. Visanio Johnson, Reverend J. S. Sykes, Dr. Charles Atkins, Senator E. Melvin Porter, Mary Pogue, Ruth Tolliver, attorneys Gene Matthews and Jay Bond, and I attended. We organized Freedom Center as a motivational and educational center that would serve as the home of the NAACP Youth Council, with Dr. Atkins as chairman.

One morning, Al Kavanaugh called me. We had been friends since the death of his son John, who had helped us during the sit-ins. After John's death, Al had promised that he would never stop helping, and he kept his word. We talked about an article in *Reader's Digest* that told the story of Dr. Leon Sullivan and the Opportunities Industrialization Center. We were trying to decide whether an OIC would be better for the community than Freedom Center at this time. I said OIC because of the larger number of unskilled people in our city. This discussion lasted for a week. He asked me to assist him in selecting a group of leaders who I felt could go to Philadelphia, Pennsylvania, and study the OIC program there so that we could set up an OIC in Oklahoma City. I called the heads of all the east side organizations and a few others who I knew would be interested, including Father McDole, Dr. Atkins, Walter Mason, Dr. W. K. Jackson, Sister Veronica, Abram Ross, and Margie. Al Kavanaugh paid all of our expenses for a week and went with us. We felt that OIC was the greatest self-help program that had been conceived by the human mind. Dr. Sullivan, its founder, was a giant of a man, physically, spiritually, and economically. He had "beheld the wall of poverty" and was doing something. So we were happy to delay the acquiring of our Freedom Center for an OIC.

A year had passed, and we had an OIC in Oklahoma City, but the NAACP Youth Council still did not have a home. The council's regular meetings were still being held in my home. Lillian and I had visited the old Mobil station at 2609 North Eastern weekly to see if it had been sold. We wanted that place and continued to watch it with passionate eyes. We had nothing but a large number of poor children and our faith in God. "Lillian," I said, "what else do we need? We might as well close the deal today." I called the Mobil Oil Company and told them that we had decided to buy their station on North Eastern. Later in the evening, Cecil Williams and I met with Mr. Goodrich and Mr. Hughes. I explained to them how we wanted to harness the energy of our young people. I showed them our purposes and outlined what we were going to do. When I had finished, Mr. Hughes said, "What about the twenty-five thousand dollars?"

"Give us an option, and in ninety days we'll have your money," I said.

The two men looked at each other and after a lengthy discussion said, "We have got to make better arrangements than that. How much are you able to pay down today?"

"Today we are prepared—"

"Yes, Mrs. Luper," said Mr. Hughes.

"We're not prepared to pay anything down today," I said.

"Then you aren't prepared to buy the place," said Mr. Hughes.

"Yes, sir, I'm prepared to buy it, but I'm not prepared to make a down payment today," I said.

"When will you be prepared to make a down payment, and what size down payment are you talking about?" he said.

"I'll be prepared in three days to pay five hundred dollars down and the rest in ninety days," I said.

"We are in agreement with your purpose, and we'll have to talk it over with our supervisor in Dallas, Texas," he said.

A telephone call was made. I was asked a few questions, and Mr. Hughes came out smiling. He said that they would go along with me, since they believed in the youth and appreciated our interest in them. But I would have to have the down payment in three days. I assured them that I would have it. They said that if we would carry our agreement, we could have it for $17,000.

I called an emergency Freedom Center board meeting at the home of Mr. and Mrs. William Hunter. The Hunters had always supported the NAACP Youth Council and had been involved in the march to Lawton. It was characteristic of Lettie Ruth Hunter, a home economics teacher, to prepare attractive arrangements of delicate refreshments for meetings. This she did.

I had worked with Mr. Hunter and had stereotyped him, but now I saw a new William Hunter. As I listened to him that night, I could understand his popularity with both Blacks and whites at Tinker Air Force Base, where he had worked his way into a top position. He said that if Freedom Center was going to be a refuge for people of all races, creeds, and colors, he would support it, and he gave the first one hundred dollars. Attorney Pat Brogan laughed and said, "Since I'm Irish, I'll give fifty dollars." Doc Williams said, "I know I'm Black. I guess I'm the blackest one here, and here's my hundred dollars." We all gave what we could. Samuel Wallace was elected treasurer, and Hunter was unanimously elected president. The board advised me to tell our story on Abram Ross's radio show, *Negroes in the News*. This I did, and in three days we had the building, and the contract clearly stated the purpose of it.

• •

Abram and Willa Ross could well be called "the Voices of the Sit-In Movement." They broadcast *Negroes in the News* at two o'clock daily from their own studio on North Alice Street and kept the people in Oklahoma informed on what was happening in the sit-ins, why it was happening, and where it was happening. They knew because one of them was always around with a tape recorder. They supported the sit-ins in every way and at all cost. They shall always remain as the two who fought to remove the walls of segregation in a way that shall always remain as the secret of the sit-ins. Without the support of Abram and Willa Ross, the Sit-In Movement could not have succeeded.

• •

Mrs. Josephine Richardson burst out crying when she found out that the NAACP Youth Council had a home.

Clementine Lawson, Harold Woodson, Lana Pogue, Reginald Irons, Nancy Lynn Davis, and the youth advisors went to the old Mobil Oil station and started working at a furious rate. We combed through dump heaps and piles of junk. We begged for money to buy paint and to remove trash. We ran into problems; Kermit Parker solved the problem of finding someone to remove the car lift. From dawn to midnight, we worked. Cleaning Freedom Center became a part of our lives: to clean, to reconstruct, to create, and most of all to work, to dream, and to work harder, day by day.

Friends came by, talked, and hurried off. It was interesting to note how some people liked to talk, but work—now, that was a different subject. Thomas Irons would have to come by and make his son Reginald go home.

We baked sweet potato pies, made chitterlings dinners, and sold Freedom pens, pencils, and ashtrays. Children came from all directions. If they needed food, we would get it. If they needed jobs, we would find them. Tutoring programs, modeling, etc., were carried on. We launched voter registration drives and "get out the vote" campaigns. It was truly a center of activity.

Everything in Freedom Center had a special history. The red rug signified the blood of all the men and women who had died for freedom. Patriotic attention was aroused. The black colors represented the Blacks who had died for freedom. The white paint represented the whites who had died for freedom, and the blue symbolized our loyal devotion and dedication to the cause of freedom.

This was our dream, and it was a reality.

Earl Sneed, the former dean of the University of Oklahoma Law School, and presently an executive of the Liberty National Bank in Oklahoma City, spoke at a regular Monday night meeting. The NAACP youth members had proudly shown him their library of books on Black history, government, and American history, electronics supplies, our primary sources of history, and over one hundred awards that they had won. Sneed's phenomenal view of people stood out as he displayed wisdom, patience, and understanding with the children.

In April 1968, things changed when Martin Luther King was assassinated. A group of white strangers came to the northeast side of Oklahoma City and offered to pay Blacks to burn down the city. There were some who bought whiskey and wine for Blacks in order that we would have some violence. There were Blacks who came in and tried to

My house was filled with NAACP'ers and advisors when I received a call from Vera Pigee on June 9, 1968. At her request, I immediately made plans to go to Clarksdale, Mississippi, to speak at a freedom rally. We had just received word that James Earl Ray, the alleged killer of Martin Luther King Jr., had been arrested in London. Nancy R. Davis expressed fear for my going to Mississippi.

organize the Blacks for violence. Our Freedom Minutemen took over, and we had nonviolent disciples placed everywhere in Oklahoma City.

We had all-day and all-night wakes at Freedom Center in memory of Dr. King. We replayed his tapes, records, and music. People came and brought food and flowers. Mrs. Esther Watson, Mrs. Josephine Richardson, Mrs. Lettie Ruth Hunter, Mrs. Nilar Jewel Phillips, Nancy Davis, Ruth Tolliver, Dorothy Stewart, and Mrs. Debra Matthews were in charge of the food. George Kerford and Calvin Luper took care of the administrative part of the building. Hundreds of people, Black and white, came by Freedom Center and mourned with us.

We staged a march in Dr. King's memory in downtown Oklahoma City. It turned out to be an all-out community effort. I left the march to go to Atlanta for Dr. King's funeral.

After the funeral, I was flooded with telephone calls threatening my life and Freedom Center. Warning notes were delivered to me. The windows at Freedom Center were knocked out four times. Each time, we replaced them. Those were difficult days. Harold Woodson emerged as a strong leader. He loved the NAACP and Freedom Center with an eternal passion and drew inner satisfaction from the mammoth achievement of doing something for the center and the Youth Council.

People came to Freedom Center and asked, "Why don't you get off of the nonviolent kick? These white people don't care anything about us. Clara, you don't own any buildings; why don't you give up or you'll get burned up. These people don't care anything about you. You're just a fool."

On September 10, after speaking to a group of women at the Westminster Presbyterian Church on the northwest side of Oklahoma City, I stopped at Freedom Center, where I was working on my memoirs. I had thousands of valuable letters, agreements, notes on conferences, and lists of contributors to the Youth Council in the building, along with all kinds of typewriters, duplicating machines, educational supplies, $1,500 worth of candy, a painting by a professional artist, and five hundred books, including sets of World Books and a complete Black history library.

I received a number of telephone calls while I was there. One irate caller said, "No aggressive civil rights nigger has any business teaching at Northwest Classen School. You aren't a schoolteacher, you are just a nigger, and you aren't fit to teach. You should have been killed like the rest of the agitators. You are just a low-down dirty communist."

"Thank you," I said, and I hung up the telephone. I had a few more similar calls that evening.

I left the center at 10:30 p.m. and went home. Shortly thereafter, my telephone rang, and a male voice asked me in a very nasty, sarcastic way, "How are you doing at the Freedom Center? Well, it's going to be bombed." He laughed and then hung up. I thought about the two white Vista volunteers who had spent the night before at Freedom Center and who had planned to stay there again that night. The older members of the Youth Council had taken them out for a late supper.

I received a telephone call about midnight from the fire department. It was to tell me that Freedom Center was on fire. I jumped out of bed and had a problem unlocking my car door. When I got to Twenty-Third and North Eastern, I saw the blaze. When I arrived at Freedom Center, Ben Tipton and Wayne Chandler Jr. rushed to my car. Tipton, a radio disc jockey and the assistant manager at KBYE Radio, put his arms around me. For minutes we stood there speechless. There were angry Blacks on the sidewalks, in the streets, and standing. There were policemen standing, some engaged in deep laughter. Tempers were high. I heard Blacks shouting, "Let's burn this old city down!"

"No, no!" Ben and I said. We started walking through the crowd, where we pleaded for nonviolence. A few heated words were directed toward the firemen. As the Youth Council members arrived, all of our grief exploded.

"The arsonist must be apprehended and brought to justice," Ben said.

Ben Tipton, fondly called the "Tall Man," was a unique personality, endowed with an ample amount of intelligence, great convictions, courage, and soothing words. Within himself, hidden in that long, tall frame, he possessed sufficient power to keep down violence the night that Freedom Center burned.

Crowds continued to come. Abram Ross, Willa Ross, Cecil Williams, the Hunters, and other members of the Freedom Center Executive Board were also there.

"A dream, and now it's just a pile of ashes."

There was no insurance. We had lost thousands of letters, over one hundred plaques that we had won, books, unpaid typewriters, printing equipment, etc. But worse was the history that was now gone, the long list of people who had given from five cents to five dollars to five hundred dollars during the Sit-In Movement and to Freedom Center.

The next few days were dark ones. There were so many questions to be answered, yet there were so few answers. The first question was: Why Freedom Center? But we also wanted to know: Who are our enemies? What have we done? Why? Why? Why? Should we go to sleep or should we just wait and watch for the enemy? What does he look like? Why can't the police or the FBI find the bomber or bombers?

A small mobile trailer had been donated, which was set up as a temporary office. George Kerford, our youthful, hardworking executive director, worked between eighteen and twenty hours a day. An inner force continued to drive him to a solution of the crime. He swung his long arms in the air in desperation and shouted, "Yet, you say, do good for evil. What has nonviolence got us? It got King a bullet in his head and Jesus a cross and a crown of thorns. Now, Mrs. Luper, do you still think you are going to be spared?" As I tried to answer the question among additional threatening calls, which had increased with the bombing, I felt an emptiness inside. What had happened to the pictures, names, and addresses?

Then an old song that my grandmother used to sing came to me, and I started repeating the words. "Nobody knows de trouble I've seen. Nobody knows but Jesus." I had no other choice but to put all of my trust in God's hands.

We started digging through the ashes. Letters, telegrams, and telephone calls came from all over the United States. Mayor Norick appointed Senator Porter and attorney Jerry L. Mash to head a fundraising drive to rebuild Freedom Center.

A "mock burial of hatred and friend-raising ceremony" was held at Freedom Center. Mal Goode of the American Broadcasting Company came from New York City and challenged Oklahomans to set an example for the rest of the nation and other nations of the world by building a new Freedom Center, one that would be more impressive than the one that burned. "They must bury hate and bigotry," he told the crowd.

A large number of whites participated afterwards. They signed a note that said:

We were white and we participated.
  And we saw the walls!

Churches, organizations, businesses, and citizens responded. Freedom Center was rebuilt. However, our involvement in the sanitation strike had led to an abrupt ending of city support, and the Committee to Rebuild Freedom Center left us without funds to complete the job.

We continue to fight not only discrimination, but crime, drugs, apathy, and ignorance at Freedom Center. Since 1968, the windows have been broken out ten times, along with other major damage. Obstacles have become stepping stones—and today we have recommitted ourselves to continue to fight.

Freedom Center's most potent rainbow may be its ability, along with the abilities of concerned citizens, to awaken the spirit, ignite the imagination, stimulate cultural appetites, and create symbols of opportunity for those who are victims of historical events. And so:

Freedom Center stands today as an evocation of man's continuous struggle to be free. It has a story.

The story is told in land, cement blocks, paneling, rocks, and historical clippings.

It is told by Mrs. S. B. Giddings Basham with an all-embracing love for children.

It is told by Harold Eugene Woodson in deep realistic immortal faith as the fulfillment of a dream.

It is told by Roshon Magnus in strong, slow-moving, highly articulated words.

It is told by Sarita Redd with sparkling inquisitive eyes and new optimism.

It is told by Noble Columbus with refreshing vigor and strength.

It is told by Reverend Brownlee with a single humble "thank you" prayer.

It is told by Sandra, Esther, Chelle, Victor, and Regina as they lift their voices in "We Shall Overcome."

It is told by Ronald Powers, O. M. Coleman, H. P. Scott Jr., and hundreds of others who were united in a common cause.

It is told by A. M. Threatt and the Mobil Oil Company as they relate their unparalleled involvement.

And finally, it is told and will continue to be told by those who will continue to see the age-old walls of segregation, discrimination, ignorance, apathy, crime, and hatred.

And in the meantime, each of us must be a Joshua—blowing our trumpet of freedom's songs. The walls will come tumbling down, and the world will right the wrong.

Station Gets New life as "Freedom Center"

Reprinted from *Mobil World*)

Oklahoma City, Oklahoma: On Saturday, August 12, more than 300 persons jammed the site of a former Mobil service station here. They came to celebrate the burning of the mortgage on the building, which is now known as the Oklahoma Freedom Center, a service organization of the NAACP. And they came to honor schoolteacher Clara Luper, a woman of unswerving faith who overcame long odds to make the dream of a Center a reality.

There were freedom songs, a parade, a rock-music band, a musical presentation, and a symbolic burning of the mortgage. A TV camera crew was there, and the event was broadcast live on a 1ocal radio station.

Charles Goin, Mobil's manager of Central Region Real Estate in Schaumburg, Illinois, was also on hand to present a $3,000 check to the Center on behalf of Mobil Foundation. "We wanted to show our appreciation for what the Center has accomplished in working with the underprivileged," says Mr. Goin, "and to help it continue its good works in the future."

In accepting the contribution, Mrs. Luper remarked she didn't know how the Center would have survived all these years if it hadn't been for the help, understanding, and patience of Mobil people.

The story goes back about ten years to 1967 when the Freedom Center decided to exercise an option to buy a vacant Mobil station and property for $25,000. From that day to this, the Center has provided services for culturally disadvantaged children, such as tutoring and counseling. It has also spurred back-to-school and voter registration drives, found jobs for hundreds of unemployed youths, and conducted classes on such subjects as electronics and cooking.

It hasn't been easy. Shortly after occupying the premises, the Center had its windows shot out and was fire-bombed. Damage was extensive. When Mobil offered to reduce its purchase price by $7,500, the Center decided to buy the property and make a $500 down payment.

After that it became a matter of raising the money over the years to meet the mortgage payments. Under the persistent guidance of Clara Luper, the Center held a variety of fund-raising activities— everything from a beauty pageant and talent show to a radiothon, and appeals to churches, individuals, and corporations.

Somehow the Center always managed to raise the necessary funds—often at the last moment. Earlier this year, with final mortgage payments in sight, a local businessman—Alonia Threatt—then stepped forward and loaned the final amount. In March, 1976, the sale was completed in the office of E. Melvin Porter, attorney and state senator.

In this excerpt from a newspaper, Clara Luper talks about the goals of the Freedom Center. "The most important thing is motivation," she said. "The first step in this is to provide young people with direct exposure to those who have succeeded, showing what they could be if they develop themselves fully. Another goal is trying to keep down violence by taking kids off the streets and getting them interested in something worthwhile."

Hugo Scott, Mobil real estate representative in Dallas, who has worked closely with the Center for several years, commented: "Everyone was pleased for the Center people and especially Mrs. Luper. We've admired and respected her dedication, and we're pleased that the Mobil Foundation grant will help the Center continue this outstanding work."

• •

16

THE FREEDOM FIESTA

After the Sit-In Movement, the NAACP Youth Council voted to com-
memorate the third week in August (marking the beginning of the sit-
ins) as Freedom Fiesta Week. The celebration would consist of parades,
carnivals, fashion shows, voter registration drives, and a worship service.

Since the churches in Oklahoma City had integrated, with the exception of Central Baptist Church, the Freedom Fiesta worship service
would alternate between Black and white churches. St. Luke's Methodist
Church was the first church contacted, and promptly refused to allow the
NAACP Youth Council to hold their service there. The second church
that was contacted was the First Presbyterian Church. The minister and
board of trustees voted unanimously not only to allow the Youth Council
to worship there, but to appoint a special committee to see to it that the
service would be a success. The Black community received this news
with new hope. In fact, Reverend J. D. Provo, the pastor of the New Hope
Baptist Church, said, "Thank God for good white folks."

In the following years, Putnam City Baptist Church, Wickline Methodist Church, First Baptist Church, and other white churches opened
their doors to the Freedom Fiesta worship service. It has led to a better
understanding of the white community and the NAACP Youth Council.

NAACP Youth Council members, including seven-year-old Ayanna Najuma (pictured fourth from the bottom), occupy "whites only" seating during the historic August 1958 Katz Drug Store sit-in. Oklahoma Journal Collection, Oklahoma Historical Society

Following the successful sit-in at Katz Drug Store, the NAACP Youth Council carried signs that read "I'm doing my Xmas shopping at Katz this year." John Melton Collection, Oklahoma Historical Society

A photograph of fifteen-year-old Barbara Posey, who helped lead the NAACP Youth Council during the Oklahoma City Sit-In Movement. Oklahoma Journal Collection, Oklahoma Historical Society

NAACP Youth Council members Barbara Posey (first from left) and Ayanna Najuma (second from left) are served refreshments after their protests helped desegregate the lunch counter. John Melton Collection, Oklahoma Historical Society

Some of the youngest members of the NAACP Youth Council are pictured leading a protest march holding signs condemning segregation. Oklahoma Publishing Company Collection, Oklahoma Historical Society

Following the successful Katz Drug Store sit-in, the NAACP Youth Council organized a sit-in at the lunch counter in John A. Brown's Department Store. Oklahoma Publishing Company, Oklahoma Historical Society

Beginning in February 1959, the NAACP Youth Council launched protests at Adair's Café and five other segregated luncheonettes. Oklahoma Publishing Company Collection, Oklahoma Historical Society

A community meeting led by the NAACP Youth Council. Oklahoma Publishing Company Collection, Oklahoma Historical Society

More than eighty NAACP Youth Council members protested segregation at S. H. Green's lunch counter in August 1960. Oklahoma Publishing Company Collection, Oklahoma Historical Society

Clara Luper (pictured nearest to the door) and members of the NAACP Youth Council block customers' access to Anna Maude's lunch counter. The NAACP Youth Council employed "sitting down" on stools or even floors as a strategy for occupying segregated establishments. Oklahoma Publishing Company Collection, Oklahoma Historical Society

Police officers confront NAACP Youth Council members for demonstrating on the sidewalk in front of Anna Maude's Cafeteria. Oklahoma
Journal Collection, Oklahoma Historical Society

An exasperated NAACP Youth Council member waits to gain entrance
to Anna Maude's Cafeteria. John Melton Collection, Oklahoma Historical Society

Clara Luper and other members of the local NAACP chapter smile for a photo as they are being interrogated by an Oklahoma City police officer during the Anna Maude's protest. Nine protesters were jailed. John Melton Collection, Oklahoma Historical Society

The NAACP Youth Council occupied Bishop's Restaurant because of a discriminatory policy that barred Black patrons from using the restrooms. John Melton Collection, Oklahoma Historical Society

The Minutemen Commandos calmly protest the lack of service at the Bouldin Café. Oklahoma Journal Collection, Oklahoma Historical Society

A Black woman, most likely Clara Luper, is dragged away by two policemen during the Wedgewood Village Amusement Park protest. Oklahoma Journal Collection, Oklahoma Historical Society

Clara Luper, regarded as the "mother" of the Oklahoma Civil Rights Movement, was arrested more than two dozen times for attempting to desegregate downtown Oklahoma City business establishments. Oklahoma Journal Collection, Oklahoma Historical Society

The NAACP Youth Council picketed the YMCA's Oklahoma City branch due to the organization's unfair treatment of Black youth. Oklahoma Journal Collection, Oklahoma Historical Society

NAACP Youth Council protesters lie on their stomachs with their hands clasped on top of their heads during the YMCA protest. Oklahoma Journal Collection, Oklahoma Historical Society

Police and Split-T Restaurant security block NAACP Youth Council protesters from gaining entrance to the restaurant. Oklahoma Journal Collection, Oklahoma Historical Society

The NAACP Youth Council participates in a demonstration at the Oklahoma State Capitol in 1964. Oklahoma Journal Collection, Oklahoma Historical Society

A multiracial group of Oklahoma City children and adults come together to demand racial change at the Oklahoma State Capitol. Oklahoma Journal Collection, Oklahoma Historical Society

A wide shot of the front of City Hall in Oklahoma City, occupied by long lines of protesters. Oklahoma Publishing Company Collection, Oklahoma Historical Society

Throngs of protesters make their way to the Oklahoma State Capitol on August 19, 1969 (Black Friday) in support of striking sanitation workers. Oklahoma Publishing Company Collection, Oklahoma Historical Society

Groups of protesters impede a sanitation truck from entering or leaving the facility during the sanitation strike. Oklahoma Publishing Company Collection, Oklahoma Historical Society

Police arrested and jailed activists protesting the city's discriminatory treatment of Black sanitation workers. Oklahoma Publishing Company, Oklahoma Historical Society

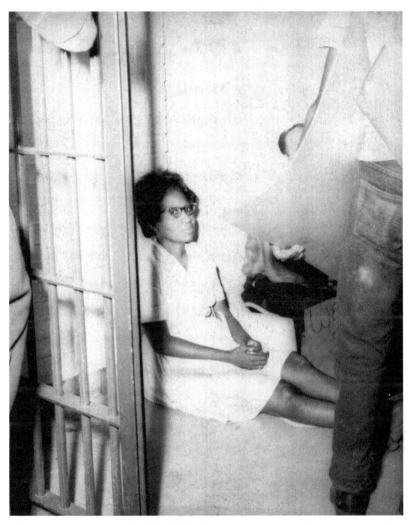

Clara Luper was arrested and jailed for her participation in the sanitation strike. Oklahoma Publishing Company Collection, Oklahoma Historical Society

Clara Luper speaks to a large crowd during her run for the U.S. Senate in 1972. Oklahoma Publishing Company Collection, Oklahoma Historical Society

The impact of Clara Luper continues to reverberate. In 2018, Oklahoma City mayor David Holt declared August 14–19 as Freedom Fiesta Week in honor of Luper's contributions to civil rights and social justice in Oklahoma. Oklahoma Publishing Company Collection, Oklahoma Historical Society

Clara Luper poses alongside a mural dedicated to Black freedom fighters that once stood in front of the historic Freedom Center in northeast Oklahoma City. Oklahoma Publishing Company Collection, Oklahoma Historical Society

In her later years, Clara Luper founded the Miss Black Oklahoma pageant, a competition that provided confidence and scholarships to young Black women. Clara Luper Collection, Oklahoma Historical Society

EPILOGUE

Behold the Walls is one of the true stories of the Civil Rights Movement. It's an unfinished story with characters and events excluded. Yet, they are there.

It's a story about people who came and did what had to be done.

They left a special binding friendship that transcends *time, distance,* and the *changing conditions* of our world.

As you read the names, remember that there were others. They were all brave, dedicated, and well disciplined. They responded with distinctive brands of courage, of persistence and faith. They fought with respect, dignity, and love.

We must remember them—

They, too, were there.

Whatever happened in those volatile times of visible segregation, it is time to remember that Ralph Adair, Cooper Lyon, and Carmon Harris, along with others, are friends today.

Friendship sometimes develops slowly, but firmly. The first years are always the most tentative, but once we have made up our minds, it is utterly impossible to separate us.

Black and white together must prepare for America's third century— knowing that the third century will be one of uncertainty, and the challenge of removing the "invisible walls" will be our greatest task.

POSTSCRIPT

The U.S. Senate Race, 1972

With a firm determination to continue the fight for freedom, I decided to run for the United States Senate in 1972. I had to face Albert D. Anderson, Dewey Bartlett, Billy Brown, Ed Edmondson, Henry Howell, Jed Johnson, Jesse D. Knipp, Charles Nesbitt, John Rogers, Al Terrill, Bill Tiffany, and C. W. Wood. I kicked off my campaign on Northeast Second Street in Oklahoma City. Geneva Smith wrote my campaign song. My students and youth gave me a twenty-five-cent rally. My highest contributor was $200, which Ella Mae Anderson sent from St. Paul, Minnesota. Mr. F. D. Moon came by and gave me $100.

I campaigned all over the state, from Sulphur, Oklahoma, to Kansas, Oklahoma. Nancy Kolb became my ace campaigner, along with my public relations director, Calvin Luper. Mr. David Threatt was my campaign manager. The people in Enid received me with open arms; whites hosted teas and luncheons for me. In Tulsa, I spoke at an apartment complex after arriving with a busload of supporters from Oklahoma City. When I finished my speech, an eight-year-old asked me, "What is a U.S. senator?"

I campaigned in Henryetta, where an emcee introduced me as "*one of us.*" I marched in parades, spoke to farmers, bankers, Indians, Blacks, and whites. I ate watermelons, safki, chitterlings, steaks, lobsters, hamburgers, fried chicken, and every kind of food. Carrie Williams, Billy Williams, and Martin Dinkins came from Los Angeles to help me campaign.

In one city, a group of whites who had never invited a Black person to dinner called me three times, because they wanted to know what I wanted to eat. I asked the lady to check the day of the week. She said Tuesday. I said, "Yes, on Tuesdays I always have T-bone steaks, and I would like to continue in that tradition of the past." This she did.

Statewide Reaction

Question: Don't you know that you can't win? You have two strikes against you. You are Black and a woman.

Answer: I'm not convinced that I can't win. I'm Black and proud. I'm a woman and I'm proud to be a woman. So I enjoy being *me*. If someone votes against me for those reasons, I don't need his vote.

Question: Do you have the support of your own people?

Answer: My people are all of the people in Oklahoma, and I, like other candidates, do not have the support of all of my people. Let me ask you, are all of the white people supporting Ed Edmondson? Of course not.

Question: What will you do if you lose?

Answer: I'll thank God that I live in a country where I can run for a public office, and I'll do like Bud Wilkinson and others who have lost. I'll just keep smiling.

Question: Do you think you could win the U.S. Senate?

Answer: Yes. Emphatically so.

Question: Why would you run for the U.S. Senate when you have two strikes against you as both Black and a woman?

Answer: Fortunately, I live in a country where the writers of the U.S. Constitution set up the criteria by which a person could run for the U.S. Senate, and fortunately, I meet the qualifications. You might see the strikes; I turn obstacles into advantages.

Question: You realize that you will be representing white people. Do you feel that you, a Black woman, can represent white people?

Answer: Of course. I can represent white people, Black people, red people, yellow people, brown people, and polka-dot people. You see, I have lived long enough to know that people are people, and that's more than I can say for some white people.

Question: Then how do you feel about intermarriage?

Answer: Of course I feel good. And I believe in *marriage*. In my travels, I have never seen an ant and an elephant having intercourse, and that tells me that when there was something that God did not want to be integrated, he made it biologically impossible to do so. I do not want anyone else to ask me about intermarriage, because if you do, I'm going to assume that you are sexually inferior and not able to compete in a market where something else is important besides the color of one's skin, because the real action takes place in a place that's completely sealed off from the public. In other words, I'm saying it's not the color, it's the thrill.

So ended my most frequently asked questions.

So it was that I ran for the United States Senate and lost the election. Like the other Democrats, I congratulated Dewey Bartlett, the winner, but won the admiration of a large number of Oklahomans, and met some of the most wonderful people in the world.

ACKNOWLEDGMENTS

It is difficult to convey my deep appreciation to my dear husband, Charles P. Wilson, fondly called C.P., who responded with patience, understanding, kindness, and encouraging words.

His penetrating words "Finish the book, Clara, not for yourself, but for unborn generations . . . They deserve to know" have made this book possible.

Thanks, C.P.!
Clara

The presidents of the NAACP Youth Council who worked to remove the walls were William C. Miles, Gwendolyn Fuller, Barbara Posey, Ruth James, Calvin Luper, Marilyn Luper, Clementine Lawson, Clifford Farmer, Linda Pogue, Lana Pogue, Gail Parker, Nancy Lynn Davis, Joyce Broiles, Harold Eugene Woodson, Charlotte Matthews, Calvin Davis, Gwendolyn Reeves, Mark Haynes, Roshon Magnus, Carolyn Germany, Sylvia Menser, Jennifer Allen, Terrye Lynn Bawcum, and Joe Relerford.

Acknowledgments and special thanks to:

The Black Dispatch Company
The Oklahoma Publishing Company

The *Oklahoma Eagle*
The *Oklahoma Journal*

Acknowledgments and special thanks to these reporters whose news reports formed the backup materials for this book:

Robert B. Allen	June Harms
Chuck Anthony	Nancy Keil
Ela Asher	Jim Killackey
George Bell	Bob Lee
John Bennett	Jackson Leonard
Jack Bickham	Wayne Mackey
Tom Boone	Tom McCarthy
Mike Brake	Bob McMillin
Larry Cannon	Phillip Morris
Ivory Coffey	Mary Jo Nelson
Claire Conley	Joe Park
David Craighead	Russell Perry
John Dunjee	Ben Poston
Kay Dyer	Donald Quinn
Mary Goodard	Jim Standard
Jim Goodlow	Jimmie Stewart
Ron Grenko	J. Nelson Taylor
John Griner	John Vornholt
Leonard Hanstein	Craig Waters

Acknowledgments and special thanks to these television stations for their news coverage:

KOCO (ABC)
KWTV (CBS)
WKY TV (NBC)

Special thanks to Goree James of KOCO and *Through the Looking Glass Darkly*, a WKY documentary.

Special thanks and sincere acknowledgments to:

Abram Ross and *Negroes in the News*	KOCY
	KOMA
KBYE—Jerry and Tom Lynch	KTOK
KFJL—Ben Tipton	

Photographic Credits:

The Oklahoma Publishing Company
The *Oklahoma Journal*
Studio '75—Photos by Calvin Luper
Oliver Murray

Don Simmons Photography
Dr. and Mrs. E. A. Owens
Ruth Tolliver
Harold Arinwine Green Photography Service

Some of the calendar historical facts are from a collection from Lillian Jones, Thelma Jones, and Sarah Jane Bells

Artwork in the original edition by Gerald Harper
Cover of the original edition by Woody Woodall—Art and Letter Service, Oklahoma City

Of those whose efforts have gone into the Civil Rights Movement in Oklahoma, each one has played an important unique, unpublicized role, and to acknowledge them is to exemplify the true beauty of friendship, love, involvement, and understanding.

Otis Abner
Jim Acres
Joan Adams
Richard Adams
Robert Adams
Adams Barber Shop
Adams Chevrolet Co.
Alan Merrell Chevrolet Co.
Alberta's Tea Room
Albert Alexander, Atty.
Leroy Alexander
Madalyn Alexander
Donald R. Allen
Edda Faye Allen
Glenn Allen
Jayce Marie Allen
Allen Chapel AME Church
Carol Allensworth
John M. Amick
Austin Anderson

Ella Mae Anderson
John Anderson
Kay Francis Anderson
Leroy Anderson
Mickey Anderson
Paul Anderson
Sherri Anderson
Verda Anderson
Lorens Andrews
Antioch Baptist Church
Ardee's Barber Shop
Almeda Arnold
Juanita Arnold
Larry Arnold
Lester Arnold
Rev. W. K. Arnold
Arrow Machinery Co.
Dr. Charles Atkins
Edmond Atkins
Rep. Hannah Atkins

LuAnn Atkins
Jimmy Ray Atkinson
Rev. I. Bacey
Bryce A. Baggett, Atty.
Scott Baird
Rev. Eddie Baker
Cordell Banks
Nun Barbee
Aster Barber
Dr. Carl A. Barclay
Anthony Barnett
Delbert Barnett
Pinkie Barnett
Tommy Lee Barnett
J. L. Barrett, Atty.
Mr. and Mrs. James Barrett
Barrett's Auto
Loren Barrie
Anna Bawcum
Hugh A. Baysinger, Atty.
Pat Becker
Clarence Bell
Don Kent Bell
James Clifford Bell
Sarah Bell
Theresa Bell
Bobby Belts
Lee Maur Benefee
Maurice Benefee
Charles Bennett
Janice Bennett
Billy Benson
Lender Benson
William Benson
Estelle Berry
J. W. Berry, Atty.
Big Chief Oil Co.
Bill's Cleaners
R. A. Bingham
Dr. Byron Biscoe

Charles Biscoe
Gay Biscoe
Floyd Blair
Blanche's Drive Inn
James Blassengill
Villetta M. Bobo
Ralph Bolen
Jay R. Bond, Atty.
Haywood Herman Boone
Thomas Williams Borden
Julia Ann Borders
Oretta Borders
Stanley Bradford
Wanda Bradley
Larry Brannon
Carolyn Bratton
Rev. and Mrs. J. B. Bratton
Marilyn Bratton
Marsha Bratton
Wynona Brent
Doris Brewer
Thomas Bridges
Robert C. Bright
Paul Brinker
Thomas William Broader
Patrick Brogan, Atty.
Bertie Brookings
Andrew Lee Brooks
Onda Lou Brooks
Albert Brown
Rev. Curtis Brown
Georgia Brown
Glendale Brown
L. C. Brown
Leslie Brown
Leslie Brown Jr.
Martha Brown
Oneita Brown
Paul Brown
Richard Brown

Rosie Brown
Sharon Brown
Franklin Bruce, Atty.
Floyd Bruner
Robert Buck, Atty.
Mrs. Robert Buck
Lillie Buckner
Buerger Brothers
Merton Bulla, Atty.
Caroline Burks
Rev. Isaiah Burleigh
Byron Butler
Nona Butler
Otis Butler
Willola Butler
Connie Byrd
Thomas Byrd
Marcus Caddell
Caesar's Florist
Ryan Caldwell
Rev. T. D. Callender
Alfred Campbell
Campbell's Grocery Store
Joe Cannon
Sylvester Carbajal
Frank Carey Jr.
Arnetta Carmichael
Ernestine Carmichael
John Carmichael
Wesley Carmichael
Cleet Carr
Jimmie Carr
Thomas Carr
Carr's Barber Shop
Jesse Carroll
Bernard Carter
Cleeta Carter
Diane Carter
Inola Carter
Patricia Carter

Robert Carter
Cartwright's Barber Shop
Willie Case
Arthur Lee Cato
Cato Oil and Gas Co.
Leon Chandler Jr.
Leon Chandler Sr.
Madge Chandler
Wayne Chandler Jr.
Charmette Beauty Salon
G. E. Chiles
Pearl Chiles
Christ United Methodist
    Church
Church of God in Christ
Church of the Redeemer
Carl Clack
Mary Miles Clanton
Blanche Clardy
LaMar Clark
Matthews Clark
Sharon Clark
Velma Regina Clark
Dr. William Clark
Clark Motor Co.
Michael Clayton
Vera Clayton
Mr. and Mrs. Williams Cleary
Cleaves Memorial CME
    Church
Bill Clifford
Wendell Clytus
Joe Bailey Cobb
Freddie Cobbs
LaVera Cobbs
El Centro Coffey
Florence Coffey
Maurice Coffey
Duayne Colbert
Rosetta Coleman

Larry Collier
Darryl Combs
Doris Combs
Eileen Combs
John Combs
Swannie Combs
Al Conner
Dr. Aubrey Cooper
Rev. C. C. Cooper
Venetta Cooper
Mr. and Mrs. Samuel
    Cornelius
Bill Cornell
Alfred Cornish
Lee Allen Cornish
Peggy Cosby
Carolyn Countee
Wendell Counter
Frank Cowan
Dr. Frank Cox
Dr. and Mrs. James A. Cox
Dr. Marcus Cox
Juanita Craft
Louise Craig
Samuel Craig
Archie Crawford
Brenda Crawford
Janet Crawford
Theodosia Crawford
Mr. and Mrs. Ira Crayton
Sam Crossland, Atty.
Dr. Freddie Cudjoe
Lance Cudjoe
Gloster Current
Jethro Currie
Rev. Morris A. Curry
Bruce Daniels
Grace Daniels
Charles Darden
Dr. and Mrs. A. I. Davis

Calvin Davis
Cress Davis
Don Davis, Atty.
Fred Davis
Joseph E. Davis
Nancy Lynn Davis
Nancy R. Davis
Ted Davis, Atty.
Eva Nell Dean
Delaney's Beauty Salon
Larry Derryberry, Atty.
R. L. Dewberry
Rita Dewberry
Mr. and Mrs. D. J. Diggs
Richard Dockery
Dolese
Susie Dooley
Dora's Beauty Salon
Dr. and Mrs. Alfonzo L. Dowell
Consuelo Vivian Dowell
Robert Dowell
Irene Drake
Brenda Dulan
Dr. Brent Dulan
Gloria Dulan
Jerry Dulan
John Dunjee
Roscoe Dunjee
Dunn's Dairy Queen
East Fourth Street Barber Shop
East Side Church of Christ—
    Clyde Mose
Ebenezer Baptist Church
Ethel Edmonson
Carolyn Edwards
Donald Edwards
Elmer Edwards
Freddie Edwards
James Arthur Edwards
Lee Etta Edwards

Rev. Leroy Edwards—St. Jude
Mae Helen Edwards
Vernon Edwards
Wendell Edwards
D. A. Elliott
Gladys Elliott
Maxine Elliott
Wanda Elliott
Wilda Elliott
James Ellis
Emmanuel Baptist Church
Gerald Emmett
Al Engle
Kittie English
Evangelistic Baptist Church—
    Rev. T. J. Roberts
Rev. Herschel Evans
Evans Furniture Co.
Arnold D. Fagin, Atty.
Fairview Baptist Church—
    Rev. J. A. Reed
Faith Memorial Baptist—
    Rev. Morris A. Currie
Alberta Farmer
Clifford Farmer
Gaylord Farmer
George Farmer
Harry Farmer
Johnnie Farmer
Larry Farmer
John Farris
Alberta Felder
Fidelity National Bank
Fifth Street Baptist Church
Dr. and Mrs. G. E. Finley
G. E. Finley Jr.
First Baptist Church—
    Dr. Herschel H. Hobbs
First Presbyterian Church
First State Bank and Trust Co.

Bruce Fisher
David Elder Fisher
Bishop William Jordan Fizer
Minnie Flowers
Sandra Flowers
Zola Flowers
Donna Floyd
Ella Floyd and Children
Henry Floyd
Henry Floyd Jr.
Jennifer Lynn Floyd
Carrie Ford
Mr. and Mrs. Anceo Francisco
Royce Frazier
Friendship Baptist Church
Gwendolyn Fullbright
Erma Fuller
Gwendolyn Fuller
Roxie Gallimore
Gandara Buick
Elwood Garcia
Roberta Garcia
Garcia's Barber Shop
Donald Garrison
Sarah Garrison
Raymond Gary
Joyce Gassoway
Robert Gates
Gates Barber Shop
James Gatewood
Alice Gentry
Barney Gerald
Anthony Germany
Betty Germany
Carolyn Germany
Clay Germany
Kennedy Germany
Patricia Germany
Vernita Germany
Willie Germany

Willie Germany Jr.
Helen Gigger
James D. Giles
Jerrie Giles
Alice Glover
Golden Oak Barber Shop
Rosie Dell Goodlow
J. R. Gordon
Claudette Goss
Grace Cleaners
Alvin Graham
Earl Grandstaff
Greater Bethel Baptist Church
Greater Cleaves Memorial
    CME Church
Greater Marshall Memorial
    Baptist Church—Rev.
    Moses Howard
John E. Green, Atty.
John E. Green Jr.
Maxine Green
Melva Sue Green
Emma June Greene
Lola Greer
Elizabeth Gresham
Eric Floyd Griffin
Colonel Grimmett
Helen Grimmett
Joe Grimmett
Charles Barnett Guylon
Alice Hall
Carolyn Hall
Dan Hall
Gov. David Hall
Dolly Hall
Doris Hall
Fidelity Hall
Ira Hall Jr.
Ira Hall Sr.
Lula Hall

Rubye Hall
Francille Hardeman
Willie Hardeman
Virginia Harding
Mr. and Mrs. Isaac Hargrove
Lanette Harkins
Adele Harris
Adrain Harris
Alvin Harris
Carolyn Harris
Doris Harris
Michael Harris
Sallye Harris
Sherman Harris
Mernoy Harrison
Ronnie Harrison
Thomas Harrison
Harter Concrete Co.
James Haskins
William Hayden
Doris Haynes
Haywood Hills Carpet
Bill Hazley
Louella Henderson
Alice Henry
Jacqueline Henry
John Hightower
Archibald Hill, Atty.
Barbara Hill
Fannie Hill
Rev. and Mrs. Forrest S. Hill
Haywood Hill
C. J. Hines
Waymond Hines
John Hinton
Raymond Hinton
Hobbs First Baptist Church
Leora Hodge
Marcellus Hodge
William Holloway

Carl Holmes
Era Holmes
Holy Everlasting Baptist
Holy Temple Baptist Church
J. R. Homsey, Atty.
Donald Hooks
James Hope
Ruby Hornbeck
Thomas Hornbeck
Paul Houghton
Saundra Houghton
Carolyn House
House of Beauty
Clyde Houston
Rev. J. W. Houston
Richard M. Houston
Rosemary Houston
Helen Howard
T. C. Howard
Rev. T. H. Hubbard—Shiloh
    Baptist
Zella Hull
John Humphrey
Humpty Dumpty
Hattie Hunter
Lettie Ruth Hunter
Willetta Hunter
William Hunter
Janice L. Ingram
Verdell Irby
Irene's Beauty Salon
Carolyn Irons
Gwendolyn Irons
Marilyn Irons
Reginald Irons
Thomas Irons
David Lee Irving
Rev. Nathaniel C. Irving
Israel Chapel CME Church
Bertha Jackson

Darling A. Jackson
Dwight Jackson
Haywood Jackson
Jean Jackson
Linda Ann Jackson
Mozella Jackson
Rev. W. K. Jackson
A. Willie James
Rev. Goree James
Mr. and Mrs. Guy James
Kermit James
Ruth James
Wayne James
Janice Jamison
Rev. Albert Janco
Ralph Jefferson
Carol Jeffries
Joyce Jenkins
Joe Esco Tire Co.
A. Visanio Johnson
Aaron Johnson
Barbara Johnson
Carol Johnson
Centrilla Johnson
Etta Johnson
Gilbert Johnson
Helen Johnson
Jed Johnson
Joanne Johnson
Rev. John Wesley Johnson
Joyce Johnson
Lawrence Johnson
Marvin Johnson
Naomi Johnson
Reginald Johnson
Roceania Johnson
Samuel Louis Johnson
Taylor Johnson
Willie Johnson
Johnson Flower Co.

Alexander Jones
Annie Jones
Eric Delbert Jones
Johnny Jones
Lynzetta Jones
Marjorie Jones
Rev. N. H. Jones
Quido Jones
Anne Jordan
Sandra Jordan
Vernon Jordan
Jordan Seat Co.
Juanita's Cut N Curl
Rev. N. E. Kabelitz
Barton Kahn
Mr. and Mrs. Al Kavanaugh
John Kavanaugh
Carolyn Kelly
Father Kelly
Roger Kelly
Mr. and Mrs. Eugene Kennard
Kennard's Red Bud
Emma E. Kennedy
John Kennedy
Mary Kennedy
George Kerford
Kerr-McGee Corp.—Robert S.
   Kerr, Dean McGee
Isaac Kimbro
Johann Kimbro
Johnnie Kimbro
Shawn Kimbro
Donna Kimbrough
Cornell King
Laverna King
Richard King
Ronald King
Sonja King
Thurman King
William King

Leroy Kirk
Sherri Kirk
Wesley Kirk
Kitty Kat Florist
Pinkie Knight
Mack Kuykendall
Lady Buick
Father John LaFarge
Lee Lambeth
Robert Lambeth
Lampkins Beauty College
Rev. R. C. Laskey
John Latta
Clyde Laviolette
Clarence Laws
Pat Laws
Clementine Lawson
Florence Lawson
Lynda Lawson
Wayne Lawson
Wylene Lawson
Richard Laymon
Le Ora's Beauty Salon
Leaf Music Co.
Elbert Earl Leake
Howard Roy Leake
Morris Harold Leake
Richard Lebenthal
Mrs. E. P. Ledbetter
Elnora Lee
J. D. Lee
Kenneth Lee
Ronnie Lee
Lee Way Motor Freight
Leo's Bar-B-Que
Chester Lewis, Atty.
George Lewis
Geraldine Lewis
Margaret C. Lewis
Lewis Barber Shop

Conway Liddell Jr.
Dick Little
Local Federal Savings and Loan
   Assn.
Robert Long
Joan Loudermilk
Laurence Loudermilk
Noble Loudermilk
Lelia Lovejoy
Lovings Beauty College
Bert Luper
Billie Luper
Bobbie Luper
Calvin Luper
Chelle Luper
Cortelyou Luper
Eleanor Luper
Marilyn Luper
Mattie Luper
Mildred Luper
Willie C. Luper
Mr. and Mrs. Henry Lurks
Verbena Jean Lusk
Alfred Luster
Malcolm Luster
Maurice Luster
Melvin Luster
Luster's Motel and Hotel
Gwendolyn Lyday
Mr. and Mrs. (Pearl) Lyons
Patrick Lyons
Dr. George Lythcott
George Lythcott Jr.
Ruth Lythcott
Stephen Lythcott
Charlotte Mackey
Kathy Mackey
Macklanburg-Duncan Co.
Billy Macon
Mark Macon

Clyde Madden
Maggie Mae's Beauty Shop
Roshon Magnus
Morgan Mallard
Rebecca Mallard
Leroy Lynn Malone
Norman Martin
McKinley Marzett
Helen Mason
Mason Furniture Co.
A. D. Mathues
Charles Matthews
Charlotte Matthews
Debra Matthews
Felecia Matthews
Renea Matthews
Darryl May
Rev. Eric A. Mayes Jr.
Cheryl McCauley
Marsha McCauley
Ruby McCauley
W. A. McCauley
Seawilla McClain
John McClellon
Lucille McClendon
Hazel McCrumby
Clara McFall
Gayle McGee
Gussie McGee
Janice McGee
Patricia McGlory
Wilton McGlory
Joe McIntosh
Howard A. McKenzie
McKerson's Drug Store
Annette McKinley
Maggie McKinley
Anthony McMullen
Boyce McMullen
Phoenix Meadows

Robert L. Medley

Williams Merritt

Karen Merriweather

Jerry Miles

Lawrence Miles

Wilburn Miles

David Miller

Jimmie Miller

Roxie Miller

Maurine Mink

Elaine Minner

John Miskelly Jr.

Alvin Mitchell

Chester Mitchell

Dr. Earl Mitchell

Howard Mitchell

John Ira Mitchell

W. B. Mitchell

Johnnie Mite

John R. Moham

Bobby Moon

Carletta Moon

Carlotta Moon

Dr. E. C. Moon Jr.

Dr. E. C. Moon Sr.

F. D. Moon

Vivian Moon

Audrey Moore

Dr. Dewey and Mrs. Moore

Herman Lee Moore

Jessee Moore

Marcus Moore

Rodney Moore

Stephanie Moore

Teletha Moore

Willard Moore

Rev. R. S. Morgan

Virgil Morgan

Louise Morrison

Deborah Morrow

A. G. Moulder

Mary Moulder

Curtis Moutrey

Mt. Olive Baptist Church

Mt. Pleasant Baptist Church

Mt. Triumph Baptist Church

Elarryo Mukes

Vincent Mukes

Eugene Murray

Oliver Murray

Lawrence Myers Jr.

Wilbert Gene Myers

Eddie Eugene Myres

Alvin Naifeh

Barbara Nash

National Conference of Christians and Jews

Rev. E. R. Neal

James Neal

James P. Nero

Shirley Ann Nero

New Bethel Baptist Church

New Hope Baptist Church

New Zion Baptist Church

Carol Nickerson

Nick's Barbecue

Jack Nickson

Guillen Nourse

Mr. and Mrs. C. M. Nunley

Robert "Bob" O'Connor

Off Beat Club

Donna Officer

Sue Officer

Oklahoma Gas and Electric Co.

Oklahoma Natural Gas

Craig Oliver

Lillian Oliver

Marvin Oliver

Roy Oliver

Dianne O'Neal

Beverly Osborne
Otwell's Grocery
Anita Owens
Charles Owens Jr.
Dr. and Mrs. E. A. Owens
Dr. Robert C. Owens
Charles Parker
Edith Parker
Gail Parker
Gladys Parker
Kermit Parker
Maurice Parker
Rozell Marie Parker
Rev. Willie B. Parker
Ebbie Parks
Ida Patmon
Marian Patmon
Sue Patterson
Carrie Pendleton
Rev. E. J. Perry
Rev. E. W. Perry
Sebrum Perry
Sylvia Perry
Petite Beauty Salon
Flossie Petty
Nilar Jewel Phillips
Doris Philpot
James O. Pierce
Vanette Pierson
Vera Pigee
Darryl Pittman, Atty.
Willard Pitts
Sharon Pleasant
Gregory Pogue
L. C. Pogue
Lana Pogue
Linda Pogue
Mary Pogue
Rev. G. W. Pointer
Pointer Real Estate Co.

Carlton Poling
Christine Pollard
Johnnie Ponds
Velma O. Ponds
E. Melvin Porter, Atty.
E. Melvin Porter Jr.
Jewel Porter
Victor Porter
Alma Posey
Alma Faye Posey
Barbara Posey
Weldon Posey
Doris Powell
Ron Power
Betty Pratt
James Pratt
Margaret Pratt
Levi Pressley
Patricia Price
Jackie Proby
Evelyn Proctor
Willie Proctor
Providence Church of the
    Nazarene
Teddy Pruitt
Pulliam's Bar-B-Que
Quayle United Methodist
    Church
Rev. L. B. Quinn
L. E. Rader—State Welfare
    Dept.
Kirby Radford
Rainbo Bread
Ram's Inn
Randolph Drug Co.
Jeff Ray
Charles Reed
Gwendolyn Reed
Rev. J. A. Reed Jr.
John Reed

Mr. and Mrs. Mitchel C. Reed
Bishop Victor J. Reed
Bell Reese
Gwendolyn Reeves
Maxine Reeves
Leo Dean Reynolds
A. C. Richardson
Barbara Richardson
Edwina Richardson
Josephine Richardson
Joyce Richardson
Lequetta Richardson
Shirley Ridge
Donald Roach
Rev. B. J. Roberts
Rev. B. T. Roberts
Rev. T. J. Roberts
Clara Mae Robertson
Jackie Robinson
Sharon Robinson
Rockwell International
James Rodgers
Dianne Rogers
Gerald Rogers
Rogers Brothers
Rev. D. W. Roland
Elizabeth Rolfe
Henry Rolfe
Henry Rolfe Jr.
John R. Rolfe
Maj. William Rose
Joe Roselle, Atty.
Mark Roseman
Abram Ross
Willa Ross
H. McKinley Rowan, Atty.
Fred Rucker
Safeway Stores
M. L. Sanders
Dr. J. W. Sanford

Satellite Ticket Agency
Williams Saxon
Deviet Scott
Theresa Scruggs
Theron Scruggs
Dr. B. B. Sears
W. B. Seldon
Shaker Club No. 2
Wayne Shannon
Debra Sharp
Sharris Cleaners
Mr. and Mrs. Jack Shaw
Shaw's Siesta Motel
Ezell Shepard
Isabel Shepard
Ruth Sherwood
James Shields
Don Simmons
James Robert Simmons
O. M. Simmons
Simmons Studio
Wendell Simpson
Rev. Isaac Sims
Rev. William Sims
Ada Lois Sipuel
Sir Knights
Charles Sledge
Connie Sledge
Roberta Sledge
Curley Sloss
Curley Sloss Jr.
Minerva Sloss
Cathedral Smith
Cragin Smith
Dorothy Dell Smith
Elmer Smith
Geneva Smith
James Smith
Jay Smith
John Smith

Leonard Wayne Smith
Loren Smith
Marie Smith
Naomi Smith
Norman Smith
Stanley Smith
Sylvester Smith
Virgel Smith
Wayne Snow
Solloway's
Sooner Savings and Loan Co.
Soul Boutique
Southwestern Bell
  Telephone Co.
John K. Speck, Atty.
Lula Mae Spencer
June R. Spivey
Ronnie Spivey
Trudy Spivey
Stewart Spraggins
Eddie Stamps
Hooks Standiver
Lucky Statum
Herman Stevenson
Lenell Stevenson
Dorothy Stewart
Mr. and Mrs. Jimmie Stewart
Jimmie Stewart Jr.
Zandra Stewart
Sheldon Stirling
Dr. W. McFerrin Stowe
George Sturm
Donald Sullivan
Carl Summers
Loren Swanson
Rev. J. S. Sykes
Syl's Deluxe Cleaners
Bernice Syrus
Tabernacle Baptist Church
Tabitha Baptist Church

Jesse Tarver
Tate's Barber Shop
Tate's Market
Agnes Taylor
Clyde Taylor
Delores Taylor
Laura Taylor
Marilee Taylor
Marjoree Taylor
Pam Taylor
Dr. R. B. Taylor
Thomas Taylor
Vera Taylor
Earl Temple
Terrace Garden Nursing
  Home
Dr. and Mrs. Boston Thomas
Irene Thompson
M. L. Thompson, Atty
Dr. M. L. Thompson
Ruth Thompson
Dr. S. J. Thompson
Saundra Thompson
Mr. and Mrs. Melvin Todd
Areda Tolliver
Ruth Tolliver
Mr. and Mrs. A. M. Tompkins
Tom's Barbecue
Tom's Market
Triangle Beauty Salon
Trinity Presbyterian Church
Patricia Trotter
True Vine Baptist Church
Curt Tull
Sheriff Bob Turner
Roosevelt Turner
Taylor Turner
Two Sisters Nursing Home
Benny VanMeter
Anthony Walker

Barbara Walker
Rev. H. A. Walker
John Walker
Larry Walker
Lillie Ruth Walker
Mildred Walker
Brenda Wallace
Mrs. Guy Walley
Alice Walls
Geraldine Walls
Ruth Walls
Eloise Walton
Geneva Warmsley
Jean Warmsley
Esther Watson
Mary Watson
Sonita Watson
Linda Webb
Gen. LaVern E. Weber
Sharon Wedgwood
Judith Wells
Rev. J. C. West
Merdine Whatley
John B. White
Wickline United Methodist
    Church
Joyce Wilburn
Wildewood Baptist Church
Dr. Jack Wilkes
Canton Williams
Cecil L. Williams
Cecil L. Williams Jr.
Charles Williams
Doc Williams
Donda Williams

Doris Williams
Fannie Williams
Gwendolyn Williams
Jackie Williams
Jerome Williams
Jim Williams
John Williams
Mr. and Mrs. Legus Williams
Martha Williams
Mary Williams
Mr. and Mrs. Portwood
    Williams
Ross Williams
Tommy Williams
Velma Williams
Vickie Williams
Zuida Williams
Capt. Clifton Willis
Dr. Frank Wilson
Fred Wilson
Wilson's Certified Foods
Hassie Winkfield
Leo Winters
D. A. Wisener
John Witherspoon
Wonder Bread
Charles Woods
James Woods
Geniece Woodson
Harold Woodson
Clabe Wright
Herbert Wright
Patricia Wydermyer
Joe Younger
Maggie Younger

LEST WE FORGET

Frank Carey can bombard, entertain, tantalize, and inform. He thinks quickly, moves cautiously, and will tell you quickly that he cannot afford to waste time on useless arguments. He always does the unexpected. At a time when it was unpopular to invite Blacks into white homes, he threw his doors open and entertained Blacks with "pomp and distinction." He neglected his lumber business by attending an endless continuous series of meetings to eliminate segregation in public accommodations. He served faithfully as chairman of a committee that had as its sole purpose the elimination of segregation in public accommodations. Oklahoma needed Frank Carey, and the work that he did must become a permanent part of our history.

William Hulsey looked like a cowboy with his famous cowboy hat, blue jeans, striped cowboy shirt, and boots. Unlike a cowboy of the West, he drove his convertible up to Freedom Center. "What's going on?" he asked.

"Trying to get it together!" I said.

Bill Hulsey had no rival in his unique combination to work long and hard hours in his business, the Macklanburg-Duncan Company. Yet he took time to visit Freedom Center, where he explained and illuminated the "need of practical common sense," as he called it. He encouraged the NAACP Youth Council members to always do their best. "The only hope for all of us is in the immediate building up of our own self-images," he said. "We must move forward."

Bill Hulsey has been a friend to all people, including minorities. This interest is not only intense, but has proved itself by his immense enthusiasm and efficiency in helping people. Thank God for Bill Hulsey.

Claude Murphy, according to some of the Oklahoma City NAACP'ers, was a handsome man, with short cropped hair slightly curled at the nape, a bold nose over delicate lips, wide, arched, penetrating eyes, and eyebrows that seemed almost artificial. His manner was gallant and charming. His dress was immaculate. His conversations were inquisitive, and he searched for minute details. He was not a yes or no man. He possessed an inner radiance and vitality that penetrated into events and personalities. He also possessed a therapeutic sense of humor and could relate blazing experiences of slum life, prison life, religious life, political life, and social life.

Murphy understood the rare art of listening, and his mind worked like a cotton gin in which he sifted out information and labeled it false or true in front of your eyes. He had been exposed to some of the great minds of the past and present. He was an avid reader and a world traveler. His personality was warm and magnetic. According to Cecil Williams, "He could talk a dog out of his bark and a lion out of his cage," and he still remained cool and calm. Melvin Porter called him "the educator."

So Claude Murphy, the nondenominational minister, came to the NAACP Youth Council office and volunteered to take on the responsibility of public relations advisor to the council. He immediately added a new dimension to our work. He assisted and organized a voter registration drive, launched a big freedom rally, and achieved participation from the League of Women Voters and the AFL-CIO. He brought in one of the greatest chaplains of all time, the honorable Dr. Earl Clayton Grandstaff from Missouri, a retired Air Force colonel and past president of the American Chaplains Association and the American Correctional Association, who delivered a dynamic and challenging address. Murphy had also invited a guest soloist, but Reverend E. H. Hill stopped the soloist, who he felt was singing a song that was prohibited by the African Methodist Church. Murphy was able to handle the situation and heal the wounds that were opened. He got the NAACP involved in some unbelievable activities, including a complete education about Alcoholics Anonymous, FBI activities, and prison reform.

Murphy understood power and used it. He invited me to a prison reform workshop at the Muehlebach Hotel in Kansas City and had the top official from National Airlines send a chauffeur to pick me up. The plane had left Oklahoma City ten minutes early, though, so Murphy had me flown to Kansas City on a special plane with one lone attendant and me as passenger.

He hosted a big steak dinner at a local hotel for his friends. They had fun, although some suffered "afterpains."

He also brought the nationally known Billy Sol Estes to Oklahoma City. Estes came to my house with a Bible in one hand and a prayer in his mouth, which echoed through the house. When people heard that he was in Oklahoma City, some went into intellectual shock. The owner of the Planet Motel called to tell me that I was the biggest fool in the world for bringing Billy Sol Estes to Oklahoma City. He vowed that he would never speak to me again, and he hasn't.

Estes spoke in a local church. He never spoke about anything but his "God" and his conversion to Christianity.

Claude Murphy talked freely about his past, and especially his stay in the Illinois State Penitentiary. We were not surprised when the *Daily Oklahoman* published a history of his past.

The role that Murphy played here cannot be overlooked. He taught his lessons well and concluded by saying that even though he was leaving, we must always remember that segregation was a psychological reaction and a public rejection of the fatherhood of God, and he wanted us to continue regardless of what happened.

Ron Powers is an extraordinary man, gifted with the rare ability to accomplish difficult tasks himself and at the same time to inspire and encourage those around him. He is a devout family man and is involved in "practically everything" in Oklahoma City. He is a man who is proud of his work with the Southwestern Bell Telephone Company. Although he has climbed the ladder of success with his company and has the respect of his employees, he has not lost his common touch, nor his million-dollar smile.

He vividly rejects segregation and deplores ignorance with a passion. For example, somewhere in the history of Freedom Center, there is a story of a time Ron Powers visited there and met an angry young Black man named Frank, who "hated all whites" and proudly described his feelings to Ron, who just so happened to be white.

Ron readily saw what I had been trying to convey to the stubborn white business community. In spite of Frank's attitude toward him, Ron had faced a "wall," and now he had to break that wall. He found out that Frank was interested in electronic equipment, and this was the hammer that broke the wall. Ron fed Frank's electronic appetite.

One day Frank came to me. He said, "I used to dislike all whites, but Ron Powers is different."

"He's white, what's different about him?" I asked.

"It's in the way that he looks at you and he treats you like you're somebody special," he said.

"Frank, there are a lot of whites like Ron Powers. We've just got to find them."

"Where do we find them?"

"Frank, they are all over America. We've just got to find them," I said.

Donald Sullivan was the executive director of the National Conference of Christians and Jews, which served as a bridge between the Black and white community. He worked to find vehicles by which both groups could develop a deep understanding and appreciation of each other. He was an ardent worker for the cause of freedom. When he left Oklahoma City, he turned the torch of freedom over to Perry Lusk, who carried it with dedication and dignity.

Danny Williams, a popular personality, is well known for his rare ability to make people "think and laugh." His voice on WKY is an integral part of Oklahoma's family life. During the sit-ins he calmly dedicated a song to me, "Walk On By" by Dionne Warwick, and proudly stated, "This is from the restaurant owners to Clara Luper." This became a laughing technique that removed a great deal of tension and hostility from the movement.

Stanton Young is a notable, perceptive, and persistent man. His record generates confidence, as he quietly discharges his role as a negotiator with zeal and distinction. He is small in stature, slow to speak, and a "giant" in human concerns. He has self-restraint and self-discretion. He is unafraid to approach hostile groups. This he did during the sit-ins and sanitation strike. It was Young's smile, his refreshing sense of humility, and his genuine desire to learn that made him an integral part of the movement. From the sanitation workers, to the mayor's office, to the business community, to the governor's office, he made his tracks— tracks that time itself will never erase.

CHRONOLOGY OF SIT-IN EVENTS
IN OKLAHOMA CITY

January 1957—The NAACP Youth Council is reorganized with Clara Luper as advisor.

May 1957—Twenty-six NAACP Youth Council members attend the NAACP Convention in New York City, where they present the play *Brother President.*

May 1957—Negotiations begin on opening public accommodations.

August 19, 1958—The first sit-in at Katz Drug Store. Several downtown lunch counters will be integrated.

September 1958—The sit-ins are suspended to see if eating places can be opened up by negotiation.

1959—Token sit-ins continue throughout Oklahoma City, with John A. Brown's luncheonette, Anna Maude's Cafeteria, Bishop's Restaurant, the Skirvin Hotel, and the Huckins Hotel as the target sites.

March 1960—Massive sit-ins continue. Governor J. Howard Edmondson convinces the adult Black leaders to cancel a planned massive sit-in at Brown's and announces the creation of a statewide committee to study and find answers to the public accommodations problem.

August 1960—The boycott of downtown stores in Oklahoma City begins.

January 1961—Nine sit-inners are arrested at Anna Maude's Cafeteria in the first legal action since the start of the sit-ins.

July 1961—The boycott ends. Three downtown lunch counters have been opened; demonstrations at the Pink Kitchen have led to numerous arrests and injunctions; demonstrations continue.

1962—Sit-ins continue daily in the summertime, after school, and on weekends.

May 1963—Oklahoma City's Community Relations Committee is organized to solve the remaining lunch counter problems.

June 1963—Legislation is enacted to establish the Human Rights Commission.

June 1963—Sit-inners have successfully integrated over twenty eating places.

July 1963—The Human Rights Commission is formed, with Major William Rose as the executive director.

November 1963—Legal dispute flares over sit-ins at Ralph's Drug Store.

May 1964—Arrests and an injunction result from the sit-in at the Split-T Restaurant.

June 2, 1964—The City Council passes a public accommodations ordinance.

July 3, 1964—Blacks test four eating places and are served at all four. The sit-in campaign ends five years and eleven months after it started.

November 29, 1967—City Councilman A. L. Dowell launches a one-man stand-in for the Fair Housing Ordinance. It will last for three months, during which time he will stand throughout the long City Council meetings in spite of swollen feet and aching knees.

March 1968—Freedom Center is founded.

September 10, 1968—Freedom Center is bombed.

June 1969—The march to Lawton.

July 15, 1969—A Fair Housing Ordinance is passed in Oklahoma City.

August 1969—The sanitation strike.

August 1978—Freedom Center's mortgage is burned.

Dear Sit-Inners,

As we sit in, we must remember the important dates in Black history.

DATES! DATES! Important dates in Black history. From the dark skies of the receding nights, a strong group of people survived. People who plucked the brightest stars and with brave hands, courageous spirits, and patriotic hearts wrote their stories on the heroic pages of history, adding a new and previously unknown dimension to American history.

The names are interwoven into the matchless history of faith and strength accomplished by those who mysteriously found a way to survive. With blood, brains, and hard work, these people won victories where defeat seemed almost a certainty.

The history of Black Americans encompassed every event in American history, often unnoticed and unwritten, yet today, Black history stands erect, clothed with a full panoply of documented facts.

As we stand today at the threshold of a new, bright, exciting day, we must constantly look back on the darkening shadows of the past. We must understand dates and events that record the energy, the determination, and the ambitions of our people.

Today Black people must face the future with confidence, knowing that dark yesterdays make today's sunshine. So today, as we sit in, we ignite the stars of progress knowing that

> Today was Tomorrow
> Tomorrow was the Future
> and
> Today is the Present
> The Present will become the Past
> The Past will become History
> Tomorrows are pregnated Todays
> and the Tomorrows will become Todays
> and the Todays will become Yesterdays
> So it was and so it is,
> So live Today
> Love Today
> Work Today
> This is Your Date with Destiny
> and
> The time is
> Today

INDEX